Rita Dove's Cosmopolitanism

Rita Dove's Cosmopolitanism

Malin Pereira

UNIVERSITY OF ILINOIS PRESS
URBANA AND CHICAGO

Library of Congress Cataloging-in-Publication Data
Pereira, Malin.
Rita Dove's cosmopolitanism / Malin Pereira.
p.   cm.
Includes bibliographical references and index.
ISBN 0-252-02837-6 (acid-free paper)
1. Dove, Rita—Criticism and interpretation.
2. Pluralism (Social sciences) in literature.
3. Racially mixed people in literature.
4. African Americans in literature.
5. Race in literature.
I. Title.
PS3554.O884Z83   2003
811'.54—dc21   2002015035

Contents

Acknowledgments

This work has been supported by grants from the University of North Carolina at Charlotte and the National Endowment for the Humanities. I appreciate the support of both of these institutions.

Many, many people have contributed to this book, although none of them are responsible for any of its limitations. Lynn Keller deserves my first acknowledgment because she was the one who introduced me to Rita Dove's poetry. Keller's careful, well-informed criticism on contemporary American poetry always provides a model to admire. Craig Werner's long-time mentoring and his early identification of me as someone who "knew" Dove's work (which was news to me) gave impetus to the first idea of this book. His on-going support and astute corrections have been invaluable. Trudier Harris-Lopez's willingness to include me among Dove scholars and further my work has also been critical.

Paula Connolly, Cy Knoblauch, Ron Lunsford, Mark West, Daniel Shealy, Lucinda Grey, Chris Davis, Fred Smith, Jim McGavran, David Amante, Marty Settle, Jonathan Barron, Meg Morgan, and Boyd Davis, each have at various times and in special ways, nurtured the project and me throughout several years. Sandy Govan dismissed negativity when I needed to hear her do so. Tony Jackson, who read many chapter drafts, served as a sounding board and tough critic. Jeffrey Leak came through with a suggestion and a book loan at a critical time. Deborah Bosley was the most encouraging lunch date imaginable. Herman Thomas, as always, assisted me with his extensive biblical knowledge. Garland Keever, during whose brief time in the Department of English at the University of North Carolina at Charlotte this project began, Kay Horne, and Elizabeth Gian-Cursio enabled my work; I am grateful for the positive attitudes and hard work of Eleanor Stafford, Jennie Mussington, and Lisa Wright, each of whom daily eases my administrative duties. Humanities librarian Judith Van Noate proved an excellent resource and a responsive colleague. The University of North Carolina at Charlotte has also supported this book with institutional know-how. The members of the 1999 NEH nominating committee, headed by Steve Mosier, and arts and science grants director Lesley Brown worked hard and provided excellent advice.

I have been teaching Dove's writing since 1993, and my students have been wonderful co-scholars. The undergraduates in my 1993 class on Gwendolyn Brooks, Audre Lorde, and Rita Dove, as well as graduate students in several African American poetry seminars that I taught, bounced ideas back and forth until we all better understood Dove's work. Former students who warrant public acknowledgment include Arlene Reilly, Lucinda Ramsey, Flower Noble, Danielle Hatchett, Jonathan Barker, Veronica Jones, Gretchen Robinson, Vincent Steele, Mack Staton, Kevin Winchester, Jenna Rossi, Kimberleigh Stallings, Melissa Daniel, Linda Hofmann, Linda Troxler, Tameya Baker, and Ilona Cesan. Thanks as well to Linda Hofmann for parsing through Dove's entry on Ralph Ellison in a German encyclopedia.

In the process of writing this book I have had to relearn a tradition I thought I knew. Scholars at conferences and journal reviewers have asked key questions that forced me to rethink my work in order to provide adequate answers. For such moments I thank Trudier Harris-Lopez, Yusef Komunyakaa, Sally Ann Ferguson, Durthy Washington, an anonymous reader for *African American Review,* Susan Friedman, and Elizabeth Zanichowsky. Susan Van Dyne's constructive comments were instrumental in developing the manuscript far past its initial promise.

Rita Dove and Fred Viebahn have been gracious and forthcoming subjects of scrutiny. I thank them for sharing some of their private life with me and for trusting me to do this work as best I could. Fred Viebahn corrected small errors of fact in the manuscript and added personal information I otherwise could not have known. For such help, and for his generous attitude, I am grateful. My editor at the University of Illinois Press, Willis Regier, aided the project with patient and kind guidance.

Finally, my friends and family have provided a context in which my work could get done and even thrive. For this I thank friends Joey Retzler, Delia Neil, Meredith Green, Fiona and Grenville Barnes, and Jeff and Ellen Ferdon. Elizabeth Evans Sachs and Shanna Greene Benjamin offered critical insights as well as much-needed, and unfortunately infrequent, diversions. Family friends Gill and Marty Heyert have been enthusiastic and informed supporters. Gill's clippings from the *Washington Post* and the *New York Times* alone supplanted hours of scholarly digging on my part. My father and his wife, Milton and Jewell Goodman, were not only interested but also useful in describing the layout of Washington, D.C. My mother, Marta McElroy Goodman, influences my work through her cosmopolitanism and keen aesthetic sense; my brother, Grant Goodman, has always been a fellow nomad. My husband, Ernest Pereira, helps make my work and life possible, and our children, Cameron, Blake, and Julian, keep us both off-kilter and a little crazy—a blessing after all this logic and argument. To everyone, many thanks.

Rita Dove's Cosmopolitanism

Introduction

Author of six collections of poetry, winner of a Pulitzer Prize, and two-term poet laureate of the United States, Rita Dove has achieved notice from both the white-dominated publishing world and the African American literary community.[1] Yet Dove remains a curiously controversial figure who, despite her impressive achievements, has yet to receive the universal acclaim of predecessors such as Langston Hughes, Gwendolyn Brooks, or even Amiri Baraka.

Dove's work creates discomfort in some readers—both black and white—in part because it expresses painful and controversial aspects of American and African American culture and history. This book focuses on how Dove's life and work pull the scabs off wounds we are bearing from the "culture wars" of the 1980s and 1990s. One of the most important elements of Dove's work, and a source of the discomfort, concerns her treatment of the role of race in shaping her—and our—identities. Dove's self-fashioned identity, both personal and poetic, challenges the black essentialism of the black arts movement of the 1960s and 1970s that carried over, often in subterranean ways, into the multiculturalism of the 1980s and 1990s. The debate swirling around essentialism can be angry and frantic, especially when it engages fundamental notions of blackness, identity, and culture. Although Dove knows that a "strategic essentialism" identifying attributes supposedly core to black identity and culture has helped ensure the survival of African Americans in a racist society, she clearly recognizes the limitations of such notions.

Dove's response to these anxieties about race, identity, and culture places her in the vanguard of American and African American letters. Both her cultural range and her aesthetic sensibility position her at the front lines of what the African American writer Trey Ellis hailed in 1989 as the "New Black Aesthetic" (NBA).[2] The key features of NBA art are:

1. Artists borrowing and assembling across both race and class lines.
2. A parodic relationship to the black arts movement.
3. A new, unflinching look at black culture, warts and all.
4. Artists comprising an elitist, avant-garde group, for now.
5. A belief in finding the universal in oneself and one's experiences.
   (Ellis 234–42)[3]

Ellis uses himself and his experiences as a model of a typical new black aesthetic artist. Explaining the predominantly white, middle-class suburban context in which he grew up, Ellis comments that at his high school (where he and his sister were the only blacks not bused in), "It wasn't unusual to be called 'oreo' and 'nigger' on the same day" (235). Such a context, coupled with his self-directed readings in black literature and culture, make him a "cultural mulatto" (235). "Just as a genetic mulatto is a black person of mixed parents who can often get along fine with his white grandparents," Ellis observes, "a cultural mulatto, educated by a multi-racial mix of cultures, can also navigate easily in the white world. And it is by and large this rapidly growing group of cultural mulattoes that fuels the NBA. We no longer need to deny or suppress any part of our complicated and sometimes contradictory cultural baggage to please either white people or black" (235). This *cultural* mulatto, someone who has had a range and mix of cultural experiences, Ellis emphasizes, is *black:* "Today's cultural mulattoes echo those 'tragic mulattoes' critic Sterling Brown wrote about in the Thirties only when they too forget they are wholly black" (235). To Ellis, this is not a moving beyond blackness in any way; rather, it is a recognition and embracing of the complex cultural milieu experienced by the children of the vastly expanded black middle class.

Although Ellis does not specifically include Dove as a new black aesthetic artist, the idea of the cultural mulatto and the key gestures of the NBA (Ellis parlays the pun with the National Basketball Association throughout his essay) are useful in understanding Dove's poetry and her position in African American poetic history. In fact, Dove, about ten years older than typical new black aesthetic artists, can be viewed as an elder sister/sister to the NBA, the first major African

American artist to articulate new black aesthetic poetics. Too young to be part of the "Third Plane" of black writers coming out of the black arts movement but developing beyond it, people such as Ishmael Reed, Toni Morrison, Clarence Major, and John Edgar Wideman, Dove is more appropriately viewed as producing the earliest artistic expression of the contemporary black aesthetic sensibility ten years before Trey Ellis capitalized on the term.[4]

The energetic and sometimes hostile response to Ellis's manifesto points to the repressed anxieties underlying the contemporary African American literary scene.[5] By adopting the term *mulatto*—traditionally used to refer to someone of mixed blood and invoking the tormented history of interracial sexual relations—Ellis forced the discussion of what literary critic Werner Sollers called "a subject likely to elicit censure and high emotions, or at least a certain nervousness" (4). The artists on whom Ellis bases his argument, including himself, Spike Lee, Lisa Jones (daughter of LeRoi Jones and Hettie Cohen), and George Wolfe, among others, share certain reservations about being, or perhaps more accurately being perceived as, cultural mulattoes. The problem, for many of these artists, is that the term implies some degree of movement away from the reality of blackness and seems to endorse a fuzzy "we are all the same" universalist posture.

Dove certainly understands the problems. But she also understands the dangers inherent in responding only to contemporary versions of the long-standing tension between black specificity and what Ross Posnock in his germinal *Color and Culture: Black Writers and the Making of the Modern Intellectual* defines as the "cosmopolitan" strain within the black intellectual tradition. Posnock identifies a continuing belief in being a "world citizen" and in using a wide range of cultural materials, as expressed in the writings of W. E. B. Du Bois, Alain Locke, Zora Neale Hurston, Ralph Ellison, Albert Murray, and James Baldwin. For Posnock, cosmopolitanism, as practiced and preached in the black intellectual tradition, maintains that culture has no color (10). Culture, especially American culture, is composite. Alain Locke argued that cultural goods "are no longer the exclusive property of the race or people that originated them. They belong to all who can use them" (Posnock 11, quoting Locke 206). Both Locke and Du Bois, Posnock demonstrates, affirm the original cosmopolitan ideal (from the Greco-Roman Stoics) of a "world citizen" (12), freely drawing upon cultural materials regardless of their source. Du Bois emphasizes a dialectical relationship between the racial particular and the unraced universal, insisting that artists and intellectuals must recognize the universal in the particular or risk "group exclusiveness and segregation" (Posnock 13, quoting DuBois 1194). Posnock brings this aspect of the tradition to the present with Samuel Delaney and Adrienne Kennedy but does not mention Dove's work. This book will show how the cosmopolitan tradition helps in understanding Dove's place in the historical trajectory of black intellectual thought and art.

One benefit of Posnock's reclamation of the term *cosmopolitan* is that it moves the discourse away from the binary vocabularies in which we have been mired—separatist vs. integrationist, black nationalist vs. universalist, Afrocentric vs. Eurocentric, and so on. Another welcome effect of Posnock's work is that it establishes, within the black intellectual and artistic tradition, a thread heretofore repressed that refuses the "fiction of cultural segregation" and acknowledges the "actuality of cultural overlap and linkage" (20). Thus, perhaps the new black aesthetic is not at all "new." The gap between the two terms—*cosmopolitan* and *cultural mulatto*—is the gap between acknowledging the anxieties surrounding the idea of cultural amalgamation (which Posnock does) and suppressing such anxieties so they emerge in inflammatory rhetoric (which Ellis does).

I understand that the term *mulatto* is inflammatory to some and impolite to others. It also participates in a binary view of race that suggests race can be determined and thus made "mixed," ideas that despite their staying power are clearly untenable. I use the term *cultural mulatto* when discussing Dove's early writings expressing anxieties about the reception of her work; in these texts the image of the cultural mulatto appears as symptomatic of these anxieties. I use the term *cosmopolitan* when referring to Dove's general attitude about her poetic identity and position in both the tradition and the contemporary period. Although Dove is cosmopolitan in her thinking, her repressed anxieties about being cosmopolitan emerge in the figure of the cultural mulatto in her early work.[6]

Throughout her career Dove has foregrounded, both thematically and stylistically, the anxieties surrounding the place of the black cosmopolitan writer. While establishing herself in a black cosmopolitan tradition in her early literary criticism on other African American poets, Dove thematizes such an anxiety in her early work through mulatto imagery and symbolism. Her repressed cultural mulatto anxiety emerges in an incest motif throughout her early nonpoetic work, culminating in the 1994 play *The Darker Face of the Earth* (which was revised in 1996). She introduces a cultural mulatto poetic persona in her first volume of poetry, *The Yellow House on the Corner* (1980). Using her work in genres other than poetry to work through anxieties about the cultural mulatto allows Dove to present her second volume of poetry, *Museum* (1983), as her first independent aesthetic statement, one consistent with the black cosmopolitan tradition. As such, it demonstrates several features of the new black aesthetic and reveals a revised universalism. Following *Museum*, Dove's poetry extends her cosmopolitan revised universalism by deploying a blues-infused nomadic subjectivity that signifies on our preconceived notions of "neighborhood" and "home." In *Thomas and Beulah* (1986), *Grace Notes* (1989), and *Mother Love* (1995), Dove indeed writes her way back home, but it is to a home and neighborhood far more cosmopolitan—and an identity far less unified or monolithic—than critics and other readers might have wished. *On the Bus with Rosa Parks* (1999) offers a bird's-eye view of her ongoing relationship to African American themes of freedom, home, and identity and reveals her journey of difference within that tradition.

Notes

1. *Selected Poems*, if counted, would bring the total to seven collections of poetry.

2. A conversation I had with Ronicka Smucker helped me make this connection between Trey Ellis and Dove.

3. Ellis also makes some offhand claims about nationalistic pride and a "commitment to disturbatory art" (239), comments that strike me more as attempts to sound politically committed rather than as key features of the new aesthetic. This perception is backed up by Eric Lott's trenchant critique of Ellis's essay, also in *Callaloo*, in which he accuses Ellis and the New Black Aesthetic of evading politics and ignoring the importance of black tradition-making. Tera Hunter's accompanying essay also denounces Ellis's failure to account for class issues. Readers of Greg Tate in the *Village Voice* or his book, *Flyboy in the Buttermilk,* will recognize many ideas Ellis puts forth as ones Tate articulated several years earlier.

4. Ellis borrows Pancho Savery's term, *Third Plane,* and says that the NBA's writers regard these writers as "icons."

5. See, for example, Lott's and Hunter's critiques following Ellis's essay.

6. Cosmopolitanism is enjoying prominence in current theory and literary criticism; see, for example, essays by Anthony Appiah and Eric Lott; work by Jacques Derrida, Charles Jones, and Timothy Brennan; an anthology edited by Carol Appadurai Breckenridge et al.; and a literary monograph by Jessica Berman.

1 ∼ Negotiating Blackness: Dove and the African American Poetic Tradition

African American poetry has exhibited the tension between Afro-Modernism and black nationalism, also seen as mainstream integrationism versus black separatism, since the mid-1940s. Ross Posnock would explain these poles in the context of the ongoing struggle between cosmopolitanism and racial purism within the tradition. Following the modernist, craft-focused poems of the early Gwendolyn Brooks, Robert Hayden, and Melvin B. Tolson after World War II and continuing into the 1960s, black arts movement poets such as Amiri Baraka (formerly LeRoi Jones), Haki Madhibuti (formerly Don L. Lee), Maulana Karenga, Etheridge Knight, Nikki Giovanni, and Sonia Sanchez rejected the values of literary formalism—the use of European-derived forms and techniques—in favor of an aesthetic centered on black culture and self-empowerment.

During the 1950s and 1960s white critics often read the formalism and modernist experimentation of Afro-Modernists as their becoming "universal," whereas black audiences—especially during the black arts movement—sometimes read such experimentation as a capitulation to the master's aesthetics. And white critics often perceived the revolutionary thrust of much black arts movement poetry, along with its emphasis on specifically African and African American cultural sources for content, as more political than poetic. Black audiences usually perceived it as engaging in black cultural pride and celebrating specifically black aesthetic forms and techniques. The two movements—Afro-Modernist and black arts—set the terms of the conversation for 1970s and 1980s' black poets who owed debts to the insights of each yet often tended to affiliate more with one than the other. Critics of Dove's poetry have sometimes oscillated between these poles of universalism and nationalism in their appraisals.

Dove's awareness of the points of conflict is conveyed in several of her early writings, including a poem about the black arts movement, "Upon Meeting Don L. Lee, in a Dream." Her 1980s' literary criticism on predecessors in the tradition also relays her anxieties about being perceived as a cultural mulatto and in the figures of Melvin B. Tolson and Gwendolyn Brooks establishes a cosmopolitan literary genealogy for her work. Dove's critical genealogy represses Amiri Baraka as a black literary father, although her early short story "The Spray Paint King," read as a *künstlerroman,* scripts a thematic place for his political legacy in the family romance of the cultural mulatto.

A feeling of navigating between Scylla and Charybdis may explain why so little critical attention had been paid Dove's wide array of work until the mid-1990s, especially attention to the relationship between her poetry and her African American identity. Early criticism on Dove was established in articles by Helen Vendler, Arnold Rampersad, and Ekaterini Georgoudaki, who address how her poetry might reflect, express, or deny her African American personal or literary heritage. In the late 1990s essays by Peter Erickson and Susan Van Dyne attempted to account for Dove's handling of race (chapters 3 and 5).

Vendler argues in a 1994 essay in the *Times Literary Supplement,* unfortunately entitled "Blackness and Beyond Blackness," that a black writer "composes both with and against racial identity" (11). Despite Vendler's enormous powers as a poetry critic, her attempt to account for blackness in Dove's poetry reprises the false universalizing many black writers fought throughout the twentieth century, the same moving "beyond" blackness against which Langston Hughes argued in "The Negro Artist and the Racial Mountain" and the same misreadings to which craft-oriented modernists such as early Brooks, Tolson, and Hayden were subjected. Focusing her praise on *Thomas and Beulah,* Vendler claims "it represents Dove's re-thinking of the lyric poet's relationship to the history of blackness" (13). In *Thomas and Beulah,* Vendler asserts, Dove makes an important discovery: "Blackness need not be one's central subject, but equally need not be omitted" (13).

In all of these statements Vendler seems to think that there is some discrete area in a black writer's psyche that is exclusively black; beyond that is a vast territory of neutral topics, perceptions, and reactions ripe for poetic plucking. She applauds going into that "beyond" in "color-neutral" poems (11). Although Vendler probably did not intend for her argument to convey such segregated psychic geography, her either-or formulation fails to recognize that one can be black and have a wide array of subject matter, ideas, and emotions, which, although they are not "marked" black (especially to a white observer), reflect one's core identity and experiences as a black person.

Peter Erickson also points out the limitations of Vendler's analysis, arguing that it is "ultimately limited and one-sided because she does not devote equal attention and sophistication to the critique of universalism. . . . In order to perceive the full scope of freedom Dove asserts with regard to race, it is necessary to present a balanced analysis of the simplifications of universalism as well as separatism" (98).

Arnold Rampersad, in an essay modestly entitled "The Poems of Rita Dove" (1986), does not try to move Dove beyond her blackness at all but rather places her squarely within the African American poetic tradition while acknowledging her primary affiliation with the Afro-Modernists. Rampersad grounds Dove's work in the black arts movement of the 1960s and 1970s "as a point of radical departure for her in the development of her own aesthetic" (53). Of her aesthetic oppositioning he notes:

> In many ways, [Dove's] poems are exactly the opposite of those that have come to be quintessentially black verse in recent years. Instead of looseness of structure, one finds in her poems remarkably tight control; instead of reliance on reckless inspiration, one recognizes discipline and practice, and long, taxing hours in competitive university poetry workshops and in her study; instead of a range of reference limited to personal confession, one finds personal reference disciplined by a measuring of distance and a prizing of objectivity; instead of an obsession with the theme of race, one finds an eagerness, perhaps even an anxiety, to transcend—if not actually to repudiate—black cultural nationalism in the name of a more inclusive sensibility. (53)

That Rampersad positions Dove against the black arts movement is an important and necessary step in understanding her relationship to the African American poetic tradition; it helps us see how to qualify Vendler's overstatements about Dove moving "beyond" race. What

Dove's work moves beyond (although it is, of course, an impossibility without) are the aesthetics and black cultural nationalism of the black arts movement, not blackness. As Rampersad makes clear, that does not entail moving beyond racial identification or cultural heritage. In readings of *The Yellow House on the Corner* and *Museum*, Rampersad demonstrates that "[a]s a poet, Dove is well aware of black history" (54). He acknowledges (at the time of his writing only those two volumes had been published) that Dove seems to publish little on "racism today" and places that issue in the context of "the trap set by race for the black writer" (55). Such a conjecture is borne out by a 1985 interview with Dove by Richard Peabody and Gretchen Johnsen in which Dove reveals that she deliberately avoided publishing in black markets early in her career because she did not want to be typecast as a "Black Poet" (6). What Dove wants, Rampersad argues, is "the complete freedom of her imagination" (56). Thus, while Vendler sees Dove as either black or universal Rampersad presents her as both African American and universal.

That Rampersad leans a little more toward the black nationalist pole of the conversation, away from Vendler's false universalizing and emphasis on craft, is not only clear in his discussion of Dove in the context of African American poetry but also in two quasi-black arts movement suggestions he makes near the end of the essay. He encourages her to loosen the technical control and also to return "to her old neighborhood" in her future work (60). That advice anticipates Dove's emerging nomadic blues subject, whose signifying poetic responses to ideas about home and identity constitute an ongoing journey through *Thomas and Beulah*, *Grace Notes*, *Mother Love*, and *On the Bus with Rosa Parks* (chapters 5, 6, and the conclusion).

A third critic, Ekaterini Georgoudaki, in an essay entitled "Rita Dove: Crossing Boundaries" (1991), tries to move beyond the universalism/black nationalism binary. Georgoudaki adopts the "world citizen" view that Rampersad rightly ascertains in Dove's values and that Posnock argues lies behind black cosmopolitanism. She articulates Dove's positioning in the literary tradition as an African American woman in the concept of "crossing boundaries." Perhaps because of her non-American vantage point (Georgoudaki is a Greek scholar who trained in the United States and has since returned to Greece as a professor), she contextualizes Dove's work as follows: "As a black person living in the predominantly white societies of the Old and New World, having entered an inter-racial and inter-cultural marriage (her husband is a German writer), and trying to forge an autonomous female poetic voice against the background of a male-dominated Euro- and Afro-American literary tradition, Dove has often crossed social and literary boundaries, violated taboos, and experienced displacement, i.e. living 'in two different worlds, seeing things with double vision,' wherever she has stayed (USA, German [*sic*], Israel)" (419). Furthermore, Georgoudaki argues that Dove's crossing of literary boundaries "overcomes" the feelings of displacement that divisions and boundaries cause (421). Offering readings of Dove's poetry through *Thomas and Beulah,* Georgoudaki convincingly demonstrates the wide range of boundaries Dove crosses in her work, thus providing a usable metaphor for her poetic sensibility.

Although Georgoudaki's perspective is useful, it is also important not to lose sight of the specifically black elements in Dove's work in addition to its breadth. Not seeking to limit her work to an African American context nor wanting to move her beyond it, this book seeks to establish how Dove's poetry articulates one of the most prominent aesthetics of the contemporary period in African American letters. She leads a new phase in African American poetic history that continues the tradition's thread of cosmopolitanism and brings it out of repression and into full expression. She thus joins the list of late-twentieth-century intellectuals Posnock identifies as rejecting cultural purism in favor of universalism, including Anthony Appiah, Julia Kristeva, Edward Said, and Martha Nussbaum, who "have chosen cosmopolitanism" (4).

This prominent aesthetic in the contemporary phase of African American poetry specifically is anticipated by the work of such Afro-Modernist poets of the 1940s and 1950s as the early Gwendolyn Brooks, Robert Hayden, and Melvin B. Tolson. It is also enabled by the racial and decolonizing cultural pride of the black arts movement, a phase that affirmed cultural particularity and gave lie to white culture's refusal to acknowledge America's indebtedness to African American cultural forms (Feher 269; Murray, *Omni-Americans* 21–22; Posnock 20). In this sense, the contemporary period's cosmopolitanism is a revisionist universalism that values racial and cultural particulars. Finally, as a movement, the "new black aesthetic" (NBA) is irretrievably associated with the 50 percent of black Americans who are middle class or above.[1]

The NBA's relationship to the black arts movement deserves further scrutiny. In his essay, Ellis figures the NBA in Lisa and Kellie Jones, the racially mixed daughters of Amiri Baraka (then LeRoi Jones) and his first wife, Hettie Cohen. In doing so, he emphasizes not only the idea of the cultural mulatto—"says Lisa, 'I had a lot of options but I chose [blackness]'" (236)—but also the NBA's debt to the black arts movement.

Little of the aesthetic Ellis describes, however, reflects Maulana (formerly Ron) Karenga's basic prescription that black art must be functional, collective, and committing (1973–74). Ellis's eagerness to claim not opposition but solidarity with black nationalism shows a filial stance unsupported by aesthetics that enact Karenga's prescriptions. In actuality, the relationship Ellis claims between the NBA and the black arts movement is solely one of the black arts movement providing a foundation of black cultural pride from which NBA artists can grow. NBA artists do not follow in the black arts movement's aesthetic footsteps. That is revealed by the new black aesthetic practice of "parodying . . . the black nationalist movement. . . . NBA artists aren't afraid to flout publicly the official, positivist black party line" (236). Ellis offers such examples as Eddie Murphy's prison poet Tyrone Greene with the poem "Cill [sic] My Landlord" and George Wolfe's play *The Colored Museum* with the character "Walter-Lee-Beau-Willie-Jones," whose "brow is heavy from three hundred years of oppression" (236). This parodic relationship suggests the black arts movement's power and influence over contemporary black artists. As Tony Jackson notes, you do not parody a failure.

Such parody of the movement's excesses is reminiscent of Dove's early poem "Upon Meeting Don L. Lee, in a Dream" (16), published in *The Yellow House in the Corner* (Lee, a key figure in the black arts movement, later changed his name to Haki Madhibuti).[2] Although Rampersad finds this poem "astonishing" in its hostility to the black arts movement (53), from Ellis's perspective it seems merely parodic, perhaps at most satiric, in its depiction of a key black arts movement poet as corrupt, decayed, and outmoded. It can be argued, however, that Ellis underplays the rejection of the black arts movement by NBA artists in characterizing it as parody and that such underplaying might indicate anxiety about affiliation. To use Baraka's arts-scene daughters as figures of the NBA, as Ellis does, supports a more psychoanalytic reading of his African American aesthetic genealogy, one which, as Harold Bloom would frame it, sees "intra-poetic relationships as parallels of family romance" (8).[3] Thus Dove's "hostile" poem on Lee can be read as exhibiting Bloom's classic "anxiety of influence," and Ellis's emphasis on the NBA parody of the black arts movement can be seen as denial of the true weight of NBA artists' "mis-readings" of black arts movement art.

The idea of a literary genealogy—inflected by race, culture, class, gender, and aesthetics—becomes critical for the cultural mulatto of the NBA and is apparent particularly in Dove's early work. In the absence of an articulated black cosmopolitan genealogy at the time (Posnock's book was published in 1998), the idea of a cultural mulatto black artist would seem to have been newly born from some interracial cultural miscegenation and thus might be of concern both to the artists and their audiences. The "hipness" of Ellis's formulation and essay—with its coffee-shop interviews, musician's gigs, and avant-garde art scene gossip—covers the pervasive anxiety just under the surface of the term *cultural mulatto,* an anxiety about "Where did I come from?" "Who are my parents?" "How did I become who I am?" "Will anyone understand me?" "How and where do I fit in?" and "Is there anyone else like me?" Although inflammatory, using the image of the cultural mulatto in this early phase of the contemporary period accurately embodies the suppressed fears of culturally mixed mulatto artists and intellectuals after the black essentialism and racial-cultural purism of the black arts movement who are concerned about being perceived as "half-white."

Dove's nonfiction prose especially reveals these anxieties about her position as a cultural mulatto articulating a genealogy for her work in African American poetry. Constructing such a literary lineage—a typical early stage for many artists—is complicated for Dove by race and gender. Hortense Spillers's essay "Mama's Baby, Papa's Maybe: An American Grammar Book" shows how African American genealogy has been shaped by the miscegenous rape of black slave women by their white masters—and thus can help reveal the complexity of, and anxiety behind, Dove's genealogical constructions. As Spillers points out, for many African Americans the father was often the white master; a denied paternity was paralleled by an undenied ownership of a child (76). Even when children were fathered by black men, paternal rights were dissolved in favor of the white master's property rights. Thus "a dual fatherhood is set in motion, comprised of the African father's *banished* name and body and the captor father's mocking presence" (80). Citing the work of Claude Meillassoux, Spillers observes, "[T]he offspring of the female does not 'belong' to the Mother, nor is s/he 'related' to the 'owner,' though the latter 'possesses' it, and in the African-American instance, often fathered it, *and,* as often, without whatever benefit of patrimony. In the social outline Meillassoux is pursuing, the offspring of the enslaved, 'being unrelated both to their begetters and to their owners . . . , find themselves in the situation of being orphans' (Meillassoux 50)" (74). Spillers argues that in the United States this situation created not orphans but black men and women "on the boundary, whose human and familial status, by the very nature of the case, had yet to be defined" (74). Dove's search to find and name her literary genealogy traverses this terrain of racial affiliation and white control and ultimately makes a place for herself and her work in African American letters.

Dove's criticism on other African American poets operates as a genealogy for her own poetry. Two particular pieces of nonfiction prose, "Telling It Like It I-S *IS:* Narrative Techniques in Melvin Tolson's *Harlem Gallery*" (1985) and "A Black Rainbow: Modern Afro-American Poetry" (coauthored with Marilyn Nelson Waniek and published in 1991), demonstrate her explicit recuperation of African American poetic forbears, what Sandra Gilbert would term her "literary father and mother." The two essays focus on Melvin B. Tolson and Gwendolyn Brooks and treat the black arts movement in black literary history as having more black psychological impact than aesthetic import.[4] A third essay, a review of Derek Walcott's *Collected Poems* entitled "'Either I'm Nobody, or I'm a Nation,'" discusses Dove's poetic negotiations in the figure of Derek Walcott, another cultural mulatto and thus a figure for many of her concerns. In Dove's literary genealogy, Walcott is a sort of elder brother whose work confirms that there is someone else like her. Together, these critical writings help in constructing the "family romance" explaining Dove's early self-imaging as a cultural mulatto, a role ultimately figured in her short story "The Spray Paint King."

The essay on Tolson is a remarkable defense of him as a black poet. Dove places his work firmly in the African American poetic tradition and bemoans its censure by black nationalists. Thus she claims an African American paternity for herself and her work, an important step in light of Spillers's articulation of the "maybe" role of black paternity in the United States as a result of slavery. The black male parent with whom she affiliates, however, is one whom some jeered as a sellout to white versions of high-modernist technique.[5] In the essay, Dove delineates the vastly differing black and white reactions to *Harlem Gallery* as indicative of the "crossfire" in which a black artist can be caught. Published in 1965, part one of *Harlem Gallery* met with "enthusiastic" response from the mainstream white audience and often angry dismissal by black critics excited by the burgeoning black aesthetic of the 1960s, which Dove defines as extolling "literature for the common people, a literature that was distinctly oral, using the language patterns and vocabulary of the street to arouse feelings of solidarity and pride among Afro-Americans" (109). Dove cites Paul Bremen's assessment as typical of African American response to *Harlem Gallery:* "'[Tolson] postured for a white audience, and . . . gave it just what it wanted: an entertaining darkey using almost comically big words as the best wasp tradition demands of its educated house-niggers'" (110). Such views, Dove argues, are unfair to Tolson's "virtuoso use of folk talk and street jive," which, as the balance of the essay shows, is central to his narrative technique in *Harlem Gallery.* Dove makes the poem relatively accessible by explaining its literary allusions and focusing on the "storytelling 'riffs' which are rooted in the Afro-American tradition" (111). She also demonstrates how, in the "controversy over racial loyalties," few were able to see that Tolson's poem drew on the complexities of the black oral tradition, just as the black aesthetic group was urging (110). At the end of a series of examples Dove finally breaks out with, "Can I get a Witness? Because what Tolson has been doing all along is testifying, which is nothing more than to 'tell the truth through story'" (114). She is testifying to the African American cultural, specifically oral, roots of Tolson's art.

Such a move makes a place for herself in African American literary history by establishing Tolson as a predecessor (she has also indicated his influence in *Thomas and Beulah,* in which she uses his

Harlem Gallery line "Black Boy, O Black Boy, / is the port worth the cruise?" as the epigraph to Thomas's section). Having located Tolson firmly in the African American poetic tradition, Dove then accounts for the cultural mix of references in his work that so infuriated black arts movement arbiters: "His references range from Balaam's ass to the game cock who thought he was chicken, from Byzantine texts to eggaroni. If anything, Tolson is deliberately complicating our preconceived notions of cultural—and by further implication, existential—order" (115). Dove could be explaining her own work in *Museum*. Her project, then, is a simple but very necessary one: In order for her work not to suffer the same rejection or dismissal as Tolson's, she must "correct" literary history in such a way that Tolson's work is made clear and its wide cultural milieu affirmed. She is "telling it like it I-S *IS*" so readers can see her work for what it is.

Dove's reading of the poem emphasizes its thematizing of the dilemma of the black artist in white America, which we can read as a mirror of her own early concerns. She sees the roles of the narrator (who, she reminds us, is a mulatto, an ex-professor of art, and the curator of Harlem Gallery) and his alter-ego Dr. Nkomo (whom she describes as "his stronger, more prideful counterpart") as playing out in their observations "a dialectic of the position of blacks—most specifically, the black artist—in white America" (111). Dove concludes her essay by reading "the lives of John Laugart, Hideho Heights and Mister Starks . . . as illustrations of the three possibilities/alternatives for the black artist" (116). These three characters from *Harlem Gallery* are emblems of the choices available to Tolson—and, by implication, to Dove herself. One can sell out to the (white) mainstream like Starks, be the "Poet Laureate of Harlem" like Hideho, or "remain uncompromising and be spurned by one's own" like Laugart (116). Dove believes that "it is John Laugart, the artist given least space in *Harlem Gallery,* who most exemplifies Tolson's own sense of artistic responsibility" (117). Like Laugart, Tolson "was misunderstood by many of those he loved most, by those to whom he dedicated his energies in the creation of his last work—the black intellectuals. No one understood this predicament better than Tolson himself" (117). In closing, she quotes Tolson's highly ironic summation of this theme in *Harlem Gallery:*

the Afroamerican dilemma in the Arts—
the dialectic of
to be or not to be
a Negro. (117)

Such a dialectic echoes Du Bois's cosmopolitan insistence on a dialectic between "the racial particular and the unraced universal" (Posnock 88). What Dove's reading of *Harlem Gallery* accomplishes is a moving beyond this dialectic to a synthesis that allows Tolson's work to transcend the debate over racial affiliation in art. In so doing, she makes a place for her own work.

∼

Recuperating Tolson, an individual artist, is one thing, but writing African American literary history is another. Dove's essay with Waniek offers a literary history for modern black poetry.[6] As such, it outlines key issues affecting African American poetry, such as audience, double-consciousness, vernacular speech, and black music, and then proceeds through the major periods of the twentieth century: the Harlem Renaissance, the post-Renaissance, the black arts movement, and contemporary poetry from the 1970s on (which Waniek and Dove stage as a "performance criticism" dialogue). In this survey Dove and Waniek emphasize the relative importance of Gwendolyn Brooks and Melvin B. Tolson, giving Brooks high praise and continuing Dove's resurrection of Tolson from the ash heap of African American literary history.

On the most basic level that is accomplished through the comparative length and depth of discussion allowed each poet. Although Langston Hughes is discussed (and fully) for six paragraphs in the Harlem Renaissance section, Dove and Waniek highly praise Gwendolyn Brooks for eight full paragraphs in the post-Renaissance section. Sterling Brown is positioned first in the post-Renaissance section but covered in only three paragraphs; in contrast, Melvin B. Tolson is discussed for six paragraphs. Clearly, Dove and Waniek see Brooks and Tolson as central and defining poets, not only in mid-century but also compared to the leading canonical figures of the African American poetic tradition as a whole. They place them with Robert Hayden, whose work the black arts movement poets attacked as too elite and not "black enough" but who merits seven paragraphs.[7]

This appreciation of Brooks and restoration of Tolson appears not only in the extended length of their discussions but also in the content. Of Brooks, they write of her "literary career most poets can only dream of." Moreover, "Her exquisite, word-intoxicated poems demonstrate her mastery of craft; her realistic portraits or working-class Black people demonstrate her insight and sympathy" (233–34). Significantly, Dove and Waniek focus solely on Brooks's early poetry and explicate only poems from *A Street in Bronzeville* and *Annie Allen*. As they explain it, "Her career took a sudden turn and fell under the detrimental influence of younger, more militant poets" (234). Later they assert, "None of Brooks' later work is equal in control or depth to the poems in her first three collections, though her willingness to experiment with poems more accessible to a Black audience is admirable" (236). These statements redefine Brooks's place in African American poetry by rejecting her post-1967 work and defining her contribution solely in terms of earlier poetry. "Her *earlier* work," they remark, "makes hers an important contribution to American letters" (234, emphasis added). Whether or not one agrees with their assessment, such a critical maneuver values craft and control over the black arts movement's emphases on reaching the people and furthering the revolution. Read through Dove's work, however, one can see her emphasis on Brooks's early poetry as constructing a necessary matrilineage for herself in African American poetic history.

Waniek and Dove's treatment of Tolson reprises Dove's analysis in "Telling It Like It I-S *IS*." They open their discussion with "Melvin B. Tolson's life as a scholar, poet, journalist, and teacher was dedicated to promoting and celebrating the cultural diversity of the Black race"; the essay continues that theme affirming his African American focus throughout (237). As in Dove's essay, they describe the black arts opposition to Tolson as "militant" and suggest it was unwarranted (239). In concluding their discussion of Tolson, Brooks, and Hayden, Waniek and Dove address the issue of "universality" that has so plagued these three: "Much has been made—often negatively—of the 'universality' of this generation of Black poets. The most striking thing about their work, when it is seen together, is the fact that by stripping their Black characters down to their central humanity, these poets made them the common denominator" (243). Rather than falsely universalizing the poets, Dove and Waniek instead recenter the universal in blackness (chapters 4, 5, and 6). Dove's project is to ensure that her lineage is read as black despite its affiliation with high modernist technique and the possible perception of being a cultural mulatto.

Given that Waniek and Dove showed their critical colors in the post-Renaissance section, it is no surprise that they entitle the black arts movement section of their volume "The Poetics of Rage" as an indication of their emphasis on the movement's psychosocial dimensions of black art. Backgrounding any technical issues in black poetry of the 1960s, Waniek and Dove foreground that poetry's role "as an important tool for consciousness-raising" (244). Ultimately, they assess the impact of the black arts movement as important because a "sense of pride in being Black remained" (255). They decenter the black arts movement away from Amiri Baraka by beginning their discussion of the period with a reclamation of Bob Kaufman, who began with the Beats and died in poverty and obscurity in 1985. Waniek and Dove applaud Kaufman's "wide" range and some of his technique (245), and Dove asserts that "his influence is coming back" (266). Waniek and Dove seem to admire Kaufman, whom they compare to Baraka: "Baraka's reaction [to racial oppression] and Kaufman's are the opposite sides of the spectrum. Baraka changed his name, killed his other self, and the anger, the rage, emerge . . . whereas Kaufman seemed to turn the rage on himself" (267). In contrast to their appraisal of Kaufman, the discussion of Baraka withholds any aesthetic appreciation of his poetry, instead emphasizing his public persona: "The most renowned Black Beat poet was LeRoi Jones" (247). Of Jones's transformation to Baraka, they observe, "Baraka's later poems are uneven and his Anti-Semitism and name-calling often embarrassing" (250). Quite a difference from the discussions of Brooks, Tolson, and Hayden.

Dove's rejection of Baraka as a poetic father deserves further discussion. It can be read with psychological, literary, and racial dimensions. Baraka and the black arts movement constitute an immediate and very influential context for Dove, who went to college in 1970, the year after Baraka's *Black Magic* was published (the volume most associated with his Black Arts phase). As she explains, "I remember, going to college in the beginning of the 70's, when there was still quite a bit of emphasis being placed on black poetry, and the fact that it had to pertain to black subjects, that it had to have lots of 'blackness' in it" (Peabody and Johnsen 6). The defining aesthetic of the time, in Maulana Karenga's words, was that black art must be "functional, collective, and committing [to the revolution]" (1973–74). Dove's rejection of this aesthetic frame for her poetry, and of Baraka as a poetic black father, can be read as constituting a "swerve" in the Bloomian sense of an overt avoidance to repress influence, a swerve that perhaps reveals anxiety about influence. One place this swerve is apparent is in Dove's poem about Don L. Lee. Rather than directly reject the central figure of the black arts movement, Dove swerves to an alternate black arts poet, Lee, thus avoiding direct acknowledgment of Baraka's connection to her poetic lineage.

The swerve also becomes apparent in Dove and Waniek's repression of the technical dimensions of Baraka's art. Their discussion fails to acknowledge his extensive affiliation with the poetic avant-garde in the 1950s, especially the influence of the Objectivist/Projectivist and Black Mountain groups of American poets William Carlos Williams, Charles Olson, Louis Zukofsky, and Robert Duncan. Furthermore, Waniek and Dove exhibit no appreciation of the technical merits of Baraka's poetry after he rejected the Beats and never discuss his adaptations of avant-garde poetics—or what William J. Harris terms his "jazzification" poetics. Such a discussion would bring Baraka's legacy to black poetry (and thus to Dove's poetry) too close for comfort. If Dove sets up a binary opposition between poetic craft and political consciousness-raising in her African American poetic history, then to keep Baraka on the side of politics refuses recognition of his technical merits as long as technique is identified with the lineage of high modernism.

Furthermore, Dove's refusal of Baraka as a black poetic father recalls Spillers's essay "Mama's Baby, Papa's Maybe," where she details the "dual fatherhood" set in motion for African Americans during slavery and "comprised of the African father's *banished* name and body and the captor father's mocking presence" (80). We can read Dove's chosen poetic patrilineage as reinscribing this dual paternity in Melvin B. Tolson and Amiri Baraka. Baraka represents the African father, whose "body" of work and influence is banished in favor of

Tolson's high modernist style that caused him to be read as affiliated with "white" poetic technique and signifies him as representing the captor's mocking presence. Dove's nascent awareness of the implications of these moves explains her anxious reclamation of Tolson as a black poet in the essay "Telling It Like It I-S *IS*." Moreover, Dove's work ultimately acknowledges Baraka's political legacy for her work, albeit in repressed forms (chapters 1 and 2).

Having established a version of African American poetic history that makes her work a reclamation of the aesthetic rigor and broad cultural sensibilities of poets of the 1940s and 1950s after the black pride of the 1960s, Dove communicates several aesthetic concerns in a discussion of Derek Walcott. In her review of Walcott's *Collected Poems*, "Either I'm Nobody, or I'm a Nation" (1987), she negotiates her concerns about poetic and racial affiliation and applauds Walcott's poetry. Walcott is emblematic of Dove's possible perception as a cultural mulatto. In using a West Indian as a vehicle for her concerns, Dove can explore from a distance those issues of racial and poetic affiliation that implicate her poetry. In using a black poet who had an English grandfather and a British education, she highlights the mulatto sensibility that her early aesthetic can be viewed as having.

Although Dove discusses Walcott as a Caribbean writer and repeatedly contextualizes his work as such, she also places him in the context of American poetry, both in this essay and in the essay with Waniek, as did Michael Harper and Robert Stepto in *Chant of Saints* (1974). Dove writes, "Walcott's poems stand out from the wash of contemporary American poetry," thus suggesting a rightful comparison with her own poetic context. Likewise, in the staged discussion section of the essay with Waniek, Dove argues that Walcott would belong in a hypothetical anthology of contemporary black American poets "because he now resides in the U.S. He's had a profound influence" (267). Waniek demurs, suggesting his influence has been mostly linguistic rather than thematic. Dove persists, however, citing his well-known poem "Sea Grapes," "which touches on the cultural schizophrenia of a Black poet" (268). Dove's comments suggest her identification with Walcott's work and his influence on her own work—especially on the theme of cultural affiliation.

Dove praises Walcott's language, calling it "boldy eloquent," "exquisite," "elaborate," and "lyrical" (49). Yet the main theme of her praise in the review focuses on the fact that he combines both of his heritages: "A true Renaissance man, Walcott has consistently resisted being cubbyholed. He has rejected neither his Caribbean heritage nor his British education" (49). The word *cubbyhole* echoes Dove's use of the word in her 1985 interview with Peabody and Johnsen, where she explained her resistance to being "cubbyholed" as a black poet: "Then you fall into a category where you're only compared to other black writers. How often have you seen blurbs like, 'This is the greatest black novel since *Invisible Man.*' I'm so tired of hearing stuff like that. Given my middle-class background, there were many experiences that I had which could not *only* have been experienced by blacks" (6). For Dove, Walcott offers a model of a cultural mulatto figure who has successfully negotiated his complex ancestry with integrity and poetic excellence. She refuses to cubbyhole him either, stating early in the review that the girth of his *Collected Poems* is "also a demand to consider the whole man—not just his skin or age or prosody or heart or mind" (50).

Dove acknowledges her affinities to Walcott in the review. In reading his volume *Another Life,* she reveals, she "recognized its major themes as chords in my own life: loss of innocence, the search for a heritage; the schizophrenia of assimilation, the writer as exile to his homeland and to his own. (Walcott's dilemma is also biological, as one of his grandfathers was British. In the oft-quoted 'A Far Cry from Africa' he asks: 'I who am poisoned with the blood of both, / Where shall I turn, divided to the vein?'). Until Walcott realizes that assimilation means embracing every culture around one, his early lyrics are often stilted and hollow" (54).

Dove's cosmopolitan view of Walcott emphasizes her own insistence on being what Georgoudaki terms a "world citizen," free to include any culture and its materials in her art. She also, unlike black arts movement artists, clearly sees assimilation as a positive force, an "embracing" of even the colonizer's culture. Such a viewpoint is apparent in a 1994 interview with Emily Lloyd. In discussing her verse play *The Darker Face of the Earth* (and affirming her cosmopolitan stance), Dove points out that although integration would have been an unrealistic goal in the antebellum South, now "I would say that integration is not only plausible but necessary if we are to survive" (1). Dove explicitly ties such cultural amalgamation to Walcott's poetic virtuosity in rejecting his earliest work, which "struggles to unite conflicting traditions," as stilted and hollow (52). She claims poetry as a life-saving order for a black prodigy, both herself and Walcott: "A prodigy and a black, [Walcott] saw his dilemma early; a poet, he knew that the iambic line, with its thumbholds of word and image, was his thread out of the labyrinth" (53).

∼

Dove's negotiations of cultural affiliation and art coalesce in her early short story "The Spray Paint King," which might be termed her portrait of a contemporary young black artist as a cultural mulatto. The story's issues—mixed cultural influences, the politics of aesthetics, and questions of racial affiliation and identification—express Dove's anxieties as a poet in the vanguard of the NBA. The central figure, a graffiti artist, is being held in a "detention home for youthful offenders" (*Fifth Sunday* 21). Dove bases the narrative on entries in the journal his psychiatrist has him keep, which readers get to read as witnesses to the classic therapeutic process of uncovering repression and getting to the "source" of the symptoms. In doing so, Dove thematizes her early repression of the blackness of the black arts movement and Baraka.

Dove erects several roadblocks to reading this story as her *künstlerroman,* roadblocks that further suggest repression of anxieties. She positions the immediate, fictional "audience" of the journal as a blonde, "down-home German girl," Doctor Severin, who is the Spray Paint King's psychiatrist (14). If readers hold any pretensions of accepting the story as a psychological window into Dove, just as Doctor Severin would read the young artist's journal as a key to unlocking his psyche, Dove makes it uncomfortable to do so. The young artist's comments to the doctor (and thus to the readers) repeatedly point out the potential for racial bias and undermine credibility as a valid reader and interpreter of his/Dove's psyche. From the beginning of the story, where he depicts her as a "[b]itch with pad and pencil doodling cocks in the margin" (14), Doctor Severin appears an embodiment of the racially pure, blonde-haired, blue-eyed Aryan fascinated by the young artist's racially mixed background and, of course, his sexuality. As an arm of the State, she "wants to ease [him] back into society" (22). By the end of the story, when the young artist predicts Doctor Severin's diagnosis, we do not trust it as fully authoritative or neutral. Imbricated with racial and national assumptions and agendas, her reading of the artist, and thus ours of Dove, seems suspect.

There are compelling reasons, however, to read the young Spray Paint King as a figure of cultural mulatto engaging history through art and thus, by extension, as an early figure for Dove's cosmopolitanism. First, all the representations of Doctor Severin's views of him are conjectured by the artist, just as Dove may be conjecturing what readers or academics may think of her. The artist guesses what Doctor Severin thinks of him, for it does not appear in the dialogue. He assumes that she cannot "look a little further than [his] crinkly hair" (14). He likes to think that "[c]ertainly Dr. Severin considers the possibility that [he] might, one day, pull her onto the shrink-couch: she considers the possibility with a mixture of thrilling curiosity and propitious dread" (18). Such views possibly say more about how he sees himself than her actual attitudes toward him. Because the young artist's thoughts seem to be (as perhaps many seventeen-year-olds are) repeatedly focused on sex, this implies that his biases may be coloring his representation of Doctor Severin's supposed sexual fascination with him. Thus, the doctor's racial and sexual obsessions can be read as functions of the perceiver rather than the perceived, of the young artist rather than any real attitudes on the part of the doctor. In this sense the narrative functions much like a Browning dramatic monologue in which we learn a great deal about the speaker by getting to "overhear" his discourse to another.

A second reason to read the Spray Paint King as a figure for Dove as an artist lies in her additions to the historical events from which the story arose. As she explains in the Peabody and Johnson interview, "The story was based on actual paintings, sprayings that I had seen around Cologne and other German cities. They caught the person finally—he was not at all a mulatto or anything like that. It was a Swiss guy who went through Europe spraying his paintings on public walls. But by that time I didn't care about that kind of verisimilitude anymore" (7). Thus the racially mixed background of the central character is purely Dove's addition, suggesting a central concern on her part about the relationship between the cultural mulatto and society/history as it appears in his/her art. In the story, Dove makes the artist a quadroon (one-quarter black). His racial and cultural mix provides the central dynamic of both his graffiti art and the story, which is the story behind his art.

The narrative charts the young artist's mixed genealogy and reactions to him as a mulatto and an artist. In 1945 his white grandmother had met the black soldier who would become his grandfather; her subsequent reaction to the "caramel-colored face of her new daughter" was "despair" (18). Being from Dresden, the grandmother "had never set eyes on a black person before" (18). Doves places this interracial contact in the context of World War II and Hitler to highlight how Aryan ideals about racial purity would shape and constrict the acceptance of blacks. Children taunt the young artist and call him "Negerlein" as his skin darkens during kindergarten (18). Displacing such an issue onto Germany allows Dove to explore an issue that affects American culture but not encounter reader resistance or assumptions. That the view of contact with blacks as defilement is a legacy passed on to the mulatto child becomes apparent when the grandmother and her daughter are placed on a U.S. Army truck: "A Negro M.P. was loading the refugees; my mother [the baby daughter] began to cry when his hands reached for her; she did not stop until, smiling, he drew on white gloves" (19). Thus the young artist's mixed racial ancestry carries a rejection of blackness as implicitly "unclean" on the part of his mulatto mother, who, unlike her son, "lightened as she aged" (18). Such lightening is depicted literally as well as figuratively, for she is twice linked to washing and soapsuds (as if trying to wash away her blackness), and she is married to a white man.

Just as Freudian theory predicts, however, what has been repressed returns. "The Negro blood is more prominent in me," the Spray Paint King observes, "in fact, than in my mother. From a very light baby with a cheesy complexion, I darkened during kindergarten. It began at the ears and descended with frightening rapidity to the neck (pale coffee). Lines appeared in my palms like lemon juice scribblings held over a flame. The hair, so fine and wispy, crinkled" (18). In this passage blackness is depicted like secret writing being revealed—"scribblings held over a flame"—thus linking the expression of repressed blackness with the process of writing. As blackness emerges in him, the young artist engages it in his surroundings, symbolized in the coal his mother asks him to haul from the cellar. At first he is "frightened," but eventually he begins to "linger" (15). The black coal fascinates him, that "blackness undiluted, one hundred percent," for it represents a part of him repressed in both his family and his nation (16). In the masturbation scene, Dove writes of the boy ejaculating against coal, which signifies his growing awareness of, affiliation with, and desire for control over the blackness within him.

The young artist's father offers a legacy in conflict with his son's black lineage, not solely because the father is white but because of his participation in the cultural processes by which the dominant culture writes history. At eleven (a year after the coal cellar visits begin), the son learns of his father's role in building the Severin Bridge. (Tellingly, the young artist dubs his psychiatrist by the same name, perhaps to indicate that he perceives her as complicit in this cultural process. The root of the name, "sever," means to cut off, and both Severins participate in a cultural "cutting off" that affects the young artist. The word also suggests an Oedipal anxiety about castration.) Searching beyond his father's "official" explanation, the boy uncovers what the dominant version of history does not tell: "Five men were buried in one of the cement pilings" (19). Their names are not prominently recorded in history. Instead, the bridge is named after "Saint Severin of the eleventh century, whose bones lie boxed in gold in a church on the south side of the city" (14). This story, like the volumes *Museum* and *Thomas and Beulah,* critiques the near-erasure and repression of the unempowered in history. The Spray Paint King's white father participates in this process, as the scene reveals. The boy says to his mother:

> "They fell into a hole while pouring concrete. The others kept pouring . . ."
> For a moment my mother hesitated, her hands quiet in the water. Then her face hardened. "That's your father's territory," she replied. "Ask him." Bending over, she attacked the laundry with renewed energy, wringing the sheets.
> "What did you want us to do," Dad said, leaning back in his armchair, "stop production and dig them out?" (20)

The scene offers a wonderful confluence of the contradictory forces of this young artist's inheritances. He discovers his father's role in burying, both literally and figuratively, five men—in the bridge and also in history, if one views history as a kind of cultural recognition. The mother knows that (her face hardens like the concrete her husband poured), just as she knows about the repression of blackness within herself and the family. Yet she is not part of the process; such public repressions of the unknown and "unimportant" are her husband's, the white man's, territory. The mother's erasures, more private and domestic, are rendered in the laundry she attacks with "renewed energy" and the sheets she attempts to clean, representing the interracial sexual unions begetting herself and her son as well as hinting at the winding sheets that wrap the dead buried in the bridge and in history. The father's nonchalant response reifies the importance of capitalist—and by implication historical and cultural, production—in his worldview. The key scene leaves the mulatto artist with a conflicted legacy. Affiliating with the white father and the black-erasing mother, although seemingly "clean," means burial of his blackness and acceptance of the burial of others who are similarly unempowered. Affiliating with the blackness to which he is drawn defiles the seeming purity and reasonableness of the parents' worldview and those of the dominant culture and the State. Such is the complicated inheritance of this cultural mulatto.

Thus, as the young artist tells it, "the itch built up inside of me, . . . I tried to ignore it at first and *act responsibly*, then learned to welcome its presence and nurture it, prime it, hone the vague desires to a single jubilant swoop, one vibrant gesture" (21, emphasis in the original). The mulatto's art, he knows, is an act of subversion against the dominant culture, the State, and a defilement of its myths of purity and reason. He begins painting his graffiti—black paint on white walls—on "the building calling with its face blank as snow awaiting defilement" (21). The paintings are a reverse of his ejaculation against the black coal and instead spray black against whiteness. One scene reveals the official response:

> Yesterday the street cleaners, under orders from the city, prepared to erase one of my sprayings with XR–3, the chemical abrasive concocted to eliminate political graffiti left over from the student movement. The spraying in question, nicknamed "Space Flower" by the press, blooms on the façade of a prominent bank; this plant with its dagger stamens and cone-shaped appendages arcs in perfect imitation of a statue poised beside it, a bronze replica of the bank's first president.

> The street cleaners moved in early—around 6 A.M.—hoping to
> avoid a confrontation. But news had leaked; already grouped around
> the statue, in a neat but impenetrable mass, were the apprentices
> from the art academy, many non-partisan radicals and some Young
> Socialists.
> Supposedly no one said a word. A fine cold rain began. After a few
> minutes, the cleaners turned on their heels and drove away. (20)

The government's response is that the Spray Paint King's art has
defiled the building, which must be cleaned. Dove links it to political graffiti through the chemical devised to remove it, and rightly so,
as the "dagger" stamens of his "imitation" of the bank president's
statue pinpoint the cutthroat nature of the banking business and the
natural, organic shapes reveal the metallic rigidity of the president's
capitalist organization. Political, indeed. The statue beside "Space
Flower," moreover, underlines the dangerous liaison between public, officially sanctioned art that reproduces the dominant ideology's
values and the institutions it upholds, such as banks. Dove neatly
highlights the differing official attitudes to the two artistic versions
of the bank president in a permanent bronze statue and in a black,
spray-painted wall that the city wants desperately to erase.

The figure of the cultural mulatto negotiates a blackness that is
not only racial but also metaphoric of the blackness of historical and
social erasure and the repression of unsanctioned, "unclean" truths.
The whiteness he negotiates is the agent of those erasures, the white-
out of repression that makes blackness invisible. Near the end of the
story, the young artist's description of how he imagines five men
falling to their deaths in cement solidifies that connection: "First there
is the blue of the air as they fall, open-mouthed, open-eyed, toward
a deeper blue. Then the red of impact, the stunned blow as their
mouths fill and capillaries pop. And then, for the longest kind of time,
the black before death and then the black of dying, the black of metal
before it is painted sea green and the black of the sea green metal
against the sun, an unfinished web" (22). Blackness becomes covered
by the sea-green "official" color of the bridge, which represents society and history's cover-up of the men's deaths and lives. It is a good
description of the limits of traditional universalism, which covers up
difference and individuality. The mulatto Spray Paint King seeks to
put the black back. As he puts it, "Oh citizens who have forgotten, I

was there to remind you, I put the stain back on the wall" (22). The stain of emphasizing production over human connection, the stain of repressing the workers' death, and the stain of oppressing blacks or "others" whose existence challenges the dominant ideas of racial, social, and cultural purity—these are truths the spray king's art seeks to make visible.

In this story Dove's early repression of the black arts movement and Amiri Baraka emerges in the blackness that the mulatto artist sprays on the wall. Dove's inheritance from Baraka and the black arts movement, to recover the unempowered in history and to stain the officially sanctioned art of the mainstream, finds representation in the figure of the Spray Paint King, in whom the blackness—and the political impulse—comes out. (In a nod to the strong masculinism of the movement, Dove images this expression in the phallus and ejaculation.) He is the return of what she has seemingly repressed in her African American poetic genealogy, a political artist who is functional, collective, and committing and whose artistic technique is deprecated by the dominant aesthetic milieu as political graffiti. Echoing Ellis's insistence that the NBA's cultural mulatto artists are black, Dove asserts that the mulatto Spray Paint King is black. When, near the end of the story, he fantasizes about going down to get coal as a child and thereby surviving the "Big Bomb" that destroys everyone else, and Doctor Severin points out, "'The coal saves you—your black blood'" (22), Dove's recognition of a black lineage is made palpable. Although she may not overtly recognize him in her aesthetic genealogy, she recognizes Baraka and the black arts movement in the thematic impulses of her earliest *künstlerroman*. Thus this story encourages a balanced understanding of her multiple, although sometimes seemingly conflicting, inheritances.

Notes

1. Dove stresses the class basis for many of the tensions surrounding her work in an interview with Therese Steffen ("The Darker Face of the Earth"). Ross Posnock acknowledges the class factor in the cosmopolitan tradition he traces, noting that the vast majority of the main figures were middle class or above. And Trey Ellis's essay overtly specifies the elite dimensions of the NBA crowd. Class issues are discussed in chapters 4, 5, and 6.

2. Both Ekaterini Georgoudaki (*Race, Class, Gender*) and Arnold Ram-

persad point out this poem and its anti-black arts movement implications but not in relation to the NBA.

3. Both Ellis and his probable source, Greg Tate, reject the possibility of "anxiety of influence" in NBA artists (Tate 207).

4. Lynn Keller's excellent chapter on Dove and Brenda Marie Osbey also surveys these important early essays, although not to construct a literary genealogy for Dove.

5. One irony Dove does not pursue in her essay is that Tolson himself was a principal attacker of Robert Hayden at the first Fisk University Writers' Conference (Coniff 487; Farnsworth 297–98).

6. One problem with Waniek's and Dove's version of African American poetic history is that it overlooks the contributions of black women poets across the century. No women poets of the Harlem Renaissance are mentioned. This may be because the article, although published in 1991, was actually written in the mid-1980s (in 1985 or 1986 according to Fred Viebahn, Rita Dove's husband, personal communication, Jan. 29, 2002), before Maureen Honey's excellent reassessment of Harlem Renaissance women poets (*Shadowed Dreams* 1989). Women, however, are not represented very fully elsewhere in the essay. The only black arts movement poets discussed are male: Kaufman, Baraka, and Knight. Across the Harlem Renaissance, post-Renaissance, and black arts movement, only two women poets receive attention: Gwendolyn Brooks and Margaret Walker. All told, they receive only nine paragraphs in twenty-six pages of text. Such a male-centered discussion of African American poetry is surprising in the contemporary period, especially when done by two women. In contrast, their overview of contemporary black poets amply includes women. Viebahn points out that Dove was aware of some of the female poets not mentioned, but they were left out because she viewed their work as meriting little attention (personal communication, Jan. 29, 2002).

8. See the *Dictionary of Literary Biography* entry by Norma R. Jones on Hayden, for example; see also Brian Coniff and Robert M. Farnsworth.

Rita Dove's verse drama *The Darker Face of the Earth* is a curious text
in her oeuvre. Curious because although its first edition publication
date was 1994, it originated, Dove says, in 1979, which places it with her
earliest work (Appendix, page 162; personal communication with Fred
Viebahn, Jan. 29, 2002). Furthermore, after its initial publication it was
substantially rewritten, resulting in what is described on the cover of
the 1996 version as a "completely revised second edition." Such a process of thinking, writing, and rewriting spanning almost twenty years
of a career offers an important view into Dove's thematizing of her cosmopolitanism in the poetic figure of the cultural mulatto.

Such a long process also suggests struggle. Although Dove admits
that some of the impetus for the 1996 revision came from putting the
play into production (Appendix, page 159), that accounts for only a
small portion—two years—of the writing process. The play's history
is a struggle between burial and expression; after writing it in the early
1980s, Dove says, she "put it away." It was only because her husband,
Fred Viebahn, "kept bugging [her] every five years or so to do something that [she] finally rewrote it and Storyline Press published it in
1994" (Appendix, page 160). Even then Dove viewed the play as a repressed text in her oeuvre, thinking "when I was dead someone would
[perform] it out of pity or whatever" (Appendix, page 160). The comment suggests an unconscious wish that the play remain buried. *The
Darker Face of the Earth* has had an extended writing process because
it presents an African American primal scene that Dove has anxiously
repressed—and symptomatically expressed—throughout her oeuvre.

Freud saw primal scenes as originary traumas explaining adult
neuroses. In "The Case of the Wolf Man" the primal scene Freud in-

ferred was that of a patient who, at the age of one and a half, had seen his parents copulating. Unable to comprehend the scene, he interpreted it as a violent castration of the mother and thus repressed the memory. Various symptoms resulted from this repression. Freud believed that discovering this kind of primal scene during the course of psychoanalytic therapy could lift repression and resolve neurotic symptoms. Discovery of the primal scene, however, is aided by the therapist, for patients' repression is such that they cannot consciously remember the event. As Ned Lukacher, in his redevelopment of the idea of the primal scene for literary analysis, asserts, in the notion of the primal scene "Freud developed a theory of the unsaid and a technique for discovering the tropes and figures that determine the shape of a patient's discourse but that the patient himself can never remember. The patient's speech 'remembers,' while the patient himself remains oblivious and utterly resists all the analyst's efforts to bring the 'memory' to consciousness" (12). Although perhaps overstating the lack of awareness on the part of the patient, that description remains useful in reading texts with an eye to apprehending their repressed primal scene. For Lukacher, the critic of a literary text plays a similar analyst role with respect to the "patient-text": "Interpretation is always a kind of listening or reading that enables one to translate one set of words into another. The voice of the text, like the voice of the patient, is a verbal mask that conceals forgotten words and the forgotten scenes they compose" (68). The critic can read the text's discourse as a key to discovering its forgotten primal scene.

Among critics who use the idea of the primal scene in literary analysis there is some difference of opinion as to the "realness" of the repressed event. Jennifer L. Holden-Kirwan writes of Beloved's experience of the Middle Passage as her primal scene in Toni Morrison's *Beloved,* maintaining a direct connection among experience, repressed memories of the horrors, and Beloved's behavior. Likewise, Ashraf H. A. Rushdy writes of the primal scene throughout Morrison's works as "the critical event (or events) whose significance to the narrated life becomes manifest only at a secondary critical event, when by a preconscious association the primal scene is recalled" (303). In contrast, Lukacher, following Freud's doubts about the reality of the repressed events, argues (paraphrasing Althusser) *"there is no subject to the primal scene"* (13, emphasis in the original). He redefines the notion of the primal scene as:

> a trope for reading and understanding. . . . In my use of the term it becomes an intertextual event that displaces the notion of the event from the ground of ontology. It calls the event's relation to the Real into question in an entirely new way. Rather than signifying the child's observation of sexual intercourse, the primal scene comes to signify an ontologically undecidable intertextual event that is situated in the differentiated space between historical memory and imaginative construction, between archival verification and interpretive freeplay." (24)

Thus, for Lukacher, the actuality of the primal scene is irrelevant, a combination of historical memory and imaginative construction. Finding the truth of the primal scene, the origin of the symptoms, is endlessly deferred in texts. For critics, the interpretive role of reading the discourse of the text, of piecing together symptoms revealed in words, plot, and imagery, is an intertextual process of constructing a narrative about a primal scene. Lukacher sees the primal scene as "always the primal scene of words. At its most elemental the primal scene becomes the primal *seme"* (68, emphasis in the original). Yet it is important to "discover" the primal scene for relevant texts, for "the primal scene is that without which the symptoms could not have developed" (33).

Lukacher's adaptation of Freud has useful strategies for interpreting Dove's work. To borrow Lukacher's phrasing, we can read her texts with an ear to "discovering the tropes and figures that determine the shape of [her] discourse" (12). In such a process the primal scene we can infer in *The Darker Face of the Earth* helps in understanding key tropes and figures persistent from her earliest work. Specifically, the trope of sexual miscegenation articulates an African American primal scene of cultural amalgamation. This primal scene has been repressed and long-deferred in Dove's work, appearing symptomatically across her oeuvre in an incest motif. That an incest motif expresses the repressed primal scene becomes clear in the discourse of several Dove texts that deploy the same figurative language in each incest scene, as well as in the ultimate primal scene in *The Darker Face of the Earth.*

Dove's incest motif, and the primal scene of cultural mixing to which it returns, is a perhaps unconscious dimension of her thematizing of a cultural mulatto poetic persona in her early work. The anxieties of presenting a cultural mulatto poetic persona are so significant for a post–black arts movement black writer—and the idea of cultural mixing so unpleasant to some in a post–black arts movement black audience—that a primal scene of such cultural mixing would be repressed, causing "neurotic symptoms" in texts. Claudia Tate, in her groundbreaking *Psychoanalysis and Black Novels: Desire and the Protocols of Race,* explains the pressures on black writers writing in a racialized society and provides a psychoanalytic dimension that can be applied to Posnock's arguments about the repression of cosmopolitanism in the tradition. Drawing on the comments of Toni Morrison, who asserts that a black writer is always conscious of representing his or her race, Tate states, "This condition marks the text, even in those instances in which the text is not otherwise racially designated. Furthermore, such works inscribe a process by which the respective author negotiates explicit, public, racial identifications—or what I am calling *the protocols of race*—with the implicit, private psychological effects of narrative subjectivity" (10, emphasis added).

Tate thus depicts African American writers as navigating a demanding terrain of racial and cultural affiliation not always congruent with their desires and subjectivities (13). When a text fails to meet the socially sanctioned protocols of traditional black literature, it and its author face racial censure; the text often becomes an anomaly that is repressed in the tradition (9). Posnock would argue that many of these repressed texts are of the cosmopolitan tradition.

For Dove, the tension between individual desire and the protocols of race plays out against the backdrop of the black arts movement. As Tate notes, although not in reference to Dove specifically, "When protest-oriented directives dominated the African American critical viewpoint, a literary work of even renowned black authorship risked intraracial censure if it failed to manifest the sociological factors of an oppressive 'black experience'" (4). Black nationalist prescriptions for literature dominant during the 1960s and 1970s included, in Maulana Karenga's words, that it be "functional, collective, and committing"— meaning that it function as a tool of the revolution, be of and for black people, and commit itself and its audience to the revolution (1973–74).

Dove came of age during this period and began college in 1970. She has commented on her feelings about the era in several interviews, most extensively in an interview with Therese Steffen in 1998. Responding to a question about the black arts movement, she said, "The insistence on black art is just a device, a way of establishing territory or generating publicity. It was necessary at one time to underscore that 'otherness' in order to get any kind of respect whatsoever, but the insistence on difference also requires one to erect certain walls or obey certain rules—all of which is anathema to the artist" (108). Dove acknowledges as well that she was "incredibly excited about some aspects of the Black Arts Movement. . . . [such as] the syncopation of jazz, the verbal one-upmanship of signifying or the dozens" (108). Ultimately, she was very concerned about the "political fray" and reveals, "I shied away from publishing early poems like 'Agosta the Winged Man and Rasha the Black Dove' because I didn't think I was strong enough to withstand the political fallout. I didn't want to have to answer questions from Black Arts people like, 'Why are you writing about a white-German!-artist?' I waited; I stepped out as a writer later, when things became more tolerant" (108). Thus the possible sanctions for disobeying protocols of black literature were potentially traumatic enough for Dove to suppress publication of a poem that might garner disapproval. Such a move suggests that unconscious repression might be operative in her art as well.

The pressures on twentieth-century African American writers generally (and post–black arts movement writers especially) to follow racial protocols, writing within the protest theme or on overtly black American subject matter, cause very real tensions. Furthermore, stepping outside such protocols can be traumatic because the writers risk intraracial attack for abandoning the race. For Rita Dove, a cosmopolitan writer presenting a cultural mulatto poetic persona at the forefront of the new black aesthetic, cultural amalgamation thus becomes an originary moment that must be repressed. To acknowledge cultural mixing openly threatens the exclusivity-of-blackness mantra dominant when she began writing.[1] Furthermore, Dove's work suggests such repression of a primal scene of cultural amalgamation operates not only on the individual level for the cosmopolitan black artist but also perhaps for African Americans generally, who may reject cultural mixing as a threat to blackness and group solidarity.[2]

The idea of cultural amalgamation—a difficult concept for which to find an image, being so intangible—finds articulation in Dove's work in sexual miscegenation, both voluntary and involuntary (rape). Her writing displaces cultural mixing onto the physical and biological mixing of races. The "open secret" of miscegenation from America's slavery past thereby offers a trope for cultural miscegenation, giving birth to the cultural mulatto figure of the late twentieth and early twenty-first century.

The title of *The Darker Face of the Earth* comes from lines in the play depicting an interracial rape: "When the pear blossoms / cast their pale faces on / the darker face of the earth" (1st ed. 76). The lines are spoken by the mulatto protagonist Augustus in a creation tale he spins in explanation of his conception. The use of the word *cast* suggests some degree of violence or force used by the "pale faces" upon the "darker face[s]," thus depicting the rapes of so many black women by white men during the antebellum period. That involuntary miscegenation is balanced in the text by the voluntary, miscegenous relationships of the white plantation mistress, Amalia, first with the slave Hector and then with her son by Hector, Augustus. Both kinds of sexual miscegenation—voluntary and involuntary—explain the creation of the mulatto Augustus. His mother Amalia voluntarily pursued a miscegenous relationship with Hector in response to her husband, Louis, raping slave girls (1st ed. 14–16).[3]

The play opens with the birth of Augustus to the white slave mistress Amalia Jennings LaFarge, who was impregnated by the black slave Hector. Augustus is clearly mixed racially; Amalia's husband Louis LaFarge is furious (even though he has been raping slave girls), so Augustus cannot be acknowledged as Amalia's child. They tell everyone he died at birth, and the doctor takes him away to be raised a slave. Hector is devastated. Twenty years later (about as long as it took for this play to develop), after an extended period of education and travel with a fatherly white master that has given him a "mix" of cultural experiences, Augustus is bought by the Jennings plantation despite the fact that it has had a recent rebellion. He and Amalia begin an affair (he does not know she is his mother, believing instead to have been born of a slave woman who had been raped by her white master). Another woman, the slave Phebe, expresses interest in a relationship with him, and the slave Scylla warns of impending doom. When Augustus becomes involved in an insurrection plot he accidentally kills Hector (whom he does not realize is his father) to prevent him from revealing the plot. In the end, he has not followed through on orders from the rebels, and his position has been compromised because he has been ordered to kill Amalia. After he does kill Louis LaFarge, thinking that he is his father, Augustus learns from Amalia that she and Hector are his parents—a fact she has just realized. How and whether he and Amalia die, or live, depend on the edition of the play.

The sexual miscegenation in Augustus' origins and relationship with Amalia is distinctly linked to Augustus' creation as a cultural mulatto. Echoing Lukacher's assertion that the primal scene is an "ontologically undecidable intertextual event that is situated in the differentiated space between historical memory and imaginative construction" (24), Augustus' biological mixing due to the historical reality of sexual mixing is inflected with Dove's early artistic anxieties about cultural mixings.[4] His cultural mixing, in the first edition of the play, causes conflicting loyalties that lead to his death. Although he knows slave culture, he also speaks of Greek and Roman gods, the French Revolution, and John Milton. Dove emphasizes that his surrogate parenting by a white master, Captain Newcastle, exposed him to travel and multiple cultures. Augustus values these experiences and tells Phebe, "[It's n]othing you couldn't learn / if you had the chance" (1st ed. 44).

That Augustus' cultural amalgamation is imbued with Dove's own early poetic self-fashioning as a cultural mulatto becomes clear in Amalia's appraisal of him as "a poet / as well as a rebel" (1st ed. 65). In "Oedipus in America," the program for the Kennedy Center production of the play in 1997, Dove expresses her sense of Augustus's nascent poetic identity and provides a parallel with herself: "In a different world, Amalia (the Jocasta figure) might have been a woman of independent means and Augustus (who recalls Oedipus) a poet" (10).

Dove's anxiety accompanying Augustus' role as a cultural, not just biological, mulatto is made manifest in the plot developments of the first edition. Beyond his dual educations, a fact established immediately upon his arrival at the Jennings plantation, Augustus' dual—and contradictory— relationships on the plantation chart a difficult course for him. The play traces the developing romantic relationship with Amalia alongside a series of undeveloped and/or truncated relationships within the slave community. Augustus engages the interests of

Phebe but does not pursue a romantic relationship with her; he rejects Scylla's prophetic warnings as irrelevant hocus pocus; instead of protecting and caring for the aging Hector (his father), he accidently kills him; and he half-heartedly signs on as part of a rebel plot yet fails to follow through on his responsibilities and is ultimately murdered alongside Amalia as a traitor. Such divided loyalties depict a problematic relationship between the cultural mulatto and the black community.

In each instance, Augustus' undeveloped or failed relationships with slaves are a direct result of his developed relationships with whites. He does not pursue Phebe because he is involved with Amalia; he perceives Scylla's voodoo with the skepticism of Western empiricism inculcated by his white master/father figure Captain Newcastle; he kills Hector while trying to silence his warning to Amalia that she is in danger, something Hector senses when Augustus speaks her name; and he does not complete his assignments for the rebels because he is sleeping with Amalia. Dove's anxieties about the price of being perceived as a cultural mulatto artist within the black literary community imaginatively construct Augustus' plot into a Greek tragedy. An exceptional, larger-than-life individual rises to great heights but suffers a reversal of fortunes because of a fatal flaw: He abandons, or is perceived to abandon, the race and is censured by other blacks. The plot indicates a cosmopolitan writer's fear of being perceived as a cultural mulatto.

It took Dove fifteen years to see this plot depicting fear about cultural amalgamation and intraracial censure—a primal scene for the cultural mulatto and an African American primal scene generally—in print. She conceived of the play during the late 1970s, but the first edition was not published until 1994. Read through the lens of the primal scene in *The Darker Face of the Earth*, two of her earliest works demonstrate the presence of the tropes and figures of this constellation of cultural amalgamation and miscegenation, although neither develops into an expression as does the scene in *The Darker Face*.

In her first volume of poems, *The Yellow House on the Corner* (1980), one poetic sequence, "A Suite for Augustus," echoes the image pattern of sexual miscegenation. Washington, D.C., the Washington Monument, and the Reflecting Pool are described as "a postcard framed by imported blossoms— / and now this outrageous cue stick / lying, reflected, on a black table" (26). That this is an image of interracial rape is suggested in the word *outrageous* and further supported by the phallic image of a cue stick "lying" on a "black table," which represents the involuntarily subdued position of a black female during rape. Two more details in this series—the poetic persona describes her heart as a "shy mulatto" (29) and Dove's use of the Augustus figure—both suggest nascent awareness of the anxieties more fully articulated in *The Darker Face of the Earth*. The second exploration of cultural mixing is in the short story "The Spray Paint King," which was written and published in *Gargoyle* shortly after publication of *The Yellow House* and later published in *Fifth Sunday* in 1985.

After these two early instances, however, Dove seemingly forgot about the issue of cultural amalgamation and its trope of sexual miscegenation for almost ten years, from 1985 to 1994. Instead, it emerged symptomatically in an incest motif that appears across the genres in her oeuvre: in the short story "Aunt Carrie," closing the collection *Fifth Sunday* (1985); in the poem "Taking in Wash," opening the Beulah section of the long poem *Thomas and Beulah* (1986); and again in the last thirty pages of her novel *Through the Ivory Gate* (1992). Finally, of course, it leads Dove to *The Darker Face of the Earth* (1994 and 1996), where the incest motif is revealed to be a symptomatic expression of a primal scene of cultural amalgamation.

The three incest episodes in Dove's work share a pattern of figuration: sheets being washed, a handkerchief ("hanky") that has a rose in its corner, and the difference in skin tones between a pale male and a dark female. In each case, acts of repression are part of the plot or character development.[5]

"Aunt Carrie"—the short story—is about a young woman visiting her aunt for some answers to a childhood moment that she has never understood and that happened in a train station. As she presses the aunt to explain, she intuits, "I was very close to the secret—if I only persisted" (62). The secret comes out slowly. When Aunt Carrie was widowed in her early adulthood, it is revealed, she moved back home and had a series of sexual encounters with her younger brother, Ernest (Ernie), the young woman's father. Their affair lasted over a spring and summer until Carrie decided it was not right and stopped it. This family "secret" of incest was later discovered by his wife, well into their marriage. Their daughter vaguely remembers the awkward scene at the train station when her mother confronted Ernest with her knowledge by bringing Carrie to the station.

The first occasion of sex between the brother and sister occurs on a day she had "been washing sheets" and hanging them on the line to dry (64). He comes to help her with them and offers to help her make the bed. Here the implication of sheets signifying sexual union becomes literally true, for it provides the opportunity for them to have sex. There is ironic tension between the clean sheets "flicking" her shins at the clothesline and then her undressing in the bathroom while she "could still feel that sheet beating against [her]" (65). Knowing that incest is an "unclean" act heightens awareness of the taboo she is violating. Furthermore, as Aunt Carrie tells her "secret" to the niece she dabs at her eyes with a handkerchief, "small and white with a pink rose in one corner" (61). As she works the handkerchief, "[s]ometimes the rose could be seen among the twisted ends of the cotton, a delicate blemish" (61). The word *hanky* connotes "hanky-panky," or naughty sexual play.[6] The feminine image of the rose, here specifically pink, acts as a figure of female genitalia, sexuality, and, ironically, idealized womanhood. That it is a "delicate blemish" suggests the sullying of an ideal, an "impurity" only "sometimes" to be "seen" among the twisted ends, just as incest (a delicate topic to be sure) or any other impurity in family history is usually kept hidden by twisted stories and lies.

A pattern of skin-tone difference is established in the first incest episode, in which the male is pale and the female is dark. Ernie, according to Carrie, "looked pale," even "ashy" (64), while the niece describes her aunt as having a "dark and wrinkled countenance" (59). Even in this unmixed relationship, the figuration of miscegenation is beginning to emerge, echoing the rapes of black slave women by white men.

The mechanism of repression is evident in the way Ernest's wife learns of the incestuous affair. Cleaning his mother's picture, she decides to put it in a new frame and discovers a note Carrie had written to him after the first time to assure him of his manhood. The idea of a note behind an image, especially an image of family stability and uprightness such as the matriarch of the clan, marks the repression of a family taboo. That his wife finds the note while cleaning highlights an ironic contrast to the "unclean" contents of the note (66). The way the incident is handled in the family also represents classic repression. As Carrie's niece realizes, *"We forgot all about you"* (67, emphasis in the original), because after that day at the train station the aunt was never mentioned. In fact, when the train pulled into the station with her father (as they await him with the "truth" his wife is about to reveal), a draft of "cool stale air swept upwards like the breath of the underworld" (60), signifying that a long-repressed truth will surface. Although for the daughter, the next generation, such revelations seem psychologically necessary to tracing her lineage—and, thus, once she's heard them she feels "very relaxed" (67)—to the older generation, including Carrie, burial is a welcome thing. In fact, she and Ernest's mother-in-law become friends in old age. The core of their rapport is, as Carrie puts it, "She told me what she knew. She didn't want to hear my story. 'Old bones, dead and buried,' she said. So we became friends" (68).

In this first incest episode in Dove's work, repressed anxieties about cultural amalgamation (the primal scene) have metamorphosed into a representation of incest. The taboo sexuality shifts from miscegenation to incest, with the racial difference between white and black appearing as an intraracial color contrast in skin tone. The sheets and handkerchief are vehicles for sexual acts and the sadness and shame that accompany the revelation (the trauma of the primal scene). Dove's extended treatment of repressions suggests self-reflexive awareness in her discourse about the story being a repression rather than being about a repression. The different attitudes toward repression, as when the young woman wants the truth known but the community and older generation seem to want to keep it buried, reveal how, for Dove, anxiety and repression operate not only on the individual level for the cosmopolitan artist perceived as a cultural mulatto but also for African Americans generally. One reason that the idea of cultural amalgamation must go underground and emerge in an incest motif, this implies, is because some in the African American community, especially the older generations, would rather keep it buried.

Incest appears for the second time in Dove's work in the opening poem of *Thomas and Beulah*, "Taking in Wash" (47). The possibility of an incestuous relationship between Papa and the speaker is implied by the identification of the speaker as "Papa's girl," which suggests that she has his special favor and attention.[7] Mama's warning at the end of the poem can be seen as a coded intervention into Papa's sexual abuse of the daughter. "Touch" takes a prominent place at the beginning of the line, emphasizing the physical dimensions of the contact Mama rejects. The daughter's nightmare in the middle stanza hints at possible nighttime traumas or acts that cause her to have "stricken eyes" and bad dreams. And Papa's "smile sliding all over" implies that it slides over the girl—it is never stated whether his smile has an object.

The imagery of sheets and hankies repeats the pattern in "Aunt Carrie." In this case, the detail of the girl standing upon the "stitched rose" of one handkerchief evokes not only femininity and sexuality but also a loss of virginity and perhaps oppression and exploitation (it is not a bud but an open rose, and it is being stood upon).

The skin tone contrast occurs as well. In the first stanza of the poem, Papa's "yellow" marks his partly "Cherokee" ancestry. That "his skin paled" in winter contrasts with the explicitly dark complexion of his daughter, who in the second stanza is represented as "Papa's girl, / black though she was." This comes somewhat closer to miscegenation than the intraracial skin tone contrast of Aunt Carrie and her brother Ernest, because it introduces a racially mixed figure. But if there is Cherokee in Papa, there is Cherokee in Beulah, so the focus remains on the incest taboo. Again, it is a pale male and dark female.

The second stanza reveals the mechanism of repression in the child's nightmare when she sleepwalks and does not recognize herself in a mirror. Instead she sees a "beast / with stricken eyes / who screamed the house awake." The implication is that she has been subjected to something that horrifies her and makes her see a beast in the mirror, something heretofore repressed and only brought out at night. In contrast, the remainder of the poem occurs while "every light hums," which suggests an artificial daytime (although it is night) in which exposure (of incest?) is imminent. The color imagery intensifies with the image of the kitchen "arctic / with sheets," relaying the whiteness of the scene as well as its deathlike coldness.

Finally, Mama's invocation of Psalm 29:5, "I'll cut you down / just like the cedar of Lebanon," suggests righteousness on her part toward Papa, for that psalm celebrates the Lord's strength and glory in his ability to break the cedars of Lebanon. The ending thus strongly implies that Papa "touching" the child would be something worthy of

God's wrath—of which Mama would be the agent. But perhaps Mama herself is an agent of repression; it is she, after all, who hides the laundry (the sheets and hankies). Perhaps she represses what Papa has done to Beulah.[8] That the poem's insinuation of incest is so coded represses the articulation of incest. In the later poems in which the father appears (all in connection with Beulah's marriage and Thomas), there are no direct expressions that an incestuous relationship has occurred. Thus, after this first poem, Beulah's entire section exhibits a code of silence about the possibility of incest; it appears that she and her family "forgot all about it," as should the reader.[9]

The third incest episode in Dove's oeuvre is a rewrite of the Aunt Carrie story in the novel *Through the Ivory Gate*.[10] The details of the episode remain the same as in the short story: a handkerchief with a rosebud in its corner, sheets, a pale male and a dark female, repression imaged in a note behind a photograph, and the family "forgetting" Aunt Carrie. The context—in this case a novel of artistic development—is more extensive than the short story and underlines the importance of reading the episode as a symptom of a repressed primal scene of cultural amalgamation. In light of Freud's connection between repression and dreamwork, it is interesting that the novel was sparked by a dream Dove had about a black woman puppeteer (Freud, "Interpretation of Dreams"; Hammer and Daub 29), suggesting the impetus of the novel as distorted expressions of repressed anxieties.

In *Through the Ivory Gate,* the protagonist, Virginia, struggles with career and dating issues. Her discovery that her aunt and her father committed incest years earlier seems unrelated to those issues unless one reads the incest as an expression of the repressed primal scene of cultural amalgamation that Virginia must acknowledge in order to understand herself and her mixed cultural heritage. Virginia, much like Dove, has a cosmopolitan background. She was raised in a black middle-class family and is a college-educated cellist who works as a puppeteer. The novel details constant amalgamations: her grandmother, who snorts, "You can't teach these white folks nothing" (60); childhood visits with Mrs. Voltz, a Hungarian immigrant and one of the last white people in the neighborhood, who teaches Greek words to Virginia and tells her that Akron means "high place" (71); her love of the cello and classical music (in one scene she realizes how to play Bach, "It was like jazz, what Ellington meant by *It don't mean a thing if it ain't got that swing.* Playing Bach, she had to put inaccuracy into every note, that supreme inaccuracy" [99, emphasis in the original]); her mother's desire that she pursue a profession such as medicine or law to "advance the race" (94); and the memory of her first straight-A report card, which, when she showed it to her white friend Karen, caused her to be shoved in the snow and called nigger.

Because of her culturally mixed upbringing, Virginia struggles with issues of racial affiliation throughout the novel, in an early episode about a black doll, for example, and later in the story in a developing romantic relationship with a black male who works as a supervisor for the county (206).[11] The novel's title, after all, is *Through the Ivory Gate,* which alludes to Virginia's one-way, no-turning-back passage through the gates of the traditionally white-identified, college-educated, middle-class. Such a title suggests that the main tension of the novel might be expressed as a question: How does one maintain racial and cultural affiliation when one has gone through the "ivory gate" and become culturally mixed? It is not as if Virginia can turn back. The word *ivory* connotes not only white culture but also value, and value her passage she does.

Read through this lens, the familial incest dealt with in the last thirty pages of the novel has the narrative effect of "explaining" a family "origin" that helps Virginia resolve some of the tensions about her life as a cultural mulatto. That the incest is a cover for a primal scene of cultural amalgamation finds force when we consider the plot logically. Why would finding out about incest between her father and his sister years earlier help Virginia decide to pursue an opportunity to do an off-Broadway play with a white puppeteer with whom she had worked and abandon a developing romance with a black man? Such a revelation becomes relevant only when read as a coded articulation of the cultural miscegenation in Virginia's upbringing. The title's sexual undertones help us see the primal scene that is symptomatically expressed (and furthermore to anticipate the switch from a pale male with a dark woman to a dark male with a white woman in *The Darker Face of the Earth,* Dove's next publication after *Through the Ivory Gate*).

To go through the ivory gate also describes the sexual penetration of a white woman, a taboo and miscegenous crossing in American culture for black men and a threshold that has been blocked until

Virginia's (and Dove's) generation. It has also been a taboo crossing culturally for blacks, one that must be repressed, at least as far as some older people in the black community are concerned. Thus, the revelation of incest near the end of the novel, in the logic of repression, validates the protagonist's passage through the ivory gate as a cultural mulatto. It explains something from her origins that shapes her to make that choice.

In all three instances of incest the episode is formative and explains the character and/or text. Dove places these scenes in key sites of beginning or ending in order to highlight their importance as originary moments that shape a life. One must either know about the incest trauma from the beginning (as in the Beulah poem) or must work back to it in order to understand the plot and the character's life (as in the two Aunt Carrie versions). These placements echo Freud's basic notion of the primal scene as an originary trauma explaining adult neuroses. One can read, in both the discourse of these episodes and their textual placements, Dove writing her way back to some originary trauma, a primal scene.

The incest in the first edition of *The Darker Face of the Earth* is portrayed as a result of the originary trauma of repression of the primal scene of cultural amalgamation as intertwined with sexual miscegenation. Augustus' incest with his mother is only possible because of the repression of his origins (on both individual and cultural levels) and the cultural amalgamation that affiliates him partially with white culture. Thus Dove critiques the repression of mixed cultural heritage. The incest motif becomes incidental to cultural amalgamation and sexual miscegenation because the originary trauma, the repressed primal scene, is articulated in the opening pages of the play's script. In that scene the literalization of the title of the novel published two years earlier is evident in the birth of the cultural mulatto Augustus through the ivory gate of Amalia Jennings's thighs. That the scene is not a sexual primal scene, although obviously the result of a sexual episode, emphasizes that Dove's concerns lie not with sexual miscegenation itself but rather with the less tangible results of miscegenous history: cultural amalgamation. The primal scene she needs to depict is the origin that explains her amalgamated and cosmopolitan artistic identity, out of which is born the figure of the cultural mulatto.

As the play opens, the slaves, especially Hector (the child's father), await word outside as the slave mistress, Amalia Jennings, gives birth in her bedroom while attended by a doctor. The baby boy is clearly racially mixed. Louis wants to kill Amalia and the baby, but the doctor restrains him. As the doctor prepares to leave with Amalia's sewing basket, in which the infant is hidden, Louis tucks a pair of riding spurs inside, hoping to end the baby's life during the rough ride.[12] It is the primal scene of Dove's discourse, and, as Lukacher would put it, situated between historical memory and imaginative construction.[13]

Drawing on historically verifiable elements of the miscegenous slave past and reconstructing them in interpretive free play inflected with her anxieties as a cultural mulatto and African Americans' more general anxieties about cultural mixing, Dove crafts a primal scene signifying an event that cannot be said to exist anywhere as an origin. It replays the key elements of Dove's incest motif discourse in displaced images, but the pattern remains. The sheets are transformed into a bed, here the bed of childbirth, where Amalia has just given birth to Augustus; the handkerchief is moved to scene five of the play; and the rose remains, both in the name of the black midwife, Rose, and in the rosettes on the sewing basket in which Augustus is taken away by the doctor. The color difference has several versions: the pale female (Amalia) and dark male (Hector, father of Augustus); the pale male and the dark female, represented by Amalia's references to Louis's rapes of slave girls (16); and the pale female and dark male color contrast apparent in the mother-son dyad of Amalia and Augustus. This suggests Dove's insistence on historical variation in the multiple racial pairings that gave rise to cultural amalgamation. That she privileges no one version of the origin constitutes a shift from the incest scenes, which were solely pale male with dark female.

The mechanism of repression in this scene is certain. Not only will Augustus' existence be repressed, but the particular racial makeup of his parents will also be in the tale the doctor will tell. In fact, Louis wants to repress it so badly that he is willing to kill the baby to keep it all quiet. The doctor convinces the LaFarges that they can say the baby is dead, but he will take the child away to be raised. Furthermore, "Everyone must think / the baby's father is the one who's white" (18), thus repressing his true origins as the son of a white woman and a black man. The slaves will be ordered to repress the scene as well and are told, "Miss Jennings wants to forget" (21). That this scene opens the play demands reading it as a formative, primal origin and essential to Augustus' character and development. On a broader scale, the scene can also be read as a figure of the repression of the cosmopolitan tradition. Dove's play is thus an articulation of an originary primal scene that must be acknowledged in order to return to racial (both white and black) and interracial health.[14]

When, at the end of the first edition of the play and after the deaths of Hector, Louis, Amalia, and Augustus (whose body lies atop his mother's in an embrace similar to love-making), the slaves shout, "We're free! We're free!" (140), Dove is proclaiming release from an originary trauma, a primal scene of cultural amalgamation. "Preoccupation with death often represents a desire to return to origins, a longing to start again, to reinstitute beginnings and reaffirm becoming" (Friedman 281). The deaths of these major characters can be viewed as a cleansing return to origins, to the truth of an originary trauma that, now articulated, sets free those who remain. The price of speaking that truth was, in the 1994 edition, the death of the cultural mulatto at the hands of the rebel blacks.

The outcome of Augustus' divided life as a cultural mulatto in the 1994 version is substantially altered in the 1996 revised edition. The revisions show Dove's continuing engagement with the tropes and figures of cultural amalgamation and suggest that she is coming to terms with the cultural mulatto, which was not possible in the earlier edition focused by necessity on articulating a primal scene heretofore unacknowledged. Generally, Dove's revisions flesh out the characters of Hector and Amalia, Augustus' parents, making them much less stock figures in Augustus' primal scene and more fully dimensional. When read through the 1996 rewrite, however, it is interesting to consider how Dove's perception of racial protocols affected the 1994 version. Along with the development of the parents, the story of their romance is elaborated. It uses imagery from Dove's incest motif, thereby strengthening the unconscious intertextual pattern between it and the text's primal scene. Finally, Augustus' fate changes dramatically in the 1996 edition, suggesting Dove's new sense of ease about the cultural mulatto.

Hector and Amalia both develop considerably as well. Hector becomes, as Dove puts it, more than just "a crazy man in the swamp"

(Appendix, page 161). The 1996 edition strengthens his Africanness, identifying him in the cast of characters as an African and commenting at several points throughout the text on his ties to Africa. One way to read this is as an underlining of blackness, similar to Trey Ellis's insistence that cultural mulatto contemporary artists are also "wholly black." Emphasizing Hector's Africanness affirms his son Augustus' ties to Africa and blackness, thus fulfilling a key protocol of racial affiliation and demonstrating Dove's desire to do so. Another way to read this is as overt acceptance of the black literary father, Amiri Baraka, and the black arts movement, from which Dove swerved in constructing her literary genealogy (chapter 1).

Amalia's character becomes multidimensional and even nurturing and loving. In contrast to Hector's development as seemingly fulfilling racial protocols, Amalia's development violates them by being sympathetic. Dove seems to no longer fear intraracial censure over such a depiction of a white plantation mistress. The changes in Hector's and Amalia's characters suggest that Dove, having articulated the primal scene of the cultural mulatto, feels freer to cross such cultural boundaries overtly rather than covertly, enacting her cosmopolitan identity as an artist.

In the second edition Dove also develops the miscegenous relationship between Hector and Amalia, making it romantic and extending some of the image patterns of the incest episodes. Thus, in Dove's earlier work incest stands in for cultural amalgamation, and *The Darker Face of the Earth* expresses the origins of the cultural mulatto heretofore repressed. Dove elaborates on the rose imagery from the incest motif, which was also present in the 1994 edition of the play but only as a minor detail. According to the 1996 version, Hector and Amalia's romance developed when, as children, they played in the rose garden. One day, she recalls, he covered her in rose petals, an Edenic scene of origins (22). When she returns home as a bride, Hector offers a rose to Amalia as a "tribute to the bride" (22). Later, Hector's mad chatter reveals his enduring memory of those scenes as he refers to the "smell" of a rose twice (66, 116). Hector's son Augustus even picks up the rose motif when he flirts with Amalia by saying,

> You can put a rose in a vase
> with a bunch of other flowers;

but when you walk into the room
the rose is the only thing you see. (93)

That Dove scripts a more loving and romantic origin for the cultural mulatto and more overt romantic imagery can be read as perhaps a sign of decreased anxiety and a lifting of repression.

Most important, at the ending to the second edition of *The Darker Face of the Earth*, Augustus lives. In the first edition his death expressed the fear of censure by blacks, which the cultural mulatto faces in the struggle over racial affiliation. Augustus chooses to affiliate with his white mother and is shot by the rebel blacks as a "traitor!" (140). In the second edition Augustus has it both ways. He affiliates with his white mother and tries to stop her as she kills herself (159); when the rebels charge in, they think he has killed her as they had ordered and so declare him a hero. They place him on their shoulders and parade him around, a victorious leader (161–62). Dove has explained how the final change developed:

> That change came about because of my daughter [Aviva], who had participated in all of the sessions at Oregon Shakespeare Festival. She loved it and would sit through all these rehearsals and make suggestions. It was great. And one night I was still perturbed at the ending. I had put Phebe in it, but I still just didn't like the way the insurrectionists came in, bang, bang, everyone was dead. So I was fiddling with it, and she came down (she was supposed to be in bed), and I said to her, "I was just messing around with this ending." And she said, "You know, I think he should live. There are worse things than death." This is a twelve-year-old who really doesn't know what she's saying, but when she said that I suddenly realized, yeah, that's even worse. (Appendix, pages 160–61)

For Dove and for her daughter Aviva, the ending now makes sense because Augustus has ahead of him a tragic life. He will know that he killed his father and had sex with his mother. The revision speaks to Dove's concerns as a cosmopolitan artist and the mother of a racially mixed child. As an artist who has resolved her literary anxieties about African American censure over cultural amalgamation, Dove by 1996 thought that a cultural mulatto artist could live. In fact, he or she could even be lauded as a hero. One can not help but wonder how much that final, ironic twist owes to Dove being noticed in African American literary circles after little attention in the 1980s amid comments that she "writes white." That the revision was supplied by Dove's racially mixed daughter provides a connection to personal life. Dove, like Amalia, has borne a mixed-race child and would, of course, want that child to live, as would the child herself. Dedicating both editions solely to her daughter speaks to the positive future that Dove envisions for cosmopolitanism and cultural hybridity and suggests that she, in the process of conceiving, writing, and rewriting *The Darker Face of the Earth,* has finally expressed what had been an artistic repression. She is able to align the personal ease about cultural amalgamation she has always found with newfound ease in her literary life.

Notes

A slightly different version of this chapter appeared in *African American Review* 36 (Summer 2002): 1–17.

1. In no way do I mean to suggest that Dove personally suffers from anxiety due to her cultural mixing. In fact, throughout her interviews and nonliterary work she exhibits a high degree of personal comfort with a wide range of experiences. Furthermore, in my interview with her she specifically challenged the word *mulatto* in Trey Ellis's term "cultural mulatto" because she felt it indicated a kind of oppression (page 178). It seems likely that she sees cultural amalgamation much more positively in her personal identity than the word *mulatto* could indicate. The anxiety and repression on which I focus is literary and due to pressures brought to bear artistically. Whatever personal ease she feels about her identity, on some level of her artistic process an unconscious disease works to create anxiety, trauma, and repression due to racial protocols.

2. Cultural mixing may be only one of many possible primal scenes operating in African American literature. Jennifer L. Holden-Kirwan's analysis of *Beloved* focuses on the Middle Passage as a primal scene, for example. Also, Ross Posnock describes a "primal scene" of "the modern intellectual's birth" enacted in the writings of several black intellectuals, including Amiri Baraka (45). He furthermore describes the famous opening of *Souls* as "a primal scene of inauthenticity" in which Du Boisian hybridity shows its "indifference to white or black fantasies of purity" (89).

3. The lines Dove quotes as inspiration for the play reference cultural mixing and colonialism—Derek Walcott's "Sea Grapes" ("The classics can console. But not enough") and a Jimmy Cliff song ("Oh de wicked carry us away, / Captivity require of us a song; / How can we sing King Alpha's song / In a strange land?") ("Oedipus in America" 8–10).

4. In making this claim, I have profited considerably from a critique of an earlier version of this essay by my colleague Tony Jackson, who urged me to separate the kinds of miscegenation, both typologically and historically.

5. Some of these are present in "The Spray Paint King" except for the handkerchief ("hanky") and incest, which eliminates it from my discussion here. But such a parallel underlines the importance of this image constellation in her early discourse and her self-presentation as a cultural mulatto artist.

6. Thanks to my colleague Paula Connolly for pointing this out in a very helpful reading of this chapter in draft.

7. Dove resists reading this poem as a demonstration of Beulah's incestuous relationship with her father, who reappears in several other poems in the section, although critics such as Lynn Keller read the possibility of incest as a likely and reasonable interpretation (Appendix, page 179).

8. Elizabeth Beaulieu suggested this possibility during a question and answer period following a panel on the poetry of Rita Dove at the George Moses Horton Conference, April 4, 1998, at the University of North Carolina at Chapel Hill.

9. I experienced this "forgetting" the first time I taught Dove in a graduate seminar in 1995, having to be reminded by one of the participants—Gretchen Robinson—that this poem had a possible incest reading, something I had noted to myself but promptly forgotten. Much of my piecing together of Dove's primal scene is an attempt to answer Robinson's astute question, "Why is there so much incest in Dove's work?"

10. Madelyn Jablon sees *Through the Ivory Gate* as Dove's *künstlerroman*.

11. The "Prelude" to the novel offers a rewrite of Toni Morrison's doll motif in *The Bluest Eye* and its interrogation of white-defined female beauty. Dove confirms this inspiriting influence (Appendix, pages 175–76).

12. The banishment of the baby in the basket recalls the Moses story in the Bible. Thanks to Elizabeth Evans Sachs for helping me see this link.

13. The opening of the play also signifies on Faulkner's bed image, noted by Eric Sundquist, in which "[t]hose beds [of Judith, Henry, and Quentin in *Absalom, Absalom!*] in figure and in fact, hide to the end the secret they appear to reveal, the secret that the whole burden of Faulkner's novel rests upon" (129)—miscegenation. As Craig Werner has observed, many African American writers have responded to Faulkner's work because of a shared "imperative to overhaul history" (32).

14. Although some could argue that Dove's rewrite of African American origins participates in what Anthony Appiah has termed "alternative genealogizing," writing different versions of origins that do not change where we end, Dove seems to believe, insofar as her text follows a psychoanalytic project, that this expression of a repressed origin frees us from a symptomology of racial binarism.

3 ～ Introducing the Cultural Mulatto in *The Yellow House on the Corner*

Rita Dove's first volume of poems, *The Yellow House on the Corner* (1980), introduces her cosmopolitan poetic in the figure of the cultural mulatto. Boldly announcing her break from the dominance of the black arts movement in a poem in the first section, "Upon Meeting Don L. Lee, in a Dream," Dove proceeds in this volume of early poems (many written in the mid-1970s as the black arts movement took its final breaths) to thematize a cultural mulatto persona and poetic in terms of imagery, structure, and theme.

A heightened awareness of how her cosmopolitanism may be received puts Dove at special pains in *The Yellow House on the Corner*— her first major public self-presentation as a poet—to control how her racial identification is perceived by both black and white audiences. In her deployment of a cultural mulatto persona, she navigates an audience that reads for adherence to a racial protocol of black affiliation as well as an audience that reads overtly black speakers and subjects as evidence of a narrow scope.

That some readers might read for blackness in a volume of poems, or distinctly look for indications that a writer moves beyond blackness in subject matter is apparent in the criticism of Dove's work. Such readings do occur, the readings demonstrate, and Dove was correct in anticipating them. Claudia Tate's focus on how a black audience might read for adherence to racial protocols (chapter 2) should be expanded to include a white audience reading for adherence to racial protocols.

Critics such as Helen Vendler, Houston Baker, and Susan Van Dyne, among others, have offered readings of Dove's poetry that explicitly search for racial markers to indicate her affiliations with, and distancings from, African American protocols. Vendler's "Blackness and Beyond Blackness" has been discussed in chapter 1. Baker's review of *Grace Notes* opens with the statement "Rita Dove is not a 'Race Poet'" (574). He implies that "the obvious absence of blatant racial signifying argue[s] strongly against" categorizing Dove as a "Black" poet. Baker is hard-pressed to place Dove in the black woman writers' tradition, although he ultimately settles on "if *Black* is the combined richness of all color, then Rita Dove is the singing blackness of blackness" (577, emphasis in the original).

Susan Van Dyne, building on Baker's concerns and pointing out his anxiety—and that of others—about the perceived lack of racial particulars in Dove's work, notes the "challenge [Dove] poses to reading 'blackness'" (70–72). In well-informed readings Van Dyne also attempts to "site" Dove the poet as within and without multiple traditions. Although she seeks racially inflected content, three times in her essay Van Dyne seems to read for racial markers and miss them. Commenting on *Thomas and Beulah,* she states that the cover photographs seem to promise "information about blackness. . . . yet within the poems race is never insisted on" (74). In discussing *Grace Notes,* she asserts that the "daughter's eye reveals what the poet's 'I' usually omits, her race" (79). And in surveying the span of *Mother Love,* Van Dyne specifies that Dove's quest in the final poetic sequence is "never represented as racially marked" (84). Although Van Dyne is correct that Dove's poetry is not often overtly marked as black, much of what follows in this chapter and in chapters 4, 5 and 6 will show how it is identifiable as coming from the perspective of a cosmopolitan black woman poet.

In *The Yellow House on the Corner* Dove anticipates and plays with such expectations about racial markers in her poetry. Her strategies sometimes yield readings demonstrating both racial affiliation and profound ambivalence. The mulatto theme is articulated in the imagery of the volume's title and cover design.[1] The yellow of the title, *The Yellow House on the Corner,* echoes the vernacular expression "high yaller" used to describe someone black who is light-skinned and racially mixed. Combined with "house," which often represents the self or one's sense of identity, the "yellow house" of the title can be read as depicting a mulatto persona.

The yellow house is positioned on a corner, which carries a number of connotations relevant to my claim. First, a corner stands at an intersection, as does the cultural amalgamation of cosmopolitanism, which intersects cultural influences. Second, a corner house stands apart from the rest of a neighborhood. In the positive sense, it is a marker (as in directions); in the negative sense, it sticks out and does not fit into the group. Furthermore, the idea of a corner implies some kind of decision about direction. One chooses, at a corner, to cross the street, to turn the corner, continue ahead, or turn back. Thus a corner offers an urban parallel to the idea of a crossroads, symbolic of identity choices, destiny, and change.

The volume's title, then, signals the arrival of a poetic sensibility developed at an intersection of cultures. The identity is different and outstanding—and may take poetry in a new direction—but does not quite fit in.[2] The anxiety accompanying such a sense of not fitting in, especially in the context of black arts movement expectations regarding blackness and aesthetics, perhaps emerges in a secondary, colloquial meaning of "yellow": to be afraid.

The first and second edition's cover designs also deploy various resonances of "yellow." Linda Gregerson points out the author photograph, black and white yet overlaid with yellow, that spans the first edition's front cover. In the second edition (1989), the yellow of the righthand house and front-yard tree contrast with the grey and white of the rest of the image. Likewise, on the back, a black and white photograph of Dove (smaller than on the first edition) is also shaded yellow. Because Dove confirms that she and her husband Fred Viebahn have had "generous input on covers—and that color is very important to [her]," it seems appropriate to read the color choice for the cover as deliberate and thematically based.[3]

Whatever artistic anxiety it may exhibit, Dove's first volume presents a culturally mixed range of subject matter, speakers, and themes. To control how this cosmopolitan poetic sensibility is perceived by her dual audience, Dove configures the volume to meet either audience's expectations, enacting a mulatto structure. Such a structure yields two seemingly contradictory readings of her intent, and the two must be combined to understand the mulatto character of its structure.

On the one hand, Dove appears to foreground poems that lack overt markers of any particular culture or contain non–African American speakers or subjects. The poems could be read as "universal" or global in scope, something valued by an (often white) audience that might otherwise cubbyhole her as a black poet. She also positions poems that have specifically African American frames (speakers who are directly identified as black or poems that explicitly take as their subject matter African American figures or topics) in such a way as to seem to diminish their prominence when the volume is read in order. Thus a simple linear reading might yield an interpretation that Dove emphasizes universal themes over her blackness, which allows her to avoid being cubbyholed as a black poet by part of her audience.

On the other hand, a synchronic (rather than a linear or diachronic) view of the volume as a whole reveals Dove attempting to center it around a specifically African American historical core from which the other poems radiate. This reading of the volume's structure demonstrates respect for racial protocols of black affiliation and emphasizes Dove's poetic identity as black. That this attempt is not particularly convincing, and an alternative center takes hold, further reveals the mulatto character of the volume. Any single reading of the volume's structure—diachronic, synchronic, or alternate center—is by itself inadequate. Together, the three reveal a volume in which conflicting audience expectations are at odds with authorial desire and subjectivity.

That Dove is aware of the possibilities of diachronic and synchronic readings of poetry becomes apparent in her discussion of puzzles and poetry in an interview with Therese Steffen. She comments:

> I think my puzzle fetish has something to do with the way poems are constructed. Poems work in temporal sense—that is, they proceed from the beginning to the end. But at the same time, there are words that reverberate throughout the poem on a different level— a more vertical axis. Words start to reverberate by virtue of their proximity to one another. That's a spatial thing as well as a temporal one. Sometimes when I get stuck working on a poem, I lay out words like they are pieces in a jigsaw puzzle and see what happens. It sounds irreverent, but it's not. I am laying out a cage, an emotional and linguistical gridwork. ("Darker Face" 107)

The volume is organized into a deliberate "gridwork" of racial self-presentation. Section one establishes and emphasizes a global scope, and section two continues that perspective, moving into a specifically American frame of reference. Sections one and two each contain two poems with specifically African American referents. In both cases they are late in their sections, the eighth and tenth poems in those sections. Section three contains "historical slave narrative" poems, as Dove has described them. The speakers are all either enslaved blacks or speak of events in slavery. Section four refuses any overt racial/cultural frames, and section five returns to the insistently global range of section one.

A diachronic structural reading could argue that the volume emphasizes the global dimensions of Dove's cosmopolitan aesthetic, deferring and delimiting her presentation of African American racial identification. In both of the first two sections, for example, the poems that specifically engage African American culture and identifying black personae are delayed until the end—numbers eight and ten. Furthermore, the slave narratives of the third section can be read as being "buried" in the middle, perhaps indicating repression. That possibility is underlined by Dove's positioning of a section of poems that are not racially marked immediately after section three and also in the return to global topics in section five, as if to reemphasize a wide range of cultural material. Nothing in sections four or five overtly continues the African American specificity of section three, which creates an initial reading of the volume that seems to deemphasize blackness in favor of the universal.

Dove encourages such a reading in the subject matter of the first three poems of the volume: "This Life," "The Bird Frau," and "Robert Schumann, Or: Musical Genius Begins with Affliction." The poems do make explicit racial and national references but not to African American culture or personae. Rather, "This Life" focuses on a speaker of unstated race who loves a Japanese woodcut; "The Bird Frau" concerns a German female persona; and, as its title indicates, the third poem concerns the German Romantic composer Robert Schumann. The poems immediately following these three do not identify their speakers racially or culturally.

In positioning the introductory poems, then, Dove seems to be steering readers away from her African American identity and deliberately foregrounding her cosmopolitanism. Thus it appears that she defers her racial specificity until the end of the first section, where the eighth and tenth poems, "Upon Meeting Don L. Lee, in a Dream" and "Nigger Song: An Odyssey," convey her African American heritage. A similar pattern occurs in the second section. Its early and middle poems are not explicitly racially marked; if they are marked, it is with non-black cultures, France and Mexico. Again, Dove appears to lead up to blackness. The eighth and tenth poems at the end of section two obliquely identify the speaker's and the main character's racial identities as African American.

Taken as they come, the poems in *The Yellow House on the Corner* appear to be arranged to defer and delimit the author's African American identity. It seems as if she hints at blackness in sections one and two, hides her black historical poems in the middle of the volume, and ends with a global perspective. When one considers the volume holistically, however, another, and very different, view emerges: Dove has placed the black historical poems in section three in an attempt to position the reality of black history as central to her identity as a poet. From that perspective, placing the slave narratives at the center of the volume makes them foundational to the volume's themes. The poems in sections one, two, four, and five, then, are intended to radiate from the center and be informed by it.

Such a view insists that whether or not individual poems specify African American speakers or subjects, Dove's cultural mulatto poetic persona is black and part of an ongoing African American tradition. At that point in literary history, she would have felt considerable pressure to attempt such a marker of racial affiliation. That the poems in the center section are among her least compelling (a point to which I will return) indicates Dove's ambivalence about such a project. It is the volume's autobiographical sequence "A Suite for Augustus" that acts as its center and furthers the mulatto theme.

The Yellow House on the Corner presents identity as its main theme, a sort of poetic bildungsroman. In several poems Dove presents a cultural mulatto persona navigating racial and historical issues in American, specifically in African American culture. The first two that appear in the ten-poem first section, "Upon Meeting Don L. Lee, in a Dream" and "Nigger Song: An Odyssey," can be read together as Dove's first poetic self-presentation of a cultural mulatto persona. As a pair they delineate Dove's distancings and affiliations within African American culture and aesthetics. The first, "Upon Meeting Don L. Lee, in a Dream," discussed in chapter 1 as an anxiety of influence poem, firmly rejects the black arts movement. Here, I offer a close reading that investigates the specific problems she sees with that movement.

In the poem, Lee is an aggressive, intimidating figure who "comes toward" the speaker, "[a]lways moving," a man whose aggression burns him alive: "his eyeballs / Burst into flame" (12). Even after his self-destruction "[h]e can only stand, fists clenched, and weep," suggesting both his militancy and impotence. Dove depicts the black arts movement as rigid, traditionally masculine, and exclusive in its blackness, noting that Lee "has never made love / To thin white boys in toilet stalls" (12). Such lines emphasize the rigidly heterosexual machismo of black power, which became equivalent with black manhood, as well as the exclusion of interaction with whites, here figuratively expressed through homosexual intercourse. Further emphasizing the gender divisions of the movement and continuing to critique its rigidity, the next stanza depicts women among "the trees, the black trees" (of course, even the trees would be black). They "stand, watching. They begin / To chant, stamping their feet in wooden cadences / As they stretch their beaded arms to him" (12). Like the trees, their chanting is wooden; as women, their static role in the movement is to support and nurture the male leaders. Such moments parody the limits of the black arts movement and signal Dove's intention to take a new direction.

Dove emphasizes that the black arts movement is over when Lee tries to talk about the past. "'Seven years ago,'" he says, but the speaker cuts him off: "Those years are gone / What is there now?" (12). Dove then horrifically destroys Lee, which allows the speaker to emerge into a cleared, safe, and fertile space: "I lie down, chuckling as the grass curls around me." The earlier solidity of the women singers is transformed as they "float away" on "brown paper wings," thus emphasizing the ephemeral nature of the black arts movement.

As a cosmopolitan in the vanguard of the "New Black Aesthetic" (NBA), for Dove such a poem parodying and destroying the movement must have seemed necessary at the time. Moreover, it was not personally directed against Lee but rather a needed "killing the father" for the emerging poet (Appendix, page 173). That Dove positions it as the first racially marked poem in her first published collection foregrounds the importance of this killing for her. In Dove's self-presenta-

tion of her blackness she makes it clear that she eschews any connection with the definitions of blackness promulgated by the black arts
and black power movements of the 1960s and early 1970s. She views
them as rigid, militant, sexist, and ultimately unproductive.

Having cleared a space for self-definition, Dove's next poem with
explicitly African American subject matter in *The Yellow House on the
Corner* comes two poems later, the final one of section one. "Nigger
Song: An Odyssey" offers a far more positive and complex portrait
of racial identification than Dove's representation of the black arts
movement and signals a cosmopolitan cultural heritage and an
affirmation of blackness. To understand Dove's self-presentation of
racial and cultural affiliations, the poem should be read together with
the Don L. Lee poem. Its title juxtaposes and conjoins two traditions,
the "Nigger Song" of African American vernacular culture and "An
Odyssey" of Western classical tradition, suggesting a journey or quest
into blackness. Read after the Don L. Lee poem, "Nigger Song: An
Odyssey" seems a next-generation response to being set free from the
black arts movement.

The poem was rejected by a previous-generation writer, Alice
Walker. When it appeared in an anthology during the mid-1970s, it
prompted Walker, whose poems were also in that anthology, to refuse to read at a book promotion in San Francisco. Dove's poem, she
felt, was "racist" (Steffen, "Darker Face" 108). As Dove explains:

> Alice objected to the use of the word "nigger," even by a black writer.
> I wrote her a letter explaining my philosophy about the word; my
> concern was to redeem the word, to reimagine it as a black concept.
> She responded with a polite, dignified letter in which she acknowl-
> edged my right to use whatever words I chose but argued we should
> not use such words in the company of white people. My immediate
> reaction was: "No one's going to put me in that kind of cage—not
> whites, not blacks, not even myself. I am trying to make the best
> poem I possibly can, a poem that will defy whatever nefarious pur-
> poses people may want to use it for." So in spite of my precautions,
> the very thing I feared—being called to task by the Black Arts Move-
> ment—happened early in my career. ("Darker Face" 108, 112)

Such an anecdote reinforces my claim in chapter 2: Dove early in her
career operated under significant anxiety about black arts proscrip-

tions regarding art.[4] Together, the Don L. Lee poem and "Nigger Song: An Odyssey" signal her intention to depart from such proscriptions. The group "we" of the poem appears to be six young people out joyriding for the night. Dove's imagery underlines blackness ("the engine churning ink") and associates racial identity with the night in "the gray-green nigger night" (14). "Green" echoes the grass of the Lee poem that fertilely curls around the speaker after Lee's annihilation, suggesting possibilities of growth. The youths avoid the limits that historically have been imposed on African Americans and drive "[p]ast factories, past graveyards / And the broken eyes of windows" (14). They even "sweep past excavation sites," a representation of the key excavatory task of so many African Americans who have repeatedly brought African American culture to light and preserved the tradition. Such an enterprise, this line suggests, has been done and is not the principal concern of this next generation.

Ultimately, the group veers "[i]nto the black entrails of the earth, / The green smoke sizzling on our tongues" (14). This generation is free, the poem suggests, to "swerve away" from the restrictions of the past, although the weeds "clutch at the wheels," free to go straight into the heart of blackness, the green again connoting potential for growth. They feel that "in the nigger night, . . . [n]othing can catch us." The final lines emphasize an affirmation of this journey into blackness, as the group's repeated "yeah" becomes the "croon" of the "Nigger Song": "And 'yeah' we whisper, 'yeah' / We croon, 'yeah'" (14). This affirmation (echoing Molly Bloom rather than reminding us of Harold Bloom as in the Lee poem) attests to black identity for the next generation. In its portrait of a group of black adolescents questing into a fertile blackness it explicitly rewrites the ambivalence of Gwendolyn Brooks's poem "We Real Cool" (1960), in which she lauds the style of seven pool players at the Golden Shovel while bemoaning their dead-end fate.

Similarly to section one, the eighth and tenth poems in section two also racially identify the subject or speaker as African American. "Planning the Perfect Evening" and "Wake" are part of a six-poem series in section two entitled "A Suite for Augustus," a poetic precursor to Augustus in *The Darker Face of the Earth*. They trace Dove's coming of age as a cultural mulatto and link her poetic identity to American national identity and history.[5] As such, the sequence is central to understanding her first self-presentation as a cosmopolitan poet.

Using the motif and structure of the suite, an instrumental form of baroque music that the *Harvard Dictionary of Music* describes as being composed of several movements in the character of dances, these poems trace a relationship "dance" between a persona and a young black man named Augustus. The persona bears some autobiographical resemblance to Dove. Beginning in 1963 (when Dove was eleven), the series charts the persona's movement into puberty, sexual awareness, and a fruitful sense of self. It includes details similar to Dove's experiences: a visit to Washington, D.C. (where Dove went as a Presidential Scholar her senior year of high school), going to Europe on scholarship (Dove went on a Fulbright grant), and references to German currency (Dove studied at University of Tübingen and has extensive experience with Germany through marriage to the German novelist Fred Viebahn). Furthermore, the persona at one point describes her heart as "shy mulatto" (25). The series "A Suite for Augustus" sketches the shaping of a cultural mulatto persona in relation to race and American culture and history.

The first poem, "1963," ties the persona's loss of innocence—the onset of menstruation and implied forthcoming loss of virginity—to the national loss of innocence with the assassination of President John F. Kennedy in 1963. The death of the president in stanza one is linked to the departure of Augustus—presumably the "you" in "[y]ou moved away" of stanza one—and loss of sexual innocence: "The cherry blinks sadly: Goodbye, goodbye" (21). Both the persona and the nation are initiated into experience. The Bay of Pigs incident is alluded to by "the violent bay," and the speaker's awakening sexuality is suggested by "under percale" and "I touch the doorknobs of my knees, begging to open / Me" (21). The bridge figure between the two, the persona and the nation, appears to be Augustus, who

> in tall buildings
> Typed speeches, each word-cluster a satellite,
> A stone cherry that arced over the violent bay,
> Broadcasting ball games and good will to Cuba . . . (21)

"Cherry" suggests both the virginity of the speaker as well as the cherry trees of Washington, D.C. Furthermore, Augustus' job appears to be in the federal government, figured in the tall white buildings and the speeches he prepares that are propaganda sent to Cuba. Augustus shares his name, after all, with a leader, the heir to Caesar, and he is tied repeatedly in the poems to authority, leadership, nationalism, and the American government. His "word-cluster[s]" are not the stuff of a poem. They are "stone[s]" thrown to Cuba by satellite and meant as tools of diplomatic manipulation. The persona's "dance" with Augustus is partly one of engaging and weighing his affiliations. As the final line describes the persona as "an erector set, spilled and unpuzzled," her sexuality is also unexplored. Exploration of that identity and sexuality will ultimately bring her into full confrontation with the national, American identity that Augustus represents.

The second poem of the series, "D.C.," drives home that connection to the national in a surreal, dreamlike rendering of the nation's capital that links Augustus and the speaker to issues of national culture and identity as well as sexual and racial union. Dove traces cultural mixing back to the Founders, and the poems share many affinities with the concerns of *The Darker Face of the Earth* (chapter 2). Divided into three numbered stanzas, the poem begins with the Smithsonian—a museum cum mausoleum—and moves in its second section to a depiction of how the Washington Monument violates the Reflecting Pool on the Mall; section three brings forth the slavery ghosts surrounding Thomas Jefferson.[6] That these scenes are perceived by the speaker, with Augustus' commentary ("you say"), overlays the dance between them with issues of the nation's foundations and history.

The first stanza details the contents of the Smithsonian: "Roosters corn wooden dentures / pins & thimbles embroidery hoops / greenbacks & silver snuff & silver" (22). The list, without punctuation and with ampersands instead of the spelled-out word *and*, suggests the endlessness of items that could be enumerated as well as the overwhelming minutiae of the collection. Sometimes called "our nation's attic," the Smithsonian is intended as a repository for U.S. history and culture. In Dove's listing, however, it seems to house trivia. The final line of the stanza particularly reinforces the age of the contents, terming them "brontosaurus bones couched on Smithsonian velvet" (22), which suggests an extinct dimension to the artifacts. The velvet authenticates and elevates the items, but they seem the stuff of a dead and buried era.

The second stanza, however, unburies a historical reality often repressed: sexual miscegenation—often rape—between white men and black women from the beginning of the nation's history. Such a reading looks back to stanza one, seeing the bones couched on velvet and the minutiae as symptomatic signals of a repressed history that needs to be spoken. Opening the second stanza with Augustus commenting on the Washington Monument as "[a] bloodless finger pointing to heaven" suggests that the nation does not acknowledge the blood on its hands.

By the end of the stanza that perception is corrected as Dove depicts the monument as an "outrageous cue stick / lying, reflected, on a black table" (22). *Webster's* defines "outrageous" as "violent; atrocious" and its root, "outrage," as "excessive violence; violation of others' rights; gross insult or indignity." Thus the outrage of the white phallic cue stick lying on the explicitly black table represents not only the general violations of slavery but also, and specifically, the rape of black women by white men as a foundation of the nation's history. Such imagery, coupled with the portrayal of the scene as "a postcard framed by imported blossoms," is reminiscent of *The Darker Face of the Earth* and Dove's figuration in literal sexual miscegenation of the cultural miscegenation required to create the cultural mulatto. In that play, too, Dove ties tree blossoms (there, pear) to interracial rape in Augustus' lines about the pear trees casting their white blossoms on the darker face of the earth. Here, Dove frames the rape scene with cherry blossoms, connecting all to the nation's capital.

The third stanza manifests the issue of sexual and cultural miscegenation through Thomas Jefferson. The third president owned slaves and reputedly had a sexual relationship with one of them, Sally Hemmings, who bore several children (genetic testing has confirmed at least one child was fathered by a male Jefferson) and outlived him. In the stanza the slavery past (supposedly dead and buried in stanza one) comes to life as ghosts from the South "play Dixie" (22). Jefferson is a sexual predator, "[l]eaving his chair" in the memorial "he prowls the edge of the prune-black water" of the Tidal Basin (which is ringed with cherry trees), imagery paralleling that of stanza two with the Washington Monument and the Reflecting Pool. That this lineage still continues appears in "[h]is slaves have outlived him / in this life too" (22); that the lineage is culturally mixed as a result finds expression in the clapping of the "gray palms" (22). Dove culminates this parallel of sexual, racial, and cultural miscegenation with national foundations in the ghost trio's "'De broomstick's jumped, the world's not wide'" (22). Invoking the ritual of slave marriage, jumping the broomstick, Dove implies that the sort of the miscegenous "marriage" in which Jefferson and Hemmings participated lies at the core of national culture and identity. It also constitutes a background for and justification of her presentation of a cultural mulatto persona.

The third poem, "Planning the Perfect Evening," returns to the theme of sexual maturation in a description of the persona's prom night with Augustus. The dance between the two of them is sexually charged, and she muses, "Ah, / Augustus, where did you learn to samba? / And what is that lump below your cummerbund?" (23). The night has fairytale proportions, indicating the adolescence of the speaker. She believes "nothing . . . can come / between us" and is "happy [her] glass sizzles with stars" (23). Drawing on this fairytale dimension, Augustus is rendered as a bear, which creates a beauty-and-the-beast type of pairing. Dove solidifies the suite motif between them in her wordplay on "suite" ("how hulking / you are, my dear, my sweet black bear!") and indicates a potentially ominous quality to Augustus' role by describing his large, unwieldy presence as "hulking," which suggests that he could overpower or block her movement. The second-to-the-last word of the poem, the eighth one in section two, is the first time that Dove explicitly identifies Augustus as being black.

The fictitious prom night with Augustus signals that this poetic series is an important coming-of-age depiction of an emerging poetic persona, for Dove has revealed that she never attended her high school prom. Instead, she was selected as a Presidential Scholar, one of the hundred best high school students in the United States, and met the president on a trip to Washington, D.C., on the same weekend as the prom (personal communication, March 5, 2000). In the series, then, Dove engages multiple issues of identity, such as Americanism, blackness, and femininity, and delineates her positions relative to each. Conflating the prom that never happened with the trip to the nation's capitol that did, she charts an important transition into an intellectual identity aware of the national, racial, and gendered implications of her experience and the culture around her. Her cosmopolitan positioning among those frames is first articulated in the series, which becomes the volume's mulatto core.

Augustus' potential to block the poem's maturing persona is elaborated in the fourth poem of the sequence, "Augustus Observes the Sunset," which specifies the extent of his nationalistic allegiances. The opening word of the poem is summative—"July"—and marks the centrality of American independence for Augustus. He is so patriotic, in fact, that he cannot observe the sunset as anything other than an American flag. He sees "[k]etchup, marshmallows, the tub of ice, / Bacon strips floating in pale soup" (24). The food items (which perhaps explain Augustus' bulk) represent the red, white, and blue of the stars and stripes. The final line emphasizes that view: "The sky shakes like a flag" (24). Dove, however, suggests a problematic dimension to American nationalism in describing the sunset as a "conspiracy of colors," implying unity of evil purpose. Furthermore, the sunset seems violent, as the "sun, like a dragon spreading its tail, / Burns the blue air to ribbons" (24). Ultimately, the poem implies a growing schism in the country (and a rift in the relationship between the speaker and Augustus). The depiction of "[e]astward, . . . / A wall of silence, growing" (24) conveys governmental silence and repression ("eastward" here meaning the falling of night in the East after sunset as well as the eastern location of the capital).

Augustus' affiliation with national leadership becomes codified in the fifth poem, "Wake," and he becomes an overt obstacle in the speaker's development. The title word's multiple meanings allow several threads to be interwoven. It suggests following in the wake of a ship (the word *hulking* earlier linked Augustus to a ship) as the persona tries to "turn eastward," following Augustus (23, 25). "Wake" also connotes endings, as in a funeral wake and to wake up, as if from a dream. Thus although the persona might follow in his wake, such a journey awakens her to the limitations of his path. Augustus represents a blind Americanism that is oblivious to its origins.

The poem begins with the speaker "[s]tranded in the middle of the nation" (25). From the Midwest, she initiates a journey "eastward." Her "heart, shy mulatto, wanders towards / The salt-edged contours of rock and sand / That stretch ahead into darkness" (25). Her journey is toward the East Coast, the nation's pilgrim origin and, it is also suggested, to the "darkness" beyond, Europe.[7]

In the second stanza, however, the speaker finds Augustus "stand[ing] in the way" and an obstacle to her journey. Blocking is explicitly linked to his alignment with American government and leadership, as he appears

> on the bank of the Potomac,
> Profile turned to sudden metal
> And your shirt-front luminous
> Under a thicket of cherry boughs. (25)

He is not only located in Washington, as "Potomac" and "cherry boughs" suggest, but also seems minted on a coin or medal that features his profile and shirt-front. The play on "capitalism" as the economic system, the affiliation with the nation's capital, and the process of being turned into capital (minted) opens in the third stanza (four of the six poems in the series contain three stanzas), a stretching of "minted." Augustus' words are like droplets "of creme de menthe," and his breath is "exalted and spearmint," denoting his elevated rank and minted quality (25). Tellingly, the speaker says, "What reaches me is not [his] words" but just his breath, which suggests that she is no longer listening to him or that, like most politicians, his speeches are high on rhetoric and low on content.

The final poem of "A Suite for Augustus" outlines the very different paths the persona and Augustus have taken and emphasizes the persona's cosmopolitan cultural identity in contrast to Augustus' rigid and limited Americanism. Entitled "Back," which can signify return to or turning away from, the poem demonstrates the persona's return to America and her turning away from Augustus and the nationalism he represents. The opening stanza parses out the two paths:

> Three years too late, I'm scholarshipped
> to Europe and back.
> Four years, a language later, and
> your 39th jet lands in Kuwait. (26)

Although the speaker and Augustus have had international experiences, they are of a very different nature; hers is educational whereas his is military. Hers has everything to do with culture, knowledge, and self-development; his is concerned with power, warfare, and acquisition. The language he learns is an acquisition ("a language later") and part of his tools of leadership rather than part of the process of intercultural appreciation.

The second stanza details with much irony how Augustus' world has narrowed substantially into one of military command in a desert, where he feels most comfortable: "you relax at last— / goat milk and scotch, no women, no / maple trees. You think: how far I've come" (26). Dove contrasts this limited result of Americanist identity with the persona's "barnstorming that led no closer to you," connoting freelance and itinerant travels. Such a journey has been quite fruitful, in contrast to Augustus' desert descent ("Down," the poem emphasizes). Dove's persona has gone to the heart of a fertile green world. Traveling, she says, "has stuffed my knees into violets, / buried me in the emerald hearts of leaves" (26). The organic imagery contrasts the infertile rigidity of Augustus' world of "columns of khaki and ribbons" with "no / maple trees" (26). Dove furthers the contrast in turning the green world imagery toward a monetary link to Augustus' coin/mint imagery in the previous poem. Yet here the leaves of the green world "are like twenty-mark bills, soft / dollars, they bring me back" (26). The soft bills suggest soft, nurturing value in contrast to the stamped, inflexible, and elevated value of coins. Contrasting values are emphasized by the phrase "soft / dollars," which implies weakened value to American currency and thereby to American culture. American dollars are juxtaposed to the German mark, promoting an intercultural and international standard of value.

Following the "Suite for Augustus," section three of *The Yellow House on the Corner* contains ten poems in which African American speakers traverse approximately sixty years of American slavery. These poems attempt to affirm African American culture and history as core to the cultural mulatto persona presented in *Yellow House,* yet they betray some degree of artistic anxiety and ambivalence.

If considered as the radiating center of the collection, the poems attempt to shift the overall focus in two ways. First, apart from the generally contemporary period setting of most others, these poems move 150 years back in history. Second, surrounded by autobiographically charged coming-of-age poems (the "Suite for Augustus" immediately precedes section three, and three poems entitled "Adolescence I," "Adolescence II," and "Adolescence III" immediately follow it to open section four), the poems shift the "I" and the eye of the volume to shared yet individual experiences of black Americans as part of the identity of Dove's poetic persona. All ten poems have first-person utterances. Eight are exclusively first-person in point of view, and the two in third person contain quotations of the subject's first-person writings (David Walker) or thought (Pamela). Thus, readers who understand Dove's "I" and eye behind the volume's cosmopolitanism are pushed toward a historicized and culturally inflected perception of that cosmopolitan identity.

The section is markedly different in tone and subject matter from the rest of the volume. In part because of their coming-of-age stance, the tone of many poems in the other sections is often one of possibility and development, such as in "Geometry" or "The Secret Garden." In contrast, the tone in section three is typically depressed and pained. Belinda, in the first poem, speaks to "plead" her "pitiable Life" (32). The house slave in the second poem "cannot fall asleep" and "weep[s]" (33). David Walker is murdered, and a newly freed slave is abducted, awakening "alone, in darkness and in chains" (36). A woman walking north to escape is found by men "smiling, rifles crossed on their chests" (39). A child being separated from his or her mother silently watches the sunrise, breaking "the water into a thousand needles / tipped with the blood from someone's finger" (40).

Dove draws painful experiences and negative tone together in the eighth poem, "Cholera," in which a cholera outbreak is controlled by isolating the slaves who are sick. The speaker reflects, "Who could say but that it wasn't anger / had to come out somehow? Pocketed filth. / The pouring away of pints of pale fluid" (41), which suggests that the sickness could be the result of repressed anger about the painful experiences of slavery. The conjurers focus on this experience as emblematic and whisper, "Here is pain . . . And it is all ours" (41). Read metaphorically, the poem implies that the pain becomes part of the healing and thus part of shared African American experience. Remaining in that pain, however, becomes a lure toward death, and the doctor orders it punished.

The two poems following "Cholera" pull back from a negative tone and depict two perspectives that might be described as making the best of a bad situation. In "The Slave's Critique of Practical Reason," the speaker explains a personal philosophy honed while picking cotton. In "Kentucky, 1833," the speaker describes a Sunday of play and community. The reality of enslavement is not effaced, however, because the poem delineates at several points the ways in which "Massa" circumscribes and controls the lives of the slaves.

The section three poems attempt to inflect the thematic focus of the entire volume. The first, "Belinda's Petition," is dated 1782, soon after the Declaration of Independence and the founding of America as a separate country. The irony that twelve-year-old Belinda points out in her petition is that although white American leaders had recently "severed / the Binds of Tyranny" for themselves, they had not done so for enslaved Africans. She requests the Senate and House to "consider the Same for me" (28). Dove counters stereotypes of cultural ignorance by specifying that the only ignorance of which Belinda might be found guilty is the evil of white imperialism. In her innocence the child asks, "How might / I have known of Men with Faces like the Moon, / who would ride toward me steadily for twelve years?" (28).

"Belinda's Petition" establishes the central theme of section three, freedom. The majority of these poems detail individual quests for freedom. David Walker, like Belinda, pleads for his and his people's freedom; Solomon Northrup, who enjoys being a freeman, is abducted; a slave girl named Pamela attempts to walk north to freedom; a wagonload of slaves breaks free; and an unnamed speaker lands in Independence, Missouri. In this section Dove continues to focus on identity but through the African American refrain of freedom.

Such reshaping is meant to resonate throughout the volume and place the book's theme of identity in a new key. In the Don L. Lee poem we can perhaps hear the poet's plea to be free to reject the black arts movement and also be free of racial protocols that demand an exclusive focus on black culture. A cosmopolitan identity wants, then, to be free to traverse the globe, migrate between black and white worlds, and engage the slave past yet also write a poem about a Japanese woodcut. As Rampersad remarks, "Dove wishes nothing less than possession of [the] wide world; she longs for the complete freedom of her imagination" (56). Section three, in its African American specificity of the historical quest for freedom, is intended to reframe the identity theme of Dove's volume.

Dove also makes it plain that black racial heritage does not always make for clear allegiances. The central poem in the section (the fifth of ten), "The Transport of Slaves From Maryland to Mississippi," details how "a wagonload of slaves broke their chains, killed two white men, and would have escaped, had not a slave woman helped the Negro driver mount his horse and ride for help" (37). The first voice is of a slave woman whose empathy with the Negro driver is clear:

> *The skin across his cheekbones*
> *burst open like baked yams—*
> deliberate, the eyelids came apart—
> *his eyes were my eyes in a yellower face.* (37)

In the final analysis she helps him because *"I am no brute. I got feelings. / He might have been a son of mine"* (37). Such reasoning refutes slavocracy stereotypes about blacks being brute animals and yet recognizes that such behavior reenslaved escapees. The Negro driver, "Gordon," rides back to the plantation for help, and the slaves are recaptured. He is not the only person with complex allegiances. He had been attacked by the slaves and "[l]eft for dead in the middle / of the road" (37). The poem thus seems a multiple-perspective riff on competing versions of African American freedom.

The final part of section three, a prose poem entitled "Kentucky, 1833," puts the section in the historical past and anticipates Dove's contemporary position. Describing a Sunday of play, the speaker ends the poem by describing a beautiful sunset. He remarks, "It's a crazy feeling that carries through the night; as if the sky were an omen we could not understand, the book that, if we could read, would change our lives" (45). Such lines position Dove's volume within the larger context of African Americans historically being denied reading and writing skills. They also emphasize the poet's valuation of the written word.

Yet viewing the historical slave narrative poems as noncontradictory and wholly positive contributions to the volume overlooks their ambivalent position within the collection and their failure to successfully recast its themes. Linda Gregerson notes that the central sequence "sits uneasily" in the middle of the volume (46). Vendler's review is likewise critical. Stylistically, these poems differ from others in the volume by emphasizing narrative story rather than non-

temporal lyric moments. The personae, while offering various perspectives, seem flat and redundant and usually serve as vehicles to
convey the negative experience of slavery. With few exceptions Dove's
typically striking imagery and complex renderings of consciousness
are subservient to the narrative needs of the poems.

Thematically, the section focuses on a simplistic version of the intertwined tropes of freedom and literacy for African Americans. By
emphasizing black experiences 150 years in the past rather than more
recent history, the poet's relationship to such experience and material remains at several arms' lengths. The poems seem an obligatory
gesture after the true core—the Augustus sequence. The perfunctory,
rote quality to the middle section—it trots out an excavated heritage
as if to profess racial affiliation—and its dissimilarities to the rest of
the collection drain the focus away from section three as a central
core and undermine the attempt to situate blackness as key to the
cosmopolitan identity.

It seems strategic that Dove follows the middle section foregrounding racial and historical specificity of African Americans with
a section that seemingly deliberately erases all signs of race or culture. Section four's poems resolutely refuse racial or cultural markers, as if to say to readers, "Ah, you thought you had me cubbyholed,
but no!" One might consider the section as the work of a young poet
who is playing with such markers, much as Toni Morrison does in
her short story "Recitatif." Race is overtly and repeatedly marked in
one section, and then race and culture are overtly unmarked in another. Such balancing between the "racial particular and the unraced
universal" ties a cultural mulatto persona to both structure and
theme (Posnock 88).

The final poem of the volume, "Ö," is usually seen as Dove's first
ars poetica, or statement of early poetics. Read as a culmination of
the issues of dual audience, cultural mulatto imagery, identity, and
freedom themes, it becomes a self-reflexive announcement about her
mulatto poetic persona and future path as a poet leading the NBA.
First, the poem emphasizes cultural mixing in its title and the opening lines, which refer to the Swedish language changing a sound, a
word, and a neighborhood. By focusing on Swedish, Dove displaces
the issues in cultural mixing onto a less charged terrain than African
American. The yellow house—Dove's image of the cultural mulat-

to—from the volume's title is transformed into a "galleon stranded in flowers." The imagery has several implications. A galleon is a large Spanish ship, typically used for commerce and war during the fifteenth and sixteenth centuries (when commerce included shipping Africans to the New World as slaves). Thus Dove sites the poem in an origin of cultural mixing.

The house/ship is stranded, run aground, and the flowers suggest that the position is not altogether unpleasant and even fertile. Yet the house/ship is stuck. The poem implies that the cultural intermixing from the opening lines somehow "keeps things going." The house on the corner, imaged as a ship, could now possibly take off "over the marshland." Dove seems to be predicting a future course for the cultural mulatto persona. It will not be "stranded" in one American neighborhood, however comfortable that might be, but take off to sea/see what there is to see, imagery that anticipates Dove's mature nomadic identity. Although "families" (an echo of Ralph Ellison's essay "The World and the Jug," in which he identifies Richard Wright as a "relative" although he connects with Dostoevsky and Hemingway as "ancestors") refuse to budge from the present, Dove's poetic identity plans to get moving, to take off. The ending is a warning to expect change: "nothing's / like it used to be, not even the future."

Notes

1. Linda Gregerson comments on these color connotations briefly in her review of *The Yellow House on the Corner*.

2. Even at this early stage in her career, Dove's outstanding accomplishments include being named a Presidential Scholar, receiving a Fulbright scholarship to study in Germany, and completing an MFA at the highly regarded Iowa Writers' Workshop at the University of Iowa.

3. Rita Dove, personal communication, Feb. 22, 2001. Fred Viebahn relates that "all the original book covers were either designed or influenced or determined by us. . . . But that is not true for the two Carnegie Mellon reprints (*Yellow House* and *Museum*), of which we weren't even informed" before they were reprinted (personal communication, Jan. 29, 2002).

4. Arnold Rampersad also expresses concern about this poem. He comments on how it causes a question about the "dubious roots" of Dove's "meagerness of racial feeling," which "surfaces disturbingly when one searches for the final meaning" of the poem (55).

5. Rampersad writes glowingly of these poems (57).

6. Many thanks to my father, Milton Goodman, and step-mother, Jewell Goodman, long-time residents of the Washington area, for help in understanding the layout of these federal monuments. Jewell Goodman was especially helpful regarding the role of the Lincoln Memorial in the poem.

7. This version of "origins" is Eurocentric as opposed to other versions focusing on native people.

4 ～ *Museum* and Cosmopolitanism

Dove's view of her first volume, *The Yellow House on the Corner,* as an "apprenticeship" work demarcates her second volume, *Museum,* as her first independent aesthetic statement.[1] After presenting a cultural mulatto poetic persona (with attendant anxieties) in *Yellow House,* she confidently unfolds a fully crafted cosmopolitan aesthetic, as the echo of "muse" in the title, *Museum,* suggests.[2] Dove's comments reveal awareness of presentation in this collection: *"Museum* was very carefully thought out in terms of a book, and the impression it would make" (Rubin and Kitchen 156).

In terms of her oeuvre, the movement from "house" in the first collection to "museum" in the second underlines the implications of her enterprise. Dove begins with necessary identity construction in the house of the self and then develops a larger world construction, as implied by the museum of the world, history, and culture. As Robert McDowell notes, "The personal turning point *House on the Corner* evolves, becoming the public Museum" (61). In *Museum,* then, Dove builds her museum from her cosmopolitan perspective.

Museum embodies many of the key aesthetic features of the "new black aesthetic" (NBA)—one contemporary articulation of cosmopolitanism—and that is also true of Dove's earlier volume *The Yellow House on the Corner.* Both employ borrowing across race and class lines, a parodic relationship to the black arts movement, a new and unflinching look at black culture, and belief in finding the universal in oneself and one's experiences (Ellis 233–51). Dove's emphasis on a worldwide range of cultures in *The Yellow House on the Corner,* the poems about the universal experiences of female adolescence, and the Don L. Lee poem critical of the black arts movement all reflect her

NBA sensibility in *The Yellow House*. Her focus in that volume is else-where, however, and intent on constructing and publicly presenting a poetic persona in the face of some intraracial censure (chapter 3). As she has commented in interviews, the volume is very much the product of her Iowa Writer's Workshop training, an apprenticeship which, although helpful, had a stultifying effect on her poetry.

Dove took a break from writing poetry between *The Yellow House on the Corner* and *Museum*. After Iowa, she produced much of her fiction—several of the short stories collected in *Fifth Sunday* and a very early draft of her novel *Through the Ivory Gate*—as well as the first draft of her play *The Darker Face of the Earth*. She left Iowa in 1977 and moved with her husband to Oberlin, Ohio, where he taught German literature at Oberlin College for two years. They also spent three months in Ireland during that time, lived in Israel for half a year in 1979, and then moved to Germany, living there from 1979 to 1981 (personal communication from Fred Viebahn, Jan. 29, 2002). Dove focused on fiction and took frequent breaks from poetry at this point because "whenever I tried to write [a poem after Iowa], it didn't sound like me" (Peabody and Johnsen 3). After this period, she began to write the poems that became *Museum*, the first major work she considers truly her own.

Reading *Museum* as an aesthetic extension of Dove's cosmopolitanism requires unpacking two intertwined concepts, universality and personal experience, as they relate to African American literature and writers. Universality in black writing, as Marilyn Nelson Waniek observes, has become a "bugbear in Black literary criticism" (Dove and Waniek 264). These tensions have a long history that became particularly high-pitched during the 1950s and 1960s. Afro-Modernist writers of the 1950s such as Robert Hayden were attacked during the 1960s by black arts movement adherents for employing what they viewed as "white" aesthetics and cultural allusions (chapter 1). Often, the same writers and texts were simultaneously applauded by mainstream critics as attaining "universality."

Furthermore, such writers frequently maintained that their personal experiences defined them, as did any shared black group experiences. Just because those experiences were not specifically or exclusively black, however, did not mean they required purging from artistic repertoires. In his definitive literary essay on universality and personal experience, "The World and the Jug," Ralph Ellison responds to an essay by a white Jewish critic, Irving Howe, on Richard Wright, James Baldwin, and Ellison himself and attacks Howe's version of literary history in which Ellison's work can only be viewed as following (or failing to follow) Wright's legacy of the protest novel. Wright, Ellison argues, "was no spiritual father of mine" (117). Instead, he was a "relative," and other writers who influenced Ellison, regardless of race, were "ancestors": "[W]hile one can do nothing about choosing one's relatives, one can, as an artist, choose one's 'ancestors.' Wright was, in this sense, a 'relative'; Hemingway an 'ancestor.' Langston Hughes, whose work I knew in grade school and whom I knew before I knew Wright, was a 'relative'; Eliot, whom I was to meet only many years later, and Malraux and Dostoievsky and Faulkner, were 'ancestors'" (140). From this one can see how Dove's use of the word *families* in "Ö" (chapter 3) evokes such distinctions.

Ellison seems particularly irritated by Howe's limited view of black *Eigenwelt* (existential being in the world). According to Ellison, "Howe seems to see segregation as an opaque steel jug with the Negroes inside waiting for some black messiah to come along and blow the cork. . . . But if we are in a jug it is transparent, not opaque, and one is allowed not only to see outside but to read what is going on out there; to make identifications as to values and human quality" (116). The metaphor of the jug is so central to Ellison's articulation of black being in the world as it relates to African American writers and literature that it becomes his essay's title, "The World and the Jug." In the sentence I have quoted, however, he only provisionally accepts the depiction ("if") so as to make his point about black interaction with the "outer" white world.

Such a construction of the world and black existence in it—black life and culture in a jug and white life and culture outside or beyond it—constitutes a dominant spatial metaphor in perceptions of blackness in American society. (More recently, Helen Vendler's essay on Dove, "Blackness and Beyond Blackness," continues that view of black being.) Ellison's conditional acceptance of the metaphor bespeaks a more complex understanding of the ultimately decentered nature of racial and cultural interaction, an understanding beyond the scope of his argument with Howe and probably beyond the state of race relations at the time of the essay, 1963.

Ellison was working against limited views of African American identity born of a legally segregated society. One of his central arguments is that Howe's overemphasis on Wright, Baldwin, and Ellison himself as Negro writers "leaves no room for the individual writer's unique existence" (130). Ellison argues that "Howe makes of 'Negroness' a metaphysical condition," a view that "leaves no room for that intensity of personal anguish which compels the artist to seek relief by projecting it into the world in conjunction with other things; that anguish which might take the form of an acute sense of inferiority for one, homosexuality for another, an overwhelming sense of the absurdity of human life for still another" (130).[3]

According to Ellison, "The individual Negro writer must create out of his own special needs and through his own sensibilities, and these alone" (130). And that personal experience, Ellison maintains, is not only individual for a black writer but also collective by virtue of a "cultural heritage as shaped by the American experience" (131). Here Ellison uses the jug metaphor to demonstrate the largeness of the "concord of sensibilities" he finds in blacks (131): "Being a Negro American has to do with the memory of slavery and the hope of emancipation and the betrayal by allies and the revenge and contempt inflicted by our former masters after the Reconstruction, and the myths, both Northern and Southern, which are propagated in justification of that betrayal. It involves, too, a special attitude toward the waves of immigrants who have come later and passed us by. It has to do with a special perspective on the national ideals and the national conduct, and with a tragicomic attitude toward the universe" (131).

Ellison continues in this vein for another page, but his main point is that African American writers cannot, and should not, be reduced to blackness as whites might define it. They, and their writings, are shaped by individual personal experiences that also include the perspective of the shared group experience of being black. In the final line of the passage, he quietly states a black writer's capacity to comment on the universe, to be universal, through existence and perspective rather than moving beyond blackness—looking "outside the jug," so to speak.[4] That comment furnishes a key foundation.

Ellison provides a useful touchstone for Dove's deployment of key features of the new black aesthetic in *Museum*. Of the four main literary features—artists borrowing and reassembling across race and class lines; a parodic relationship to the black arts movement; a new, unflinching look at black culture, warts and all; and a belief in finding the universal in oneself and one's experiences—the first and last are most important in relation to *Museum* and other cosmopolitan works. These features, transcultural references, and a revisionist universalism reflect the cosmopolitan sensibility underlying the idea of a new black aesthetic.

Dove borrows and reassembles across race, class, and all sorts of other boundaries, a hallmark of her aesthetic from the beginning. As in *The Yellow House on the Corner,* she deliberately foregrounds her poetic identity as a poet of the world and writes from perspectives that cross history, cultures, genders, socioeconomic positions, races, and ethnicities. Many, including Robert McDowell, have noted that Dove does so; Ekaterini Georgoudaki has detailed such boundary crossings throughout Dove's four volumes of poetry, including *Museum* ("Rita Dove"). Writers of the 1950s who crossed boundaries received intraracial censure during the 1960s because they were perceived as trying to move beyond blackness and write outside the jug. Although Dove has felt similar pressures, her view of blackness and African American literature does not fit the world and the jug model that Ellison provisionally offered as a correction to Howe. Instead, Dove sees no jug of containment for black experience and being. Her wide experiences across a range of cultures have become part of the personal experience that shapes her perspective rather than being a world "out there" that she regards through a glass wall. Thus, for her, no gulf exists between the transcultural personal experiences she has had and the "concord of sensibilities" Ellison identifies as shaping a uniquely African American perspective. In discussing Derek Walcott's mixing of traditions in his use of both patois and traditional English, for example, Dove comments, "I think it's a wealth rather than a problem, and it's so ass backwards to say that there is a black way of writing and then there is a white; this is madness. Every black person that I know speaks at so many different levels all the time, and why not use all of that? All of it. Why not?" (Appendix, page 172). Dove identifies multiple language uses as a transcultural feature of black experience rather than having some be within the jug and others without.

Such a decentered, uncontained view of black being restructures universality as available to African American writers through personal experience rather than by accessing the outer, white world. This cosmopolitan belief is one of the central features of Dove's *Museum*. Dove presents a museum of the world that comes from her perspective, including personal experiences sometimes circumscribed by race (and sometimes not) as well as that "concord of sensibilities" Ellison outlines of an African American point of view. *Museum* constitutes Dove's *Harlem Gallery*, but the locus includes the world and all history as seen through Dove's perspective.[5]

This revisionist universality is typical of writers of Dove's generation. As Waniek observes, "One of the things our generation is achieving is that we are not saying, 'Look at me, I'm human too'—which is what most of the generations before us had basically been saying—but: 'Look, I'm human, and my humanity is the common denominator. Not that I have to be integrated into your humanity. *My* humanity is what you must find in common with *me*'" (Dove and Waniek 265).

Dove reprises Waniek's assertion in an interview with Therese Steffen. In response to the question, "What do you think about 'universalism' and the literary imagination?" Dove replies, "I don't think a universalism that lacks a sense of the specific can be very powerful; at the same time, any culturally drenched perception isn't going to be powerful if it doesn't have some kind of universal reverberation. I guess what I am saying is that 'the universal' is a bogus concept. We've come to believe that being 'universal' is to transcend difference—again, the incredible trauma of difference in modern society has made us yearn for conformity. Why can't we find the universal in those differences?" (123).

Dove's definition of the universal resembles Posnock's characterization of Du Bois's goal of negotiating "the racial particular and the unraced universal" (88), of having cultural specificity and also a sense of shared experience. Beyond that, Dove challenges any notion of obliterating difference through the universal. Instead, she values a universal focused on exploring difference. This is much the same as Michel Feher's definition of cosmopolitanism (used as part of Posnock's argument). Cosmopolitanism, Feher asserts, "entertains curiosity about . . . differences. It is 'color-curious' rather than color-blind or color-bound. . . . a cosmopolitan perspective calls for a dynamic of mutual transformation" (276).

Museum's structure makes clear that its transglobal, transcultural, transhistorical, transracial, and transgendered stances and the recurring themes of the underside of history (Rubin and Kitchen 156; Taleb-Khlyer 356); the representation of artifacts; the misjudgment of beauty and ugliness; and the abuses of power spawned by cultural difference—in short, its universality—emanate from the perspective of an African American middle-class young woman. *Museum*'s four sections avoid attempting a core section like that of *The Yellow House on the Corner*. Yet Dove's arrangement of poems in sections two and three, the middle part of *Museum*, insistently marks the universal perspective of the volume as originating in the worldview of a cosmopolitan African American writer who shares sensibilities with other blacks of similar experience in America and whose point of view has been shaped by personal and familial experiences.

Museum's forty-one poems divide somewhat evenly into four sections. Section one, "The Hill Has Something to Say," contains twelve poems, although two form pairs with two others (the two on Catherine of Siena and the two involving Boccaccio and Fiammetta) thus make the section read like it has ten poems. Section two, "In the Bulrush," has ten poems; section three, "My Father's Telescope," includes nine; and section four, "Primer for the Nuclear Age," contains ten. The two poems most critical to Dove's cosmopolitan project of finding the universal in herself and her experiences (the twenty-first and twenty-second) lie directly in the middle of the volume in section two: "Agosta the Winged Man and Rasha the Black Dove" and "At the German Writers Conference in Munich."[6] These, not coincidentally, are followed by a series of personal poems involving Dove's relationship with her father (section three) and then a "universal" section (four).

In "Agosta the Winged Man and Rasha the Black Dove" (hereafter "Agosta and Rasha"), Dove inverts the objectifying gaze to which museum or cultural artifacts are exposed as she subjectifies the two German sideshow entertainers. Inversive subjectification offers details and information about those being objectified and is a key stage in creating a revisionist universalism. They become subjects who have perspectives that readers can share. That the inversion is central to the collection's enterprise as a whole is obvious not only in the central placement of the poem (twenty-one of forty-one poems) but also in the recurrence of the same inversive subjectification throughout the volume.

From the beginning of section one (the initial poem is "The Fish in the Stone"), Dove turns the tables on the objectifying gaze of history and culture. The first poem, for example, presents a fossilized fish's point of view. He is:

> weary
> of analysis, the small
> predictable truths.
> He is weary of waiting
> in the open,
> his profile stamped
> by a white light. (13)

In other poems a hill has something to say, a wife talks back to her husband, and we are invited into the stream-of-consciousness thoughts of a blues singer.

"Agosta and Rasha" represents the apex of Dove's subjectifying inversions for reasons other than the poem's central placement in the volume and Dove's choice of the painting of Agosta and Rasha as the collection's cover.[7] In the poem, which follows the process of German artist Christian Schad's composition and execution of a portrait of Agosta and Rasha in 1929, Dove offers a doubled portrait of her position as both artist and artifact. Although other poems in *Museum* also concern artists (Boccaccio, Champion Jack Dupree, and a cellist) and three present specifically African American characters, only in "Agosta and Rasha" does Dove present the issue of an artist representing a black woman. Her comments on her experience as a Fulbright scholar in Tübingen, Germany, help demonstrate how the character Rasha reflects Dove's experience. In Europe, Dove says, "I became an object. I was a Black American, and therefore I became a representative for all of that. And I sometimes felt like a ghost. I mean, people would ask me questions, but I had a feeling that they weren't seeing *me,* but a shell" (Rubin and Kitchen 156). Rasha, "so far from Madagascar" (41), parallels Dove's familiarity with feeling that she is a visual object.

The motifs of seeing and objectification by the gaze run throughout the poem.[8] Schad is depicted at the beginning as pacing his studio and then "staring" (41). Both sideshow entertainers, Agosta and Rasha, are first developed through others' visual objectifications. Dove describes Rasha's performance with a boa constrictor through Schad's recollection of the scene and how "spectators gawked." Likewise, Schad thinks of how Agosta described being observed by medical students, "his torso / exposed" (42). Schad seems concerned to distance himself from repeating these objectifying moments in the artistic representation. As he notes, "The canvas, / not his eye, was merciless." It is as if the demands of artistic representation (the canvas) might gaze mercilessly upon them but not him (his eye) (41). Ultimately, however, Rasha and Agosta invert the gaze, described by Schad in the painting as

> [w]ithout passion. Not
> the canvas
> but their gaze,
> so calm,
> was merciless. (42)[9]

The inversion of perspective and the gaze by the end of the poem is accomplished through Dove's deliberate subjectification of the two characters. She offers information and details that provide their point of view and make them subjects in the poem and thus the painting. All of that happens in Schad's mind, which suggests Dove's point. The artistic process of representation, or the cultural process of constructing history, need not objectify people into artifacts. Metaphorically speaking, we can hear what the hill has to say "if we would listen!" (19). In "Agosta and Rasha" the poet-Dove represented through Schad (who is distinct from the personal-Dove represented through Rasha) attends to the subjectivities of Agosta and Rasha. Schad recalls how Rasha, after her show (where the spectators gawked), "went back to her trailer and plucked / a chicken for dinner" (41). Later in the poem, he remembers:

> [o]nce,
> she brought fresh eggs into
> the studio, flecked and
> warm as breath. (42)

Both descriptions personalize Rasha in the process of depicting her. After being viewed as a sideshow freak, she goes home—like anyone else—and plucks a chicken for dinner. The descriptions also link Rasha to sustenance and nurturing. The eggs in particular connote fertility and life, even if cooked and eaten. Likewise, Agosta's objectification is inverted when Schad relays how Agosta, with "lip curled," spoke to him

in wonder of women
trailing
backstage to offer him
the consummate bloom of their lust. (42)

Such derisive amazement offers a dimension of subjectivity to Agosta that is unavailable through the medical gaze or spectators gawking. Dove plays with the idea of taking off and putting on appearances; Agosta and Rasha are both objectified visually through physical appearance. Schad describes Rasha as moving slowly, "as if she carried / the snake around her body / always" (42). Even without the boa constrictor, she is still a snake charmer. Agosta can cover his misshapen torso, but when Schad paints him he will have "the black suit jacket / thrown off like a cloak" (42). Dove's specific mention of blackness seems a nod to the black skin color, unmentioned, that Rasha also cannot remove. The play with appearances becomes a triangle of reference among Rasha, Agosta, and Schad with Schad's reflection that

[h]e could not leave his skin—once
he'd painted himself in a new one,
silk green, worn
like a shirt. (41)

That suggests the possibility of escaping one's physical appearance (and its concomitant objectifications) through art. Dove plays with crossing boundaries of individual perspectives in this triangle of reference, suggesting that readers can do so as well by taking on various perspectives, and taking them off, via art.

Ultimately, the poem rests with the conviction that one is welded to appearance—whether skin color, physical aspects, or accessories such as snakes—and those things are inseparable from identity. Schad concludes after painting himself wearing a green shirt, "He could not leave his skin" (41); Rasha "moves slowly, as if she carried / the snake around her always" (42); and Agosta can cover but never leave

his torso
. . . its crests and fins
a colony of birds, trying
to get out. (42)

Although the imagery of "leave," "always," and "trying to get out" suggest a trapped feeling, appearances in the poem are also linked firmly to identity. The title is, after all, "Agosta the Winged Man and Rasha the Black Dove," the same title as the painting's. The two sideshow entertainers' appearances become part of their names and identities. The connection to Dove herself in Rasha's title (she is the Black Dove) further supports reading Rasha as a partial commentary on Dove's stand on blackness and identity. (That her husband Fred Viebahn's first book—seven years before he met Dove—is entitled *Die schwarzen Tauben* [The Black Doves] makes this resonate more deeply.) Dove's habit of using her last name in her poetry as a word and in bird imagery connects both Rasha the Black Dove and also Agosta the Winged Man to Dove's artistic identity as it relates to aesthetics in *Museum*.

In this poem, then, Dove as artist inverts objectified depictions of herself as a black woman (and others similarly objectified); furthermore, she returns the "merciless gaze" back on the observer. The poem's final moment, in which Agosta and Rasha look out from the canvas, states the perspective of the entire collection: Artifacts and the marginalized gaze onto both the culture and those who objectified and buried them. And Dove's gaze, or perspective, is behind it all. Thus she enacts a revisionist universalism in *Museum*.

Dove pairs this poem with the one that follows, "At the German Writers Conference in Munich," by linking imagery and theme. Unlike "Agosta and Rasha," which is experienced through Christian Schad's consciousness, the second poem uses no persona other than Dove's poet-persona; the experience presumably comes from her attendance at a conference in Munich. The perspective of the poem, then, is unabashedly Dove's, as the first stanza reveals:

> In the large hall of the Hofbräuhaus
> above the heads of the members
> of the board, taut and white
> as skin (not mine),
> tacked across a tapestry
> this banner. (43)

Dove's parenthetical denotation of her race points out the assumption of "universal" acceptance of white when no markers are given to denote other skin colors. The words "not mine" are slipped in as if they are a minor aside, but in reality they turn the perspective of the entire poem, just as in "Agosta and Rasha." The image of skin, of course, also ties back to the preceding poem and is a reminder that skin color (and other facts of physical appearance) is interwoven with identity. Thus the perspective of the volume is again underlined as being that of a black woman.

The poem sounds Dove's theme of repression of aspects of history, with the focal point being a medieval tapestry partially covered by a large white paper banner that states the organizing group of the conference. The banner obscures most of the tapestry, yet the "tapestry pokes out / all over," expressing the eruptions of repressed history (43). The substance of the poem details reading the tapestry's parts, which represent history outside a frame. Dove's parenthetical insertion of her skin color "(not mine)" acts as a similar eruption of history and culture in the text of *Museum* (43). As such, it becomes a central statement of aesthetic perspective that refuses to "paper over" a false presentation of skin color as "universally" white. At this moment in the text, Dove asserts a universally relevant vantage point that comes from an African American perspective.

After the two central poems in *Museum,* Dove's new black aesthetic of finding the universal in oneself and one's experiences finds expression in the structural interplay between the last two sections. The third section, "My Father's Telescope," concerns the poet's father and their relationship. The fourth section, "Primer for the Nuclear Age," ranges across the globe and throughout the contemporary era. As Dove explains some of the connections between the two sections:

> The entire third section deals with my father. . . . I was trying to look into the fourth section with the telescope so that it becomes much more; it becomes the technological age, the scientific age, the nuclear age, that I'm looking forward to. . . .
>
> Rubin: And finally you have the "Primer for the Nuclear Age," which extends the theme, as you said, to everything.
>
> Dove: Yes, looking outward again after going to the father. I also didn't want the father poems to appear too early in the book. . . . But after two sections where there's nothing personal at all, I wanted to go into the personal poems and then explode out of them into

the nuclear age. And I do believe that the kinds of events which are formed by the cruelty of Trujillo or the carelessness of nuclear escalation nowadays start at very personal levels. (Rubin and Kitchen 159)

Dove here confirms that, for her, the personal undergirds the global. Thus in section four her move to the global or "universal" comes only after, and is fundamentally informed by, her individual perspective as reinforced by section three. She makes this structural interplay apparent in the poem "Anti-Father" in section three, in which she speaks back to a father—both her personal father and also the father of "universal law"—and asserts,

> [c]ontrary to
> tales you told us
> . . . .
> —the stars
> are not far
> apart. Rather
> they draw
> closer together
> with years. (54)

"[W]oman to man," she tells him, "outer space is / inconceivably / intimate" (55).

Dove's revision of the universe—and the universal—from her perspective (in this poem specifically female) helps readers understand "Parsley," the final poem of section four and the volume, as also informed by her individual perspective. Rafael Trujillo, the Dominican dictator who is said to have had twenty thousand Haitian canefield workers killed because they could not pronounce the word *parsley* (*perejil*) in Spanish, represents great evil to Dove because he refuses to appreciate difference (78).[10] Instead, Trujillo kills because of a repressive universalism that enforces the dominant party's culture and experience over those of others. As the workers note, in El General's version of universalism, "He is all the world / there is" (75). Because his mother "could roll an R like a queen," such linguistic ability should be a standard of humanity, and Trujillo will kill to enforce it. Dove condemns such oppressive universalism and contrasts it with revisionist universalism such as her own, which depicts subjects enacting a dynamic of mutual transformation because of cosmopolitan curiosity about difference.

～

Several among Dove's contemporaries in African American poetry could be named as cosmopolitan, among them Yusef Komunyakaa, Toi Derricotte, and Cyrus Cassells. Of the younger generation, Elizabeth Alexander, who studied with Derek Walcott, could also be identified. To what extent they might also consider themselves part of any new black aesthetic is debatable. Komunyakaa, for example, might agree to being cosmopolitan but would certainly insist that his work is founded on a blues and jazz aesthetic.[11]

Other aesthetics were also evident in African American poetry during the 1980s and 1990s. Cheryl Clarke, for example, in *Living as a Lesbian,* writes in a deliberate refusal of traditional aesthetic poetic values, as Melissa Daniel notes. Brenda Marie Osbey's work offers a New Orleans–specific narrative poetic that eschews the figurative.[12] And Wanda Coleman's blunt, energetic poetry attacks the evils of racism, sexism, and classism in a style insistently oral and polemical. Furthermore, a new generation's interest in performance or "spoken-word" poetry, which has connections to hip-hop culture, is another dominant poetic aesthetic; individual wordsmiths now appear on CDs and in published anthologies (Anglesey; Wannberg).[13]

Cosmopolitanism is assuming a centrally important role in academic circles for several reasons, especially class differences. Ellis notes the vastly expanded black middle class as a factor behind the black arts of the 1980s. As the twentieth century came to a close, fully 50 percent of the black American population was middle class or above. With such economic advancement came an array of educational and cultural experiences and a concomitant entrance into institutional positions of power.

African American cosmopolitan poets come from graduate programs such as those at the University of Iowa, Brown University, and New York University and have bachelor's degrees from institutions such as Stanford, Wesleyan, and Yale universities. They tend to have traveled extensively and have lived abroad for extended periods, for example, in Germany, France, Senegal, Italy, and Vietnam. They have academic appointments, often at prestigious universities such as Columbia University, the University of Virginia, and the University of Chicago. They also are generally well published, having found acceptance in key venues such as the *American Poetry Review, New England Review, Bread Loaf Quarterly,* and the *Kenyon Review* as well as the preeminent journal for African American literary arts and criticism, *Callaloo.* Their books appear with major publishers such as Norton and Random House as well as with well-respected poetry presses such as Copper Canyon, the University of Virginia's *Callaloo* Poetry Series, and Wesleyan University Press. They also have been successful at winning grants, fellowships, awards, and residencies to support their work from institutions such as the Ford Foundation, the National Endowment for the Arts, the Academy of American Poets, the Rockefeller Foundation, the Lannan Foundation, the National Humanities Center, and the Fulbright, Guggenheim and Mellon Fellowships. Both Yusef Komunyakaa and Rita Dove have won Pulitzer Prizes for Poetry.

Thus, in terms of institutional sanction by African American, American, and international culture brokers, cosmopolitan poets are prominent in the generation of African American poets who were born after 1940 and published throughout the 1980s and 1990s. Although Wanda Coleman has complained that she could not find enough money to bury her son and that she has been shunned in African American poetry circles, cosmopolitan poets are generally well funded and well fêted, indicating their high stature since the 1980s.[14] When the George Moses Horton Society for the Study of African American Poetry (founded by Trudier Harris-Lopez of the University of North Carolina at Chapel Hill) held its inaugural conference in 1998, for example, the three poets of focus included one "elder" in the tradition, Margaret Walker, and two cosmopolitan poets, Komunyakaa and Dove. In addition, when the Academy of American Poets finally relented in the face of overwhelming criticism of their all-white chancellors' group (thanks to an aggressive campaign by Fred Viebahn following a written complaint by Toi Derricotte), they appointed Komunyakaa a chancellor along with Lucille Clifton, whose work is more representative of the previous generation. Dove has received a high degree of public attention in her two-term appointment as poet laureate and her authorship of the "Poet's Choice" column (begun by Robert Hass) in *Book World.* If we agree with Michel Feher and Ross Posnock, who argue that cosmopolitanism has been repressed in the black intellectual tradition, it is apparent that the 1980s and 1990s represented a two-decade emergence into prominence. It is worth reflecting on the politics of this academic prominence. If 50 percent of black America is middle-class or above, then the other half is not (Raymond). Henry Louis Gates, Jr., and Cornell West have identified the bifurcation in African American culture as a key issue for the twenty-first century, a continuation and redefinition of Du Bois's articulation in 1903 that the problem of the twentieth century is the problem of the color line. The problem of the twenty-first century appears to be the class line within the community. Gates comments that "Dr. King did not die so that *half* of us would 'make it,' and *half* of us perish" (xvii, emphasis in the original).

Spoken-word poetry, with its connection to hip-hop popular culture, often urban and overtly political themes, and frequent protest of racial and class oppression, is the aesthetic vehicle for those outside the black middle class. The aesthetic itself is slowly gaining academic and institutional recognition by teachers, scholars, and established poetry organizations. It appears prominent in popular culture—more students know it than know the work of Rita Dove. The prominence of cosmopolitanism in academic culture thus may be born of privilege and the class schism in African American literature. In general, the youngest poets who garnered academic attention during the 1990s—Elizabeth Alexander, Melvin Dixon, and the Dark Room Collective—all seem to be from the half that "made it." Poets such as Angela Jackson, who is committed to the people of Chicago's South Side, are almost completely unknown. When including more popular poetry in our sights, cosmopolitanism seems only one of several current threads in African American literature; that encourages scholars and institutions to broaden their understanding.

Notes

1. In an interview with William Walsh, Dove remarked that *Yellow House,* "like many first books is a hodgepodge of techniques and visions. . . . 'Ö' [the last poem of that volume] felt like a very different poem, one that signaled the end of an apprenticeship" (150).

2. Thanks to Ilona Cesan for this insight.

3. One cannot help but wonder if Ellison intended these three specific cases to correspond to Wright, Baldwin, and Ellison directly.

4. Ross Posnock's take on the problem with universalism is white refusal to acknowledge black contributions to the larger culture (20). From that perspective, the universal is composed of everyone; it is only the fiction of cultural segregation, perpetuated in the interests of white dominance, that makes people believe otherwise.

5. Although Dove has pointed in interviews to the German *Mausoleum* by Hans Magnus Enzensberger as an inspiration for *Museum*, it seems likely that a model or influence closer to home is Tolson's *Harlem Gallery*, especially given Dove's essay on it within two years of *Museum*'s publication (Peabody and Johnsen; Taleb-Khyar).

6. Robert McDowell also pairs these two poems (65).

7. It is also notable that Dove, in this early poem, deliberately suppresses her apprehensions about an attack from black arts movement adherents (Steffen, "The Darker Face" 108).

8. Although I have in mind some of the ideas about the male objectifying gaze first promulgated by Laura Mulvey and later the subject of some degree of feminist theorizing, I am not directly drawing on the gender implications here as much as the mechanism of visual objectification.

9. McDowell notes the shift of their gaze outward at the end of the poem (65).

10. Fred Viebahn notes the correct date of this mass murder is 1937 rather than 1957 as originally footnoted in *Museum* (personal communication. Jan. 29, 2002). Historians offer differing interpretations of the causes behind the massacre. Robert Crassweller, for example, posits that Trujillo, who had been plotting to overthrow Haiti, ordered the massacre in retaliation for the killing of his underground agents in Haiti. Crassweller perceives no "general prejudice" or "color prejudice" toward Haitians on the part of Dominicans (149). In contrast, Eric Roorda argues that the "Dominican nationalism promoted by Trujillo emphasized Hispanic culture and demonized Haitian, African-derived culture" (129). Trujillo's attempts to reduce Haitian influence and border-crossings were revealed to him as unsuccessful during a tour of the border in August and September 1937 (130–31). On October 2, 1937, he announced his intent to permanently eliminate the Haitian presence in the Dominican Republic (131). Although Crassweller mentions the pronunciation of *perejil* as a test (155), neither historian considers it a cause of the massacre.

11. Thanks to Craig Werner for helping me articulate this distinction.

12. See Lynn Keller's balanced and informative study of Osbey in *Forms of Expansion*.

13. Thanks to Veronica Jones, a spoken-word poet herself, for introducing me to the next generation.

14. Wanda Coleman's letters to E. Ethelbert Miller appear in *Callaloo*.

5 〜 *Thomas and Beulah:*
Starting at the "Source"
of the Blues Nomad

Dove's cosmopolitanism, and the revisionist universalism it leads her to promulgate in her major new black aesthetic volume *Museum* (1983), complicates her positions—as a poet, a woman, and an African American—and forces her to consider, with acknowledgment of increasing complexities, the ramifications of aesthetic self-fashioning in relation to her (poetic) subjectivity. Having demonstrated global breadth in *Museum,* Dove asks herself in the volumes that follow, "Where is my home?" Unlike the anxiety behind *The Yellow House on the Corner,* in which the tensions surrounding her cosmopolitanism focus on the issues of identity through the figure of the cultural mulatto, following the cosmopolitan confidence of *Museum* Dove faces the challenge of imagining a home or location for a cosmopolitan identity.

Her answer comes in an evolution that signifies on "writing her way back home" in *Thomas and Beulah* (1986), *Grace Notes* (1989), "In the Old Neighborhood" in *Selected Poems* (1993), *Mother Love* (1995), and *On the Bus with Rosa Parks* (1999). In his eerily prescient "The Poems of Rita Dove" (1986)—which justly and carefully characterizes her differences from the generation of black arts poets preceding her—Arnold Rampersad ends by reflecting on where Dove's "great talent" might take her during her "major career": "I believe that, paradoxically for someone so determined to be a world citizen, she may yet gain her greatest strength by returning to some place closer to her old neighborhood." He adds, "Very carefully, I do not say her 'home'—much less her 'real home' or her 'true home.' Such terms, made shabby by the hucksters, are millstones to a poet like Dove; for her a house is not necessarily a home. In the end, she may yet as a poet redefine for all of us what 'home' means. Dove herself would probably benefit in her own way as an artist from this active redefinition" (60).

Given that in the pages preceding these remarks Rampersad has charted Dove's "meagerness of racial feeling" and "possession of the wide world" as opposed to a stance of "racial indignation" (55, 56), his comments about a return to "her old neighborhood" are freighted with racial implications.[1] He is, on one level, inviting her back to a black homeplace; at the same time, he is recognizing that her definition of that homeplace may be new and even contradictory of established definitions.[2] More generally, he is encouraging her to explore personal concerns.

Dove's three volumes following *Museum*—*Thomas and Beulah*, *Grace Notes*, and *Mother Love*—all chart a path back home in the sense of a return to family origins, autobiography, personal experience, and family life. After the very public and global *Museum*, the apparent subject of Dove's poetry has seemed to move progressively closer to intimate, more personal material. *Thomas and Beulah* initiates this development from the distance of a generation with a focus on Dove's maternal grandparents; *Grace Notes* moves closer with poems on the immediate experiences of Dove's family of origin and the family she has made with her husband, Fred Viebahn; and *Mother Love* explores the mother-daughter bond.[3] Published between *Grace Notes* and *Mother Love*, Dove's poem "In the Old Neighborhood" participates in the trek back via self-reflexive comment (and perhaps even direct reference to Rampersad's article in the title).[4] In detailing a family moment at her parents' home, Dove recreates a flood of memories.

Furthermore, Dove's comments in interviews near the beginning and ending of this period (from 1986 to 1995) draw attention to her return home. In a 1989 interview with Steven Schneider, "Coming Home," she notes, "Now, when I look back on the three books that I have done and see how they move, I understand that old adage about coming back to your own backyard" (115). When Schneider asks if *Thomas and Beulah* seems different than her earlier books, she responds, "I think it is a departure from my other work—rather, I came home" (118). And in a 1994 interview with Emily Lloyd, who asks about Dove's move from history into the personal and whether the

focus on the personal in *Grace Notes* was a result of finally feeling safe
about her reputation as a poet, Dove explains:

> It wasn't so much that I felt safe in my reputation as it was that I felt
> secure enough in my craft as a poet to write about the personal with-
> out the personal becoming too self-indulgent. I was really conscious
> of the fact, when I began publishing, that there was a lot of poetry out
> there that assumed the writer's personal life was intensely interesting.
> I'd rather that the personal not be so self-indulgent; instead, let it be
> only a lens for seeing the world more clearly. Also, I was working my
> way back home, learning about myself by learning about the world
> around me. Like a child does, you try to figure out how the world
> works and then you understand your relationship to the world. (22)

That explanation accounts for Dove's "personal reference disci-
plined by a measuring of distance and a prizing of objectivity" in her
early poetry (Rampersad 53). What came from the personal in her
earliest work, such as the adolescent poems in *The Yellow House on
the Corner*, was subject to tight poetic control. Later, Dove feels she
attained more poetic skill and therefore is less concerned about using
the personal in her poetry. After *Museum*, she has allowed herself, as
she sees it, to move closer to home in her choice of subject matter.

Significantly, Dove describes a unique role for the personal: as a
lens for seeing the world more clearly. Such an attitude constitutes
an extension of revisionist universalism (chapter 4), in which many
post–black arts movement writers insist on the universality of their
perspectives.[5] This role is inherently cosmopolitan and overtly global,
an expansion and revision of the world and the jug metaphor Ralph
Ellison debated with Irving Howe. They are the world and the world
is them, as Dove indicates by the titles of a pair of lectures she gave
as poet laureate that were published as the two central sections of *The
Poet's World* (1995): "Stepping Out: The Poet in the World" and "'A
Handful of Inwardness': The World in the Poet."

If taken at face value, however, Dove's expression of a journey
home seems overly simple when compared to her actual treatment
of the idea of home. Instead, her work signifies on the concept of
home and neighborhood, refusing any sort of nostalgic embrace of
one location for poetic identity. Her idea of home, for example, stands
in stark contrast to that of Amiri Baraka in his essay "Home," where

he charts his artistic process as a moving into his "blackness" (10). The essay, an introduction to his collection *Home*, ends, "By the time this book appears, I will be even blacker" (10). Dove's redefinition of home, however, moves beyond identity politics—whether based on race, class, nationality, or gender—and practices an enlarged, cosmopolitan interplay between home and identity that radically expands the sense of what home or neighborhood means and is.[6]

Dove's self-fashioning in her post-*Museum* work is that of a blues nomad. The blues emanate from acknowledging the partial losses inherent in a cosmopolitan identity, and the nomadic stance reflects her multiperspectived, global, "rhythmical displacement[s]" from any one home (Braidotti 22).[7] Nomadism, Rosi Braidotti observes, is a

> theoretical figuration for contemporary subjectivity—out of the phallocentric vision of the subject [that represents a] situated, postmodern, culturally differentiated understanding of the subject in general and of the feminist subject in particular. This subject can also be described as postmodern/industrial/colonial, depending on one's locations. In so far as axes of differentiation such as class, race, ethnicity, gender, age, and others intersect and interact with each other in the constitution of subjectivity, the notion of the nomad refers to the simultaneous occurrence of many of these at once. (1, 4)[8]

The nomad works well as a figure for Dove in her mature work because it allows simultaneous expression of her perspectives as an African American and American as well as a woman, poet, cosmopolitan writer, world traveler, and mother.[9] The idea of the nomad incorporates Dove's revisionist universalism and involves "radicalizing the concept of the universal rather than doing away with it" (Braidotti 12). Thus, Dove's poetic persona evolves from the anxious cultural mulatto figure in *The Yellow House on the Corner* into a nomadic stance in work after *Museum*. Undergirding all is cosmopolitanism. Such a development suggests that perhaps Trey Ellis's cultural mulatto is not an enduring figure for writers' cosmopolitanism, although it may reflect their initial anxieties. Instead, their mature poetic identities are culturally nomadic.

Identifying the nomad as a polyglot with "polymorphous perversity," slipping between and among languages or discourses within one language (13–15), Braidotti sees a nomadic style as based on "compassion for the incongruities, the repetitions, the arbitrariness of the languages she deals with" and "a process of undoing the illusory stability of fixed identities, bursting open the bubble of ontological security" (15). Braidotti specifically differentiates the nomad from the migrant or exile. The migrant moves specifically from one location to another and is often fixed in the lower class; the exile, however, is forever displaced and in a sense "countryless" (21–22). Braidotti's nomad "does not stand for homelessness or compulsive displacement; it is rather a figuration for the kind of subject who has relinquished all idea, desire, or nostalgia for fixity" (22). Thus, my use of the term *nomad* specifically differs from critics—Ekaterini Georgoudaki (*Race, Gender, and Class Perspectives*) and Therese Steffen (*Crossing Color* and "Beyond Ethnic Margin")—most directly—who have used the terms *exile, displacement,* and *migrating* in describing Dove's perspective.

Nomadism is not without pain, however, as the blues motif running from *Thomas and Beulah* to *On the Bus with Rosa Parks* reveals. Dove's embrace of cosmopolitanism, her "rhythmical displacements," her refusal of nostalgia, and her head-long focus on contradiction, uncertainty, and gaps all give her poetry a blues background that is not always readily apparent, because Dove typically pulls back from using overt blues idiom.

Dove's poem most apparently in the blues tradition is "Shakespeare Say" from *Museum*. The black vernacular speech of the title continues in the depiction of blues singer Champion Jack Dupree, often in his voice directly, with lines such as

Shakespeare say
man must be
careful what he kiss
when he drunk. (90)

Early in the poem Dove nods to the dominant twinned themes of the blues and loss of love and/or money ("Champion Jack in love / and in debt" [89]). Dupree experiences the stuff of the blues, from the hardships of the German winter—

Munich was misbehaving,
whipping
his ass to ice

while his shoes
soaked through. (89)

—to problems with love—

In trouble
with every woman he's
ever known, all of them
ugly. (90)

—all the way to complete breakdown by the end of the poem—

my home's in Louisiana,
my voice is wrong,
I'm broke and can't hold
my piss; my mother told me there'd be days like this. (91)

Dupree, of course, succeeds most at the blues when he utterly falls
apart, because he transforms that experience into the art of the blues
(Appendix, pages 184–85). Even though he is miserable, by the end of
the set depicted at the close of the poem he is "winning / now, so even
the mistakes sound like jazz" (90). Thus Dove marshals the blues
idiom and its themes in the use of black vernacular and classic blues
subjects and also represents Dupree's music and voice—all in ways
very similar to Langston Hughes's poem "The Weary Blues."

The Dupree poem, however, is atypical of the blues in Dove's oeuvre, which revoices the blues on a black, middle-class cosmopolitan
note. Dove is no "poet laureate of Harlem," as Hughes was fondly
dubbed, but rather the first African American poet laureate of the
United States, a different position and perspective indeed. Yet that
vantage point does not eliminate her or other black poets from the
African American poetic tradition, as she insisted in a series of critical essays in the 1980s and early 1990s (chapter 1).

In a discussion of Jessie Fauset and Nella Larson, Ann duCille vig-
orously defends the blues as a space for middle-class expression and
maintains that they sang a "bourgeois blues," their own brand of
"somebody done somebody wrong" songs (67). DuCille argues that
a valorization of the vernacular is exclusionary: "Too often writers
whose expressive geographies are perceived as lying outside the blues
space are not remapped but demapped" (68). As she notes, the term

"'middle class,' when applied to black artists and their subjects, becomes pejorative, a sign of mortgaging one's black aesthetic to the alien conventions of the dominant culture" (71).

DuCille, like Dove and Posnock, argues against the repression of cosmopolitanism and defends the inclusion of black middle-class experience and expression within the African American literary tradition. Dove's bourgeois, cosmopolitan blues embraces a broad range of cultural experiences of alienation, loss, and pain. The blues, as Dove's poetry shows, is not always about losing your woman (or man) or having no money. As Albert Murray writes, "[T]he blues statement, regardless of what it reflects, . . . *expresses* . . . a sense of life that is affirmative. The blues lyrics reflect what they confront, of course, which includes the absurd, the unfortunate, and the catastrophic; but they also reflect the person making the confrontation, his self-control, his sense of structure and style; and they express, among other things, his sense of humor as well as his sense of ambiguity and his sense of possibility" (208, emphasis in the original). Dove's poetry, in its confrontation of contradiction, abjuring of sentimentality, and sense of humor about the human situation, presents a blues perspective. She confronts and affirms cosmopolitanism, acknowledging its benefits and its costs.

Yusef Komunyakaa further explores the range of resonance of the blues in his short essay "Blue," where he asserts, "The first abyss is blue. An artist must go beyond the mercy of satin or water—from a gutty hue to that which is close to royal purple. All the seasons and blossoms in between. . . . . The blue of absence. The blue of deep presence. The insides of something perfect" (3). Many of Dove's poems mine these nether regions of experience as she regards an abyss that others will not inspect. Komunyakaa's emphasis on a range of blue shades suggests that a broad repertoire of blues expressions is possible.

Craig Werner's framing of the "blues impulse" in *Playing the Changes: From Afro-Modernism to the Jazz Impulse* also adds to an understanding of how Dove's poetry reflects a blues sensibility. Drawing on blues thinkers such as Ralph Ellison, Werner outlines a three-phase process: brutal experience, lyrical expression, and reaffirmation. It is ironic that Dove, a relatively privileged member of the black middle class, seemingly lacks the "brutal experience" necessary for the blues. She confronts that irony in *On the Bus with Rosa Parks*. Although she, as the title suggests, links herself with Rosa Parks in poems that focus on the struggles of civil rights leaders, Dove is careful not to elide her experience as a black American with that of a previous generation or with blacks who are not middle class. Nearing the end of the last section, "On the Bus with Rosa Parks," is the poem "QE2. Transatlantic Crossing. Third Day," in which Dove sketches her experience as different. After describing the luxurious environment of the *Queen Elizabeth II,* she writes:

> Here I float on the lap of existence. Each night
> I put this body into its sleeve of dark water with no more
>
> than a teardrop of ecstasy, a thimbleful of ache.
> And that, friends, is the difference—
> I can't erase an ache I never had.
> Not even my own grandmother would pity me;
> instead she'd suck her teeth at the sorry sight
> of some Negro actually looking for misery.
>
> Well. I'd go home if I knew where to get off. (84–85)

Dove's argument appears to be that the civil rights movement is no more her home than any other experience is. As a beneficiary of the gains the movement has made possible, Dove lacks the "ache" (or brutal experiences) of her forebears and those who have not benefited. With characteristic self-deprecating blues humor, however, she points out how lack of misery disqualifies her from traditional blues expression. In addition, the poem unsentimentally identifies the source of her blues: "I'd go home if I knew where to get off" (85). For her, nomadism—even middle-class privilege—is partly a loss that brings on the blues. Werner's three-stage blues process, then, is apparent in Dove's sense of a painful experience of loss—of one home or place— and also in her lyrical expression of that loss. I shall return to the third stage—reaffirmation—in chapter 6.

On the most apparent level, Dove's blues is signaled through the covers of the paperback volumes of her poetry between 1987 and 1995. *Thomas and Beulah* is solid, dark blue, almost navy, and *Grace Notes* features Georgia O'Keefe's watercolor *Blue #2,* composed of several shades of that color. *Selected Poems* offers an author photograph carefully mounted between bands of blue; she wears a blue dress, blue-violet eyeshadow, and a multicolored necklace of blue, green, red, and violet beads. The beads reappear in small bars that surround the type on the front and back of the cover and also in the words of the title. The overall effect is a violet-gray, cornflower blue. *Mother Love*'s cover is also predominantly blue, but with a significant proportion of green in the photograph of Romare Bearden's *In a Green Shade.* Blue colors the sky in the background and also the foreground's pool, leaves, and birds. Dove was "adamant" about using the Beardon print. As she says, "Once I found 'In a Green Shade,' I knew that was the cover," and Albert Murray has identified Beardon as someone who painted "the visual equivalent to blues composition" (*The Blue Devils of Nada* 115).

Dove acknowledges that her "instincts" have led her "to prefer designs that featured blue" for the volumes published between 1986 and 1995. A pattern in cover designs for most books would be accidental or result the ideas of people other than the writer. Dove confirms, however, that she takes an active role in the design process for the covers, and both artwork and color are "very important" to her.[10] She and Viebahn collaborated with editors on the cover of her first collection, *The Yellow House on the Corner,* and found and secured the rights to the Christian Schad painting on the cover of her second volume, *Museum.* They completely designed the cover of *Thomas and Beulah,* as Dove writes, "down to the shade of blue and the placement of photographs (which are from the family album) on the page." Dove's editor at Norton, Carol Houck Smith, found the O'Keeffe watercolor for *Grace Notes,* but Dove "lived with the painting for a week or so and discussed the cover with her before they went ahead." The color blue also permeates the books' subject matter.

The text for which Dove won the Pulitzer Prize in 1987, *Thomas and Beulah,* has garnered the most critical attention. Structured as two narrative sequences of lyric poems, the volume traces the experiences of Dove's maternal grandparents, Thomas and Georgianna (whose name Dove changes to Beulah) from young adulthood and marriage to death, as she told Grace Cavalieri. Critics generally concur that its two most distinctive features—aside from its strikingly well-crafted poems—are its treatment of race and history. Ekaterini Georgoudaki demonstrates how Dove "crosses boundaries" of race and gender and notes her self-stated interest in the "underside of history" evident in the volume ("Rita Dove" 419). Patricia Wallace emphasizes Dove's preoccupation with American history—a preoccupation she does not let diffuse her passion for literary language (5). Lisa Steinman, Robert McDowell, and Helen Vendler each specify that Dove's interest in history in the volume is partly in personal history. Therese Steffen carries such a point further, arguing that "Dove's reclamation of her ancestors' lives represents both an aesthetic and an eth(n)ic act of historical recovery" ("Moments of a Marriage" 181).

Both Steffen and Vendler sense that *Thomas and Beulah* marks an important phase in Dove's poetry. Vendler proposes that it "represents Dove's rethinking of the lyric poet's relation to the history of blackness" ("Blackness and Beyond" 13). This "important discovery—that blackness need not be one's central subject, but equally need not be omitted" in *Thomas and Beulah*—has governed Dove's work since then, Vendler observes (13). Steffen, citing Hayden White's idea that history is our creation of a past from which we would like to be descended, claims that Dove is "not only fictionalizing her past but forging her own history" (181).

Although *Museum* is a significant text in Dove's oeuvre because it confidently presents her fully crafted new black aesthetic, *Thomas and Beulah* represents a landmark in that it is *Museum*'s necessary counterpoint and corrective response. In it, Dove writes her source, the roots that allowed her to have wings, as the folk saying goes. *Thomas and Beulah* begins Dove's deployment of a blues nomad persona, something entirely absent from the volume's poems. Allowing specifically African American historical experiences to be much closer than the arm's length of the slave narratives in *The Yellow House on the Corner,* Dove writes about the core sources beneath her cosmopolitanism, including displacement of blacks from the rural South to the urban North during the Great Migration in the early twentieth century and the restrictions of racial discrimination and gender role expectations on both Thomas and Beulah. Such self-sourcing creates a home from which to launch a blues nomad and initiates the ongoing signifying—Dove "writing her way back home"—that extends from *Thomas and Beulah* through *On the Bus with Rosa Parks.*

Thomas and Beulah, on one level, rewrites the epigraphic nondedication of *Museum:* "for nobody / who made us possible." With the portrait of her maternal grandparents, Dove begins to focus on the "nobodies" who made her possible, revealing them to be "somebodies." This begins her process of writing more personal poetry. As Dove describes it to Mike Hammer and Christina Daub,

> When I finished *Thomas and Beulah,* I said to myself: "It's taken you three books to get back to your own backyard." And even earlier, when I was working on *Museum,* I'd wonder why I couldn't write about the community I grew up in—especially since I felt there were very few books out there that addressed the black middle class existence. I just wasn't ready or able to write about it then. But I managed to get back to Akron, Ohio by writing about my grandparents, and when *Thomas and Beulah* was off to press, I remember thinking, "Now I can write more personal poems." One of the reasons why I titled my next book *Grace Notes* is because I felt that grace—and I don't mean this religiously or anything—grace had been afforded me. Something opened up inside; it was as if I had undergone an apprenticeship and now was ready to write those poems. (33)

Thus, *Thomas and Beulah* is Dove's first step into writing her way back home. Originally planned as a third part to the volume (Steffen, "Movements of a Marriage" 191), the city of Akron, Ohio, functions as a place Dove can name as a family home. Throughout the volume she balances such sourcing of roots with a concomitant sourcing of her wings, identifying the elements of her origins and lineage that provided the wings and thus a cosmopolitan, nomadic identity. Furthermore, Dove's volume resists the easy nostalgia of home, roots, and origins and plays a blues theme of loss and pain throughout Thomas and Beulah's poems. *Thomas and Beulah* is, as Peter Harris mentions but does not elaborate upon, a "blues book" (272).

The volume announces itself as a turn to home and family roots. Critics have noted the use of personal family photographs on the cover (Steffen, "Movements of a Marriage" 180; Van Dyne 74), a man and a woman standing before a car, presumably their own, in 1952.[11] The photograph does not depict Dove's grandparents, Georgianna and Thomas, as some critics have assumed, but an aunt and uncle from her father's side of the family.[12] The year is significant in that it is the year of Dove's birth, leading one to speculate that perhaps the picture was taken on the occasion of a visit to the Dove family to see the newly born Rita. The image is credited to Ray A. Dove, the poet's father. The photograph of Dove in the early to mid-1980s on the back cover was taken by Fred Viebahn, who has been responsible for most photographs of Dove used in her published volumes.[13]

Thus the family photographs emphasize the personal dimensions of the volume. In interviews such as those with Steven Schneider and Grace Cavalieri Dove has explicitly marked the personal, biographical elements behind the poems, identifying Thomas and Beulah as her maternal grandparents, explaining how and why she changed Georgianna's name to Beulah, discussing the genesis of the volume in stories her grandmother and mother would tell her about Thomas, and revealing how Beulah/Georgianna's stories insisted on being told. Furthermore, she dedicates the volume to her mother, with whom she spent hours on the telephone, learning more details of her grandparents' lives.

At the beginning of this "origin," Dove identifies a racially specific experience that shaped Thomas and Beulah's lives: the Great Migration of rural southern blacks to the urban North during the beginning decades of the twentieth century. The first six entries in the volume's chronology detail this movement, note how both Thomas and Beulah were born in the South, and relate that each came north with the thirty thousand workers who migrated to Akron (78). As Lynn Keller argues, the migration shapes Thomas's section. Janet Jones Hampton places the Great Migration in the context of a diasporan people's feelings of exile. Dove's story of origins recognizes a racially specific experience of migration as a source of her nomadism and also refuses the nostalgia of fixity common in identifying one's roots. Dove may be able to identify Akron as a place that was and is home for her and her family of origin, but that placement adheres only for three generations. Her nomadism thus seems a natural extension of the migration of her forebears.

Race and gender define, and occasionally constrain, many of Thomas and Beulah's life experiences. Thomas is shown as vulnerable to racist violence. "Nothing Down," for example, details his recollection of hiding in the woods from lynchers with "[e]very male on the Ridge / old enough to whistle" (22). Racial tensions were also behind an experience he had while driving in the South: a "carload of white men / halloo[ed] past them on Route 231" (23). The racial prejudice to which both are subjected is made official in the Werner Encyclopedia that Thomas buys. Negro children, the book asserts, develop "indirection and laziness" at puberty (38). Such prejudice causes Beulah's reciprocal prejudice against whites. *"Nothing nastier than a white person!"* she mutters (63, emphasis in the original).

Limited job choices, intermittent poverty, and unfulfilled dreams are all part of African American experience as lived by Thomas and Beulah. Likewise, both find that the gender roles of the period define their opportunities. Thomas becomes the breadwinner, giving up his riverboat wanderings and freedom for family life, and Beulah becomes a homemaker and mother, giving up her dreams of Paris and travel.

At the same time, Dove refuses to reduce either Thomas or Beulah to the limits placed upon them. Both draw on rich cultural traditions that give their lives meaning and fulfillment, for example, Thomas's music and ability to tell stories and Beulah's domestic talents and interest in cooking and fashion. Thomas may at times feel stifled by his life as a family man, as detailed in "Compendium," but the poem ends with the image of his daughters "fragrant in their beds," which conveys the almost undefinable pleasures of having four girls. Similarly, in "Sunday Greens," Beulah's "wants" are unmet. Although she has scant food with which to cook and a house that smells, the poem ends with a memory of her mother

> lost in blues,
> and those collards,
> wild-eared,
> singing. (69)

Thomas and Beulah are blues artists who sing the pain of brutal experience with lyrical expression. Dove "plays the blues" throughout the volume's themes and imagery. Blues, and the sense of loss with which it is synonymous, are the central mood of Thomas's section; even the predominant color image is of blue (a color mentioned six times). Thomas loses Lem, leaves the South, gives up the mandolin, never has a son (a gender identified with the color blue), loses a blue car due to the depression, and repeatedly feels a loss of masculinity. All these are the stuff of the blues.

The poem "Straw Hat" nicely sums up Thomas's blues. They begin when he realized that "no one was perfect" (15)—an insight per-

haps borne of the drowning of Lem, Thomas's best friend. The blues
he sings reflects the internal pain of loss and the grief of a hard life
of labor, a grief "spread around" (and thus shared with others as well
as exacerbated by them) by the blues muse that visits with his music.
In other poems as well, Thomas's life at times seems to be a blues refrain as his experiences provide a feeling akin to "despair" (31). Avoiding being lynched leaves him eyeing a blue flower while the "air was
being torn / into hopeless pieces" (23); a mid-life attempt at playing
the mandolin results in blisters and Thomas threatening to himself
"Some day, / . . . I'll just / let go" (29, emphasis in the original). Even
his final moments carry a blues sensibility—he laughs to keep from
crying. While dying, he wonders whether he should sound the horn
of the car in which he sits but thinks, "What a joke— / he couldn't
ungrip the steering wheel" (43). Looking at the car's glove compart-
ment, which has a prescription inside, "he laughed as he thought *Oh
/ the writing on the water*" (43).

While apprehending Thomas's blues it is important not to over-
look Beulah's.[14] Her section refers to blue or the blues five times, only
one less than Thomas's. The alliteration of her name plays with the
word *blues* ("Beulah's blues"), and the first four letters of her name
are an anagram of "blue." It is Beulah who chooses the color—blue—
of Thomas's car. Her blues are inflected by specifically female experiences, including father-daughter incest, and align closely with Ann
duCille's articulation of the bourgeois blues of Fauset and Larsen, a
blues of female romance and domestic concerns.

The figure of her father is particularly associated with the color
blue and with Beulah's blues. He wears a "blue serge" suit at her wedding, carries a "blue worry bead" (59), and gives her wedding-day advice that suggests how to deal with painful experiences: *"Each hurt
swallowed / is a stone"* (51, emphasis in the original). That he has been
a source of painful experience (i.e., incest) for Beulah is implied as
she thinks about the advice: "If that were the case / he was a mountain of shame" (51).

The blues dimension that childhood incest creates in Beulah's life
can be seen in the poem "Anniversary," which, tellingly, is not about
Beulah's twelfth wedding anniversary or her marriage to Thomas as
much as it is about her father. He puts his blue worry bead "into his
mouth" and remarks, *"The trick is to swallow your good luck, too"* (59,

emphasis in the original). The inappropriate eroticism of the moment is underlined by the last two lines: "Last words to a daughter . . . / and a wink to remember him by" (59). The lurid wink and the image of swallowing one's hurt and good luck provide insight into the blues that underlies Beulah's life. Scarred by her father's sexual abuse of her as a child, she has swallowed her hurt, which weighs her down. That she has a "wink" to remember him by indicates that the painful memories of his abuse will remain. But just as the blues affirms life while recognizing the pain of brutal experiences, Beulah can choose to accent the positive, the "good luck" of her marriage to Thomas. "Company," later in Beulah's section, suggests that she has taken that part of her father's advice when she thinks, *"listen: we were good, / though we never believed it"* (74, emphasis in the original).

While singing the blues of racial and gender-specific experiences in Thomas and Beulah's lives, Dove also writes of the roots of her cosmopolitanism by implementing revisionist universal depictions of both characters. The Thomas section, "Mandolin," for example, ties Thomas's particular experiences—the bachelor life, questing, fatherhood, job issues, war, and concerns about masculinity—to archetypal and supposedly universal patterns in male experience. At the same time it specifies that Thomas is a black man. Thus Dove negotiates "the racial particular and the unraced universal" (Posnock, on Du Bois, 88). Allusions in the section link Thomas to Odysseus (18), Jonah (24), and the Kingfisher (27), as Gretchen Robinson notes. Motifs relayed by repeated imagery include that of fate, time, and water.

Although Dove declares Thomas a "Negro" from the first poem (11), places his quest in the context of the Great Migration, and specifies moments of racial oppression that cause his blues, the poems also seem to concur with Dove's belief that "we're more alike than we are different" (Lloyd 22). Thomas's concerns about his manhood—including having four daughters and no sons, being labeled too frail for combat, and having trouble getting work and providing for his family—are male concerns generally. That Dove writes of them from the perspective of a black male enacts a revisionist universalism that is characteristic of cosmopolitan writers.

Likewise, Beulah's section, "Canary in Bloom," connects Beulah to archetypal patterns in female experience such as courtship, the possibility of incest, marriage, domesticity, pregnancy, and motherhood.[15] At the same time, it details Beulah's specifically African American culture (e.g., in "Pomade" [65–66]) and restricted position due to racism ("The Great Palaces of Versailles" [63–64]). Among the allusions in the section are those to the Bible, John Donne, *Pilgrim's Progress,* and Freud.[16]

The racial particular and the unraced universal are carefully balanced in "Wingfoot Lake," in which Beulah attends a Goodyear company picnic with her daughters. It is Independence Day of 1964, and the independences are multiple. Beulah is now a widow (Thomas died in late July the previous year); African Americans are pursuing greater civil rights; and the daughters seek independence from the views of their mother.[17] Dove inscribes racial and cultural issues in the poem, including the segregated eating arrangements at the picnic, the televised March on Washington, the daughters celebrating their African ancestry, and the Goodyear symbol (a racially specific white foot). At the same time, Dove connects across the divisions and anticipates her contemporary nomadic stance.

The tensions and ironies of race relations in the 1960s are apparent throughout the poem. Dove contextualizes the scene with an introductory stanza detailing Beulah's experiences with having a restricted position due to race and class. Thomas takes her to see a swimming pool—her first—and she reacts nervously to viewing the privilege of "high society"; she rolls up the automobile's window and tells him to "drive on, fast" (72). The swimmers' privilege is linked to their race, as their "white arms" jut out of the water (72). Segregation continues in the next stanza, which shifts to a company picnic in 1964, "white families on one side and them / on the other" (72). Class differences seem somewhat diminished for this next generation as each family unpacks "the same / squeeze bottles of Heinz, the same / waxy beef patties and Salem potato chip bags" (72).[18]

But the racial divide remains, and Beulah has not forgotten her experience with class privilege (stanza one). The fact that the daughters are "dragging her" to the picnic conveys her reluctance to confront race and class privilege. The daughters seem to view the excursion as an *"act of mercy,"* a phrase that becomes ironic when viewed through Beulah's perception of race relations during the 1960s. They may feel it is good for her to get out and see the "progress" being made (Joanna exclaims, *"Mother, we're Afro-Americans now!"*), but

Beulah responds with fear. Seeing the March on Washington—and standing as if on alert while she viewed it—had "scared her," just as viewing the privileged, white people's swimming pool had frightened her years before (72). To Beulah there is nothing merciful about such changes. Even invoking African roots makes her wonder, "What did she know about Africa?" (72).

Although Dove centers the poems on the distinct race- and class-inflected perspective of Beulah, she also links across race and class via imagery and word choice. The repetition of "the same" at the ends of the two lines describing the picnic food emphasizes a connection perhaps undiscernible to the picnickers at the time and echoes Dove's belief that people are more alike than different.

Such ironic connections across race and class also appear in the link between the depiction of white swimmers at the beginning of the poem ("white arms jutting / into the chevrons of high society") and the mostly black March on Washington ("a crow's wing mov[ing] slowly through / the white streets of government. That brave swimming" [72]). A crow's wing has the same shape as a chevron, and the march is described as swimming. Although the swimmers are clearly privileged and the marchers are protesting for basic civil rights, the two groups are connected via Dove's use of shared imagery. Even the racial exclusivity of the Goodyear company symbol ("a white foot / sprouting two small wings") becomes an ironic and difficult connection. It is unabashedly white, conveying the racial exclusivity of its creation and early policies that excluded blacks—such as Dove's father—from professional jobs until the 1960s. Yet in "sprouting" wings it potentially can connect the crow's wing to the march. "Sprouting" implies new, potential growth and suggests that the marchers will take flight, leading to a connection between the races and a possible sharing of privilege.

That Dove ends the poem, the third to last in the volume, with an image of "two small wings" sprouting from a white foot can be read as a self-reflexive commentary on *Thomas and Beulah*'s role as a "sourcing" in which Dove writes about the roots that gave her wings. Although "where [Beulah] came from / was the past," the nomadic future of her granddaughter, Rita Dove, is suggested as one of potential flight, a recurring "mascon" of freedom throughout the African American literary tradition.[19]

In implementing a revisionist universalism in *Thomas and Beulah,* Dove uses associational devices with both characters that conveys the complex relationship among the specifics of race, class, gender, or historical moment and their universality. Both associations anticipate her nomadism and thus create a source or home for her cosmopolitanism. For Beulah, that device is a desire for international travel, particularly to France; for Thomas, it is his Werner Encyclopedia. Each association recurs throughout the character's section and demonstrates the thematic tension between cages and freedoms that Dove began to sound in *Thomas and Beulah* and the poem "In the Old Neighborhood" and that she continues through *Grace Notes* and *Mother Love.*

References to other countries abound in Beulah's section. She thinks of France most often (49, 63–64) and also makes reference to Turkey (66), Africa (72–73), and China (77). For Thomas, connection is supplied by the purchase of a Werner Encyclopedia (33), which he subsequently uses in storytelling with his grandchildren (37–38). These symbols of connection demonstrate how, for both characters, the "mind is free" (62) and reflect freedom despite the cages in their lives. For example, Beulah reads about the Palace of Versailles, and Thomas looks up descriptions of the opossum and also considers illustrations of orchids.

Unfortunately, these vehicles of connection and freedom also reveal the cages that surround Thomas and Beulah. For Beulah, the apparent contrast between her real life and the life she imagines in other places increases to the point that she finally rejects the existence of the other places, thinking in the final poem, *"There is no China"* (77, emphasis in the original). Although at the beginning of her life she is certain that "she would make it to Paris one day" (49), the closest she comes to doing so is ironing alterations that emit "Stale Evening of Paris" (69). "The Great Palaces of Versailles" critiques the converging forces of race, class, and gender privilege that have conspired to keep Beulah from her dream. Likewise, in Thomas's experience with the Werner Encyclopedia, racism stultifies the connection. The encyclopedia claims that African American children, at puberty, develop "indirection and laziness" (38). Thus Dove underlines that—for this generation—cages generally outweigh freedoms, and Thomas and Beulah both know that racism has narrowed their range of choices.

Dove takes care, however, through these devices and elsewhere in the volume, to position Thomas and Beulah in relation to historical, cultural, and social forces beyond their immediate perception, thus revealing their home to be much larger than merely the home or neighborhood in which they live. The volume's chronology offers a complex and wide nexus of contexts for Thomas and Beulah, ranging from their origins in the South and the migration to Akron and then on the Great Depression and workers' rights (78).[20] The chronology also connects them to global concerns in its mention of war relief work and their daughter Rose's marriage to a veteran (79).

If Dove begins to write her way back home in *Thomas and Beulah*, it is to a place positioned as part of one that is larger and shared. Although Thomas and Beulah are enriched by their black heritage and restricted due to racism and gender roles, they seek connections with the global world and are connected via shared national and global forces and events. Dove places her grandparents as ancestor figures in a transcultural lineage that has made her possible. Just as she established an African American literary lineage that allowed her a cosmopolitan stance (chapter 1), so, too, in *Thomas and Beulah* does she establish a personal lineage that can accommodate her transcultural life and work. As Therese Steffen notes, "[Writers such as] Rita Dove create their own pluricultural and transcultural realm in which they embody and cultivate both 'métissage'—i.e. the fusion of different races—and 'créolisation'—i.e. primarily the blending of languages and cultures. Out of this hybridity emerge artistic 'empires' that seek to migrate around the world at will" (227).

Although I would question the use of the terms *empire* and *migrate* in relation to Dove, Steffen's view of her as a cultural hybrid comes close to my sense of Dove's nomadic, cosmopolitan movement among multiple cultures and perspectives, a movement that eschews the fixity of any one place or home. *Thomas and Beulah* constitutes an important beginning to Dove's signifying on home, for she is trying to demonstrate that her personal cosmopolitanism has roots in the African American culture and experience that preceded her generation. Thus, she is not deviating from the tradition as much as embodying one ongoing aspect. It is important groundwork to lay for her next volume, *Grace Notes*, in which Dove is unabashedly, deeply, and graphically personal.

~

Before turning to *Grace Notes* and *Mother Love*, I want to discuss a poem that Dove places in the introduction to *Selected Poems*. The self-reflexive "In the Old Neighborhood" provides an overview and frame for Dove's post-*Museum* project. Signifying on the idea of returning to the old neighborhood, the title encourages the reader to view Dove's work in *Selected Poems* as doing likewise.

As Peter Erickson argues in his insightful reading of the poem, Dove's employment of "deceptive understatement" leads the reader to take the poem superficially as a descriptive rendering of the occasion of returning home for a sister's wedding (96). Yet Erickson convincingly reveals a much more complex level of reflection, demonstrating a web of metaphor and association in which the poem comments on the weight of racial stereotype and discrimination on Dove in her poetic career. Having assembled the poem's references to black-gloved raccoons, Othello, a white rock on a black lawn, Dakar, and the father's feelings of failure—all evidence of an undercurrent of commentary on the racialized social forces that impinge on creative consciousness (94–97)—Erickson culminates his reading by identifying the poem's "final drama" (the death of a bird in the home's attic fan) as an "outlandish parody" of Paul Laurence Dunbar's poem "Sympathy" (97). Thus he reads the poem as an "exploration of a problematic inheritance" (97).

I would like to expand upon Erickson's sketch of the poem's undercurrents. The poem elaborates a general tension between cages and freedoms that becomes pronounced throughout Dove's poetry after *Museum*. The events and memories in the poem illustrate the contradictory interplay between cages and freedoms in life; what cages one often constitutes an occasion of freedom as well. The cages in the poem, for example, have to do with the poet-persona's upbringing: being taught how to read the newspaper; feeling trapped in a tent during a backyard campout; following childhood rituals of eating certain foods with certain books; filling the roles of matron of honor and firstborn daughter; and, as the poem ends, folding up kitchen trash for burning "properly" (xxvi). Although none of these are extreme or abusive cages, being in the family of origin, in the old neighborhood, in some ways does cage one. Likewise, the racial stereoptypes and discrimination Erickson reveals function as potential cages for the poet-persona.

Yet for each cage Dove writes in a loophole, some way in which the cage enables freedom. The newspaper she reads offers datelines that "snare" her, connecting her imagination to the larger world (xxiii). Her mind freely travels, such that she "never finished" reading the newspaper as she was instructed (xxiii). Likewise, the other reading she describes—that of the household library, which includes Shakespeare and The Iliad along with Brenda Starr—is a free-ranging oeuvre of her own compilation and desire. As she notes in the introduction, "In books, I could travel anywhere, be anybody, understand worlds long past and imaginary colonies in the future" (xix).

She also finds sustenance and comfort in food rituals while she reads. Furthermore, Dove constructs the "dutiful daughter" role as a performative persona, put on at will whether by "pretending" to read the newspaper as she had been taught (xxii) or seeming to listen to her mother's "chatter" while a six-stanza-long reverie of childhood memories occupies her mind.

As she stands in her mother's kitchen, awash in the sounds of the "pressure cooker" of wedding preparations (xxiv), she nonetheless feels, in the echoing sound of the pressure cooker, "whole again whole again now" (xxiv). Ultimately, Dove refuses to classify the neighborhood and her childhood as cages and her adult life as one of freedom. Rather, she obligates readers to see freedom in the cage and vice versa. Even when describing the escape offered by newspaper datelines, the speaker admits the "names [are] as / unreal as the future / even now" (xxiii). Thus the speaker refuses to privilege Dove's adult globetrotting life as being more real than her childhood.

Yet there is one cage that Dove explicitly contrasts to her own freedom: the black starling chopped up in the attic fan. Here my reading of the poem departs from Erickson's. Where he aligns the (Dove) persona of the poem with the bird, and thus sees the "cruelly macabre farce of the starling's demise [as Dove's rueful acknowledgment] of the lingering force of the stereotype she has had to overcome" (97), for me it is a deliberate contrast of fates. Of course, Dove's use of "birdplay" throughout her poetry to comment on her surname invites viewing the starling as somehow linked to her own identity or at least that of the Dove family. Erickson also seems correct in identifying the allusion to Dunbar. Given the interplay between cages and freedoms in the poem, however, this is the sole cage that lacks a freedom loophole. Dove makes that especially clear in the "anonymous" disposal of the bird's remains: "a switch / flipped on reverse / to blow the feathers out" (xxv).

This passage (and thus the poem) seems to be Dove's reflection on having avoided that cage—or "cubbyhole" as she has termed it— of being silenced by the forces of racism, whether in the form of having to spend energy fighting discrimination, feeling she must write literature in the service of the race, or being labeled a black poet. In the autobiographical mini-narrative just before the poem she muses on how she came to be a poet. "[E]ach of us would have taken a very different path in our life with little effort on our own," she observes, "if all the roadblocks and unmarked junctures we encounter constantly had assumed a slightly different constellation. The mystery of destiny boils down to the ultimate—and ultimately unanswerable— questions: How does where I come from determine where I've ended up? Why am I what I am and not what I'd thought I'd be? What did I think I'd be? Where do I reside most completely?" (xxi). Suggesting that her poetry, at times, attempts to answer such questions, Dove introduces the poem as being "about the old neighborhood—its physical topography as well as the spiritual and aesthetic terrain" (xxi).

"In the Old Neighborhood" implicitly contrasts Dove's fate to that of the fatally caged starling. When the children drop their books and run to see the "first tragedy of the season," they each think, *"At least I'm not the one"* (xxv, emphasis in the original). Thus, the poet-persona and her siblings are contrasted to the starling. The poem does not suggest that any particular action on Dove's part has saved her, but a generational pattern does emerge. Throughout the poem the father is repeatedly associated with many cages; not only does he shape his "mutant" roses but he also shapes his children. It is the father who "insisted" that they remain in the backyard tent; it is the father who turns on the attic fan that kills the starling (xxiv); and it seems probable it is also the father who taught the children how to read the newspaper and then to fold it "properly" for disposal (xxvi). The mother, in contrast, seems a beneficent force, benignly worrying and producing large quantities of food. Dove has explained that her mother "is a very sweet woman, and I haven't written very much about her simply because there's no friction" (Peabody and Johnsen 5).

When the poet's dreamy reverie turns to imagining the father's denunciation of his garden plants as *"all weeds,"* the connection between the cages and the fate of creativity becomes apparent. Dove describes this section of the poem as a "psychic landscape through which the speaker can travel and discover the subconscious significance of familial relationships" (Erickson 91). It appears that the constellation of caging behaviors on the part of the father is associated with failure of creativity, represented in the dream of the failed garden, and also the death of creativity, represented in the figure of the starling. That the death of the starling immediately follows this passage reinforces the connection.[21]

Writing this poem in 1993, as she put together *Selected Poems,* Dove is reflecting on how she came to be at that particular place in her life—a winner of the 1987 Pulitzer Prize in Poetry, the poet laureate of the United States, and a writer of enough stature and poetic output to justify a volume entitled *Selected Poems.*[22] "In the Old Neighborhood" charts her awareness of the cages and freedoms of her upbringing and how each helped shape her destiny or fate. It also specifies that the preceding generation of black Americans, as represented by the father, had a rather different fate. The stereotype and discrimination Erickson reads in the poem as impinging on the poet actually impinges more severely on the father. The cages of his era—discrimination and more rigid codes of personal conduct—are ones that consign him to despair. Yet the poem both acknowledges the fruitful role this upbringing played in shaping her destiny and demarcates her fate from that of the previous generation.

This is, the poem insists, the old neighborhood, not the present one. The epigraph suggests that it is a leave-taking, being pulled up "by your own roots" and having a "last meal" in the old neighborhood (xxii). The poem ends with the poet-persona folding bones and eggshells, symbols of death, into an *old* newspaper, to be burned as if on a funeral pyre. Thus Dove suggests a cleansing release of the old neighborhood's traps and the previous generation's fate. Had she remained (aesthetically or spiritually, the introduction qualifies), perhaps she would have been chopped up like the starling—a sort of dismembered madwoman in the attic. Perhaps the old home or neighborhood is not exactly where Dove might wish to return, at least not to stay very long, although it does represent her roots.

Notes

1. Susan Van Dyne reads this passage as a "mild racial admonition veiled as esthetic judgment," and characterizes Rampersad's comments as reflecting "his desire that her talent ought to be used to make her particular, historical, autobiographical blackness culturally significant for black readers" (69).

2. Houston Baker employs the term *homeplace*, which comes from bell hooks (*Yearnings*), in relation to Dove (567).

3. Van Dyne reads Dove relationship to Rampersad's critique somewhat differently (80), seeing *Mother Love* as a sudden shift in her trajectory after the movement toward home in earlier volumes.

4. Given that an excerpt from Arnold Rampersad's article is featured on the back cover of Dove's *Selected Poems,* and in light of Dove's interest in the cover design of her volumes, it is quite likely that she had read his essay before writing "In the Old Neighborhood."

5. Several black writers not mentioned in this study, such as Robert Hayden, Michael Harper, Alice Walker, and Lucille Clifton, have also used the personal in their writing and insist on the universality of their perspectives, although not necessarily from a contemporary cosmopolitan perspective.

6. Rampersad seems to foresee this possibility.

7. Thanks to Linda Krumholz, who introduced me to Braidotti's work.

8. Kevin Stein's essay on multiple perspectives in Dove's poetry shares this insight.

9. Braidotti notes that nomadism does not require actual travel as much as "the subversion of set conventions" (5).

10. All of the quotations in this paragraph are from a personal communication with Rita Dove, Feb. 22, 2001.

11. Steffen remarks upon the dialogue between "documentary fact and historic metafiction" implied by the photographs ("Movements of a Marriage" 180), while Van Dyne reads them as "promis[ing] authentic, even autobiographical information about blackness" (74).

12. Fred Viebahn relates that they chose the image for several reasons: "It was taken in their Akron working class neighborhood in 1952, Rita's birth year; it depicts relatives of about her grandparents' age at the time; it shows pride in the possession of a car; and it shows both a family home and the industrial setting (two Goodyear factory chimneys) of their life" (personal communication, Feb. 8, 2002).

13. In the photograph for *Thomas and Beulah* Dove wears the same sweater and earrings as she did for the *Fifth Sunday* (1985) picture. Because her appearance is unchanged, presumably the photographs were both taken at the same time, before or during 1985. Some press photographs of Dove appear in *The Poet's World,* published by the Library of Congress, and a professional photograph spans the cover of *Selected Poems.*

14. John Shoptaw maintains that Beulah lacks a loss comparable to Thomas's loss of Lem (378).

15. Susan Van Dyne notes that Dove's poems on motherhood are often cited as "universal" (72–73).

16. Patricia Wallace identifies this allusion in "Sunday Greens" in the lines "Ham knocks / in the pot, nothing / but bones, each / with its bracelet / of flesh," which she maintains revises Donne's "a bracelet of bright hair about the bone," cited in T. S. Eliot's "The Metaphysical Poets" as a brilliant figure of language (8). Lynn Keller points out (132) that in *Pilgrim's Progress* "the land of Beulah" is a place of rest and peace. The poem "Motherhood" possibly alludes to Freud's case of the Wolf Man (58).

17. The chronology in the original edition of *Thomas and Beulah* incorrectly stated April 1963 as the month of Thomas's death, a detail corrected in *Selected Poems* (personal communication from Fred Viebahn, Feb. 8, 2002).

18. The squeeze bottle for catsup had not been developed by 1964. The package supplier to Heinz, Pechiney Plastic Packaging, was established in 1979 as a plastic bottle business and created the "world's first squeezable ketchup bottle (for Heinz in 1990)." Its Web-site, <http://www.pechineyplasticpackaging.com/products/bottles_na_euro.asp>, was accessed on October 6, 2002.

19. "Massive concentration of black experiential energy" (MASCON) is a critical term developed by Stephen Henderson in *Understanding the New Black Poetry*.

20. Lynn Keller's chapter on Dove demonstrates the centrality of the migration in Thomas's section. She also offers a nuanced and aware reading of how the volume balances literary, racial, and gender concerns.

21. Erickson, in an endnote, introduces biographical information about Dove's father, specifically the discrimination he experienced in the rubber industry as a chemist (he was first hired as an elevator operator despite his M.A. degree in chemistry), which perhaps explains the sense of failure Dove expresses in this passage.

22. In the opening lines of her review of Derek Walcott's *Collected Poems* ("'Either I'm Nobody, or I'm a Nation'"), Dove reveals awareness of the significance of such milestone's in a poetic career: "A celebrated poet reaches a point in his career where there needs to be a retrospective consideration of the work. Several choices can be made. A *Selected Poems* demands rigorous excerpting from previous books. A *New and Selected Poems* is a way of ensuring the public that one is not yet an institution. A *Collected Poems* is like tossing in one's lot with the gods" (49). Dove was forty-one when *Selected Poems* was published.

Beginning with *Thomas and Beulah* and continuing through *Grace Notes* and *Mother Love,* Dove's sensitive balancing of the racial particular and the unraced universal, a revisionist universalism in which her perspective (whether as a woman, an African American, or a cosmopolitan world traveler) provides a lens through which to see the world. A pattern emerges: As her poetry becomes increasingly personal, it also becomes increasingly mythical in the sense that it connects to the archetypal patterns of human experience. In her call to see the universal, mythical dimensions of personal experience, Dove universalizes specifics of race, gender, and class.

The extended interplay between the personal and the mythical to some degree evident in *Thomas and Beulah* becomes even more pronounced in *Grace Notes* and *Mother Love.* In both volumes, Dove "begins with" personal experiences as the occasions of the poems. Many of the poems in *Grace Notes* draw on her experiences, and Dove's personal life as a daughter and a mother contributes to the poems in *Mother Love,* as the epigraph ("FOR *my mother /* TO *my daughter*") conveys. Yet in *Grace Notes* the momentum of personal poems moves toward mythical patterns, whereas the mythical poems in *Mother Love* turn toward the personal.

Such patterns are most discernible in the volumes' structures. Each section in *Grace Notes* ends with death, a key archetypal pattern, and the final poem is about a retirement home in which everyone is "waiting here" for death. In *Mother Love* the structure moves in the opposite direction, with the early and middle poems, written from mythic Persephone and Demeter personae, giving way in sections five and six to an array of "real life" personae and in section seven to the poet's personal experience during a trip to Sicily.

Thus in *Grace Notes* Dove moves from the personal into archetype, and in *Mother Love* she moves from myth into the personal.[1] The constant coupling of personal and mythical becomes a dominant strategy in her cosmopolitan, post-*Museum* revisionist, universalism. Houston Baker sees this dynamic specifically in her treatment of race, which, he notes, "is poetically transformed into an uncommon commonality; it makes its appearance in an uncanny and stunning field of reminiscence that strikes readers as somehow 'archetypically' *true*" (575).

The blues nomad identity of *Thomas and Beulah* takes flight in *Grace Notes* and *Mother Love,* whether in the blues of death (*Grace Notes*) or the blues of loss and of patriarchy (*Mother Love*). Furthermore, *Grace Notes* contains Dove's post-*Museum,* nomadic *ars poetica,* which is conveniently and unsentimentally entitled "Ars Poetica" (48). Of all her volumes of poetry, *Grace Notes* is the one that plays Dove's theme of signifying on the idea of home in a major key; *Mother Love,* however, transposes that theme into a minor key.

∼

Dove articulates a cosmopolitan, nomadic identity most fully in *Grace Notes,* identifying the "rhythmical displacements" characteristic of her experience and poetic perspectives. *Grace Notes* is very much an identity volume and intensely personal. The back of its jacket announces that "intimate concerns [are] expressed" in the poems and promises the poet's exploration of "autobiographical events." Dove dedicates the volume to her husband and daughter, and many of the poems involve them. Identity is, of course, one's ultimate home, and the theme of home extends from the identity focus. The words *home* or *house* appear seventeen times in the volume. Moreover, many poems are set in a home or house, such as on a front porch or in a backyard or kitchen, although they might not specifically use the word *home.*

Divided into five sections, the poems focus mainly on the poet's relatives, familiar places, and experiences. Except for section five, in which persona poems proliferate, Dove's voice dominates. Her poems in *Grace Notes* reflect a nomadic intellectual style that Rosi Braidotti characterizes as "not so much in being homeless, as in being capable of recreating your home everywhere. The nomad carries his/her essential belongings with her/him wherever s/he goes and can recreate a home base anywhere" (16).

Thus, *Grace Notes* depicts a multiplicity of homes and neighborhoods, whether for Dove or for other personae. There are moorings, places where "space [is] stapled down" and the persona has connections with people or memories (43). Homes of friends and family members, memories of childhood, and significant relatives all offer significant points of connection. These homes, ultimately, transcend place, although they are occasionally tied to places. As the epigraphs to the five sections emphasize, Dove presents the idea of home as a nexus of identity, place, homes, origins, and memory. *Grace Notes* insists on a roving internationalism. It is a global stage of being where the poet is a "traveling x-marks-the-spot," that is, a nomadic identity (48). It is the world, Dove reveals, that is her neighborhood.

The blues provides the overarching philosophy of *Grace Notes* as its poems meditate on questions of life's meaning, pain, and death. The word *blue* is repeated eleven times in the volume, along with related words such as *indigo, blueberry,* and *purple,* and a "blue feeling" can be inferred through repeated water imagery and weeping. Dove's blues focuses upon moments of loss, the transience of existence, and—especially—death. Such a mood intensifies in section five in the persona poems of loss, such as Billie Holiday in "Canary" (64).

The poem "Lint," in which "[b]lue is all around," sums up the "blues attitude" of the volume (68). "Lint" sings the blues of isolation, ephemera, and insignificance. Although there are moments of beauty and potential meaning in life, such as the "awkward loveliness" beneath the "wing of a mallard," there is also the alternate view that life is composed of "noise" and "lint" rather than being meaningful (68). The final lines are almost surreally existential: "How good to revolve / on the edge of a system— / small, unimaginable, cold" (68). That it is "unimaginable" and "cold" makes such an existence or perspective frighteningly unknown and lacking in the warmth of human connection. Such moments of awareness, although painful, constitute the "grace notes" of life.

Allusions to other poets' reflections on existential moments of awareness further reinforce the attitude. "Ozone" echoes Dylan Thomas's "Rage, rage against the dying of the light" in its opening line ("Everything civilized will whistle before it / Rages" [28]). And "Genetic Expedition" alludes to Elizabeth Bishop's "In the Waiting Room" in the poet's description of her breasts "each day resembling more the spiked fruits / dangling from the natives in the *National Geographic* / my father forbade us to read" (42). The poem ends with an existential experience similar to that Bishop described: contemplating her and her daughter's physical similarities yet differences as well, the poet-speaker states, "I'm sucked into, sheer through to / the gray brain of sky" (42). Vendler's idea of "Ozone" as the real *ars poetica* of *Grace Notes* makes sense if one sees this as a blues volume lamenting the central loss that is at the core of life—death. I shall return to "Ozone" in my discussion of individual sections.

The blues Dove sings in *Grace Notes* has an intensely personal as well as professional dimension. Her blues attitude (chapter 5) can be tied to her awareness of the partial losses inherent in eschewing any fixed location for her poetic identity and also in her relatively privileged position as a member of the middle class. Although Dove acknowledges that she perhaps lacks the "brutal experience" Craig Werner notes as characteristic of the vernacular blues, she insists on participating in a blues that are revoiced to include black middle-class experiences. Werner's three-stage process of brutal experience, lyrical expression, and reaffirmation can be applied to Dove insofar as brutal experience can be expanded to include experiences beyond racist violence and poverty.

The last stage, reaffirmation, becomes key to Dove's blues in section four of *Grace Notes*. There, she reflects extensively on her position within the multiple traditions she nomadically traverses. Read through the epigraph, the section elliptically comments upon Dove's lack of affirmation within the African American literary tradition. She quotes Claude McKay, "I know the dark delight of being strange, / The penalty of difference in the crowd, / The loneliness of wisdom among fools" (45). Like Dove, McKay traveled widely, made a place for his work within the white-dominated publishing world, and employed traditional poetic techniques. He insisted upon poetic excellence and social relevance rather than the latter at the expense of the former. Invoking McKay's sense of being marginalized speaks to Dove's blues of exclusion within the African American poetic tradition.

It seems that Dove's work has been far more widely and enthusi-
astically accepted among the white-dominated, "mainstream" American and contemporary European literary traditions than the African
American.[2] *Thomas and Beulah* has been included in survey courses
on American literature, and her poetry is frequently taught in poetry
classes, both creative and interpretive. Such widespread acceptance
within what are still white-dominated canons gives some credence
to the comment that she "writes white" in the sense that her work fits
easily into white-dominated aesthetic standards. Although the poems
have been included in some anthologies of African American literature, that partial degree of acceptance has not been mirrored in
African American literary criticism. Scholarship on Dove's work is
finally proliferating, but it is predominantly that of white American
and European critics.[3]

That the first book on Dove was by a Swiss scholar, Therese Steffen, who is white, indicates the level of attention paid her work by
white critics; if this book is the second, my point is even more clearly
made.[4] Whether it is a case of people not reading Dove or simply not
responding to her, one cannot say. The lack of attention among black
scholars leaves Werner's last phase of the blues process—reaffirmation—noticeably absent, at least in terms of black affirmation. In
Murray's sense of the blues, the blues itself, its lyrical expression of
pain, is the affirmation of life. The poet/artist, in the blues, reaffirms
life in all its complexities. In that sense, Dove's work affirms itself.
But Werner's sense of the process emphasizes the community's role
in the blues process. The lyrical expression is a call that encourages a
response. From that perspective, Dove's blues throughout her volumes since *Museum* seems a call the African American literary community has either not heard or failed to answer. Her blues continues,
however, and asks for an "amen."

The opening poem of *Grace Notes*, "Summit Beach, 1921," which
Baker reads as less "an epigraph than a frontispiece and signature for
the volume's five sections of verse" (575), plays a similar role to that
of "Dusting" in linking *Museum* and *Thomas and Beulah*. "Summit
Beach, 1921" connects *Grace Notes* to the Beulah section of *Thomas and
Beulah* and at the same time sounds the signature theme of home in
Grace Notes. If "Summit Beach, 1921" is read after *Thomas and Beu-
lah*, its connections to Beulah's character become salient, as does the

fact that Dove has moved from articulating her roots to spreading her nomadic wings. In the poem, the year is 1921 (Beulah is seventeen), and a young woman sits at a party on the "Negro beach." She refuses to dance, in part because she broke her leg as a child and in part because she does not want to be "fast" in courtship (3). The poem seems easily another version of "Jiving" from *Thomas and Beulah*, although from Beulah's point of view. In "Jiving," Thomas arrives

> in Akron, Ohio
> 1921,
> on the dingy beach
> of a man-made lake. (14)

There he plays his mandolin and impresses the ladies. In "Summit Beach, 1921," the "Negro beach jumped to the twitch / of an oil drum tattoo and a mandolin" (3). Although the mandolin player does not approach the young woman in the poem, her reticence about courtship is reminiscent of Beulah's behavior in "Courtship" in *Thomas and Beulah*. Another line further connects the character to Beulah. The dancers on the beach have "the finest brown shoulders / this side of the world" (3). This echoes Beulah's fascination with "the other side of the world," a motif throughout her section and expressly articulated in her final poem, "The Oriental Ballerina" (75).

It would appear that "Summit Beach, 1921" is a Beulah poem that did not find its way into *Thomas and Beulah*. The way in which it does not quite fit that volume, however, is how it sets the stage for *Grace Notes*. The final lines reveal how the character broke her leg as a child: "she climbed Papa's shed and stepped off / the tin roof into blue, / with her parasol and invisible wings" (3). Earlier, "[h]er knee had itched in the cast / till she grew mean from bravery." By withholding information on how the character broke her leg until the poem's final lines, Dove pushes the focus from how the broken leg confines the character onto her moment of impossible freedom, when she takes flight from her father's shed. Throughout *Thomas and Beulah*, Beulah dreams of taking flight—whether to Paris or just in her imagination—but in "Summit Beach, 1921" the character actually does so. Beulah, however, succumbs to cages, eventually "relinquishing . . . her fantasies about 'the other side of the world' where life is dramatically different and more beautiful" (Keller 135). In contrast to Beulah, whose life ends with the thought *"there is no China"* (Dove, *Thomas and Beulah* 77), the character in "Summit Beach, 1921" has taken flight and holds on to her feeling of freedom:

> She could feel
> the breeze in her ears like water
> like the air as a child when
> she climbed Papa's shed and stepped off
> the tin roof into blue. (3)

The poem ends with an emphasis on her "invisible wings," an echo of the "sprouting wings" of the Goodyear symbol in "Wingfoot Lake" of Beulah's section (72).

Thus the opening poem of *Grace Notes* provides a connection to the personal lineage of Dove's family's past—her roots—and also moves readers into an exploration of her personal past and present as she spreads her cosmopolitan wings. The character's flight introduces flying and the bird imagery that dominate *Grace Notes* as figures of Dove's nomadism and freedom. That she steps off "into blue"—and seems to have the blues—continues the blues motif that runs throughout her post-*Museum* work and is especially prominent in *Grace Notes*.

"Summit Beach, 1921" continues the complex tension between cages and freedoms apparent in *Thomas and Beulah* and expressed by "In the Old Neighborhood." It also introduces the signifying focus of *Grace Notes:* home or neighborhood. Taking place on the "home turf" of the beach, the action—dancing—takes place in a neighborhood of sorts. The other action—the character jumps off her father's shed—happens in the past and at her childhood home.

Most of section one of *Grace Notes* contains snapshots of childhood, many of which are, presumably, Dove's experiences. The epigraph from Toni Morrison—"All water has perfect memory and is forever trying to get back to where it was"—establishes that the section's theme involves a quasi-return to origins (which are fleeting and hard to hold onto) and emphasizes "trying to get back to" them. The settings of the poems are explicitly homes, houses, neighborhoods, and vacation spots.

The final poem of the section, "Poem in Which I Refuse Contemplation," makes clear the complex internationalism of the Dove's adult life. She arrives at her German mother-in-law's house "six hours from

Paris by car" (19) and reads a letter from her mother that conveys various news from home, including the murder of her cousin, Ronnie, in Washington, D.C. The poem demonstrates that the nomadic poet-persona has multiple homes and moorings. She is connected both to America and to her present home in Germany, where her daughter "hops on Oma's bed, / happy to be back in a language / she knows" (19). Upset by the news in the letter, the speaker wants to withdraw to her inner home, to "pull on boots and go for a long walk / alone" (19). Unable to do that (it is "one A.M."), she lashes out in anger at elements of the multiple homes. When the mother begins describing how the garden at home is doing, for example, the speaker reacts,

> Haven't I always hated gardening? And German,
> with its patient, grunting building blocks,
> and for that matter, English, too,
>
> Americanese's chewy twang? (20)

Separated by distance, time, and place, the speaker tries to reconnect with the cousin via memory, a possible shared home. As the letter describes a raccoon invasion, she remembers things in snatches that are interspersed with her mother's news:

> *Raccoons*
> *have taken up residence*
> we were ten *in the crawl space*
> but I can't feel his hand *who knows*
> anymore *how we'll get them out?* (20)

The unemphasized words convey a trace of a memory, one partially lost because she can no longer feel his hand. The title, "Poem in Which I Refuse Contemplation," refuses to glamorize or idealize the nomadic stance into a fecund plurality of locations and homes. The speaker refuses to contemplate Ronnie's murder and/or her position, perhaps because it is too painful to do so or perhaps because it is beyond grasping.

Negative imagery of death and disconnection runs throughout "Poem in which I Refuse Contemplation" (the final poem of each section of *Grace Notes* references death). The speaker is menstruating, it is night, Ronnie has been killed, the speaker wants to go off and be alone, she angrily rejects both languages available to her, and raccoons have invaded her parents' crawl space. Despite its proliferation of negative imagery, the poem ends with a reality of everyday existence: "I'm still standing. Bags to unpack. / *That's all for now. Take care*" (20, emphasis in the original). Although Ronnie is dead, the poet is not, and her connection to the love of her mother via letter is still standing as well. Such an ending deploys a blues attitude in which voicing despair is cathartic and affirms life despite life's hardships. Dove places Ronnie's death into a larger, archetypal cycle: Life goes on despite how one individual life ends.

Section one of *Grace Notes* establishes the complex interplay between the poet's roots (which now reside mostly in memory) and wings, focusing on the home of relatives and family. Section two emphasizes place and identity. In that way "Poem in Which I Refuse Contemplation," by moving into the poet's identity in relation to the idea of origins and memory, provides a transition to section two. As the epigraphs to the second section suggest, place is a conduit to (and forum for) identity. The first epigraph ("The legendary forbidden fruit is the self") is by David McFadden, and the second ("To inhabit was the most natural joy when I was still living inside: all was garden and I had not lost the way in") is by Hélène Cixous (21). Both—the former from McFadden's book on Lake Huron and the latter from the French feminist psychoanalyst—emphasize identity in relation to place. Section two traverses the places of Dove's cosmopolitan identity, including the Mississippi, the desert (possibly Arizona), Alabama, Europe, Jerusalem, and Germany, and maps her nomadism. As Braidotti notes, maps are a central image of nomadism; nomadic status engenders a need to draw maps (16–22).

A central poem, "Ozone," particularly sums up the existential feel of the section. Its epigraph is from Rilke: "Does the cosmic / space we dissolve into taste of us, then?" (28). The poem details how we

> wire the sky for comfort;
> we thread it through our lungs for a perfect fit.
> We've arranged this calm, though it is constantly
> unraveling. (28)

The human impulse is to make place permanent with identity, to sing "memento mei." Dove ties the drive toward certainty and a fixed place to the creation of neighborhoods and ends with a negative, potentially violent image:

> The sky is wired so it won't fall down.
> Each house notches into it neighbor
> and then the next, the whole row scaldingly white,
> unmistakable as a set of bared teeth. (28)

The poem graphically depicts a rigid, frighteningly conformist existence within the conventional neighborhood, an existence Dove's nomadic stance rejects. In contrast, her poet-persona wishes in the last stanza,

> If only we could lose ourselves
> in the wreckage of the moment! Forget
> where we stand, dead center, and
> look up, look up,
> track a falling star . . .
>   now you see it
>   now you don't (29)

The poet presents a cosmopolitan sense of place—if one defines "cosmopolitan" as in the *Random House Dictionary:* "1. not limited to just one part of the world. 2. free from local, provincial, or national ideas, prejudices, or attachments." The desired self in "Ozone" can forget being the center and become an agent of perception for time and space. That is reminiscent of Dove's hope of using the personal in her poetry and avoiding self-indulgence. As she told Emily Lloyd, she strives to "be only a lens for seeing the world more clearly" (22).

"Ozone" also acknowledges how frighteningly close to the abyss such an existential and ego-less stance brings people. Again the word *blue* appears, here in a center line: "A gentleman pokes blue through a buttonhole" (28). The blues in "Ozone" admits that the emptiness of death is fought by the human spirit, which is driven toward permanence, fixity, and forms of supposed immortality. Dove portrays such reactions as a trap or cage, and people must free themselves from that confinement despite their fears. The final lines offer no reassurance for the timid, as the poem trails off into the nothingness it recommends.

Dove recognizes this existential, ultimately cosmopolitan ideal as partial and improbable in the final two poems of the section, "Your

Death" and "The Wake," which are addressed to her late father-in-law. Humans inhabit places, times, and spaces; identities, to some measure, take possession of them. The father-in-law's death is of such impact ("Your Death") that "the day changed ownership" (32) for Dove and her husband, despite being miles apart from him and having just learned of her pregnancy. In "The Wake," the lack of his presence leaves palpable gaps in the house. His "absence distributed itself" as "the green hanger swang empty, and / the head of the table / demanded a plate" (33). The speaker feels his presence in the space she inhabits:

> When I sat down in the armchair
> your warm breath fell
> over my shoulder.
> When I climbed to bed I walked
> through your blind departure. (33)

The father-in-law's reality even after death has an impact on the speaker's possession of place and time. When "the day changed ownership" she reacts: "I felt robbed" (32). Although the couple had begun the day by reveling in her new pregnancy, once they learn the bad news,

> [e]ven the first
> bite of the tuna fish sandwich
> I had bought at the corner
> became yours. (32)

Thus Dove acknowledges the ego involved with identity. It is not something one can control, the last lines of "The Wake" suggest: "I slept because it was the only / thing I could do. I even dreamed. / I couldn't stop myself" (33). Dove ties her father-in-law's death to the archetypal cycle of life and death by linking the beginnings of her pregnancy with the end of his life. In so doing she universalizes her personal experiences and perceptions.

Having tied identity to the homes of family origins, memory, and place in sections one and two, Dove turns to her current home and family in section three of *Grace Notes*. Most of the poems in that part concern her daughter, Aviva, despite Dove's claim in 1985: "I haven't written a single [poem] about her and I don't think I'll ever do it"

(Peabody and Johnsen 11). The transition from Dove's past to the future and her daughter are summarized in the apt title of the first poem in the section, "The Other Side of the House." Again, the final poem of the previous section provides a segue to Dove's pregnancy, which during the wake provided a refuge:

I lay down in the cool waters
of my own womb
and became the child
inside, innocuous
as a button, helplessly growing. (33)

The pregnancy results in a child who now inhabits home and place with her. In "The Other Side of the House," the poet-persona reflects upon "the dim / aggression of my daughter on the terrace drawing / her idea of a home" (37). The daughter adds another dimension, or "side," to the house of identity Dove maps in *Grace Notes*. The speaker wonders, then, "Where am I in the stingy desert broom?" (37). The answer comes in the next stanza: "Many still moments, / aligned, repair / the thin split of an afternoon" (37). The speaker's identity seems transient and uncertain but then is anchored, "repair[ed]" by moments of home and family such as the daughter drawing "her idea of home" (37). In a place where "[t]he sand flies so fast, it leaves no shadow," such moorings offer connection and continuation (37). The desert, Braidotti notes, is the space that is representative of the nomad and ideal because it has no boundaries (26–27).

The poem's epigraph is Dorothy's exclamation in the film *The Wizard of Oz*: "*But it wasn't a dream; it was a place. And you . . . and you . . . and you . . . and you were there!*" It draws upon notions of home and is a reminder of Dorothy's refrain "there's no place like home," which she must believe and repeat in order to get home. What Dorothy learns, however, is fundamentally contradictory—she never left home, and her home went with her, in herself. An orphan, she makes her family from those around her. Dove riffs on Dorothy's nostalgic song about home, "Somewhere, Over the Rainbow," in the final line of the fifth stanza, which she ends with a dangling "somewhere" (37).

Dove thus places an orphaned girl's naïve longing for home and family in counterpoint to the reality of a fleeting sense of having a mooring. Fantasies about having a fixed home or family "some-where" become apparent as just that—fantasies. In this short section (seven poems, the fewest of the five sections), Dove both presents an aspect of identity, parenthood, and also problematizes its status as not being in any way absolute, monolithic, or inherently grounding. This portrait refuses sentimentality at the same time that it ac-knowledges parenting as an identity force.

The central poem of section three portrays children as "the trail-ings of gods. Their eyes / hold nothing at birth then fill slowly / with the myth of ourselves" (40). Such a rendering of the parent-child re-lationship (furthered by allusion to Wordsworth's "Intimations of Im-mortality") reflects the desire of many parents to make a child in their own image. "The Breathing, the Endless News," while evoking that desire, undercuts its reality with the word *myth*. Even as parents seek to make their children like themselves, there is slippage between iden-tity and myth. Dove further pulls away from nostalgia with the end-ing of the poem, where children line up their dolls and shoot them.

The poems in section three generally draw connections between the mother and child and at the same time complicate those connec-tions. "After Reading *Mickey in the Night Kitchen* for the Third Time before Bed" links the poet-persona and her daughter in gender; *"We're pink!"* they say of their vaginas. The poem also specifies their separate colors: "black mother, cream child" (41, emphasis in the original). "Ge-netic Expedition" invokes an African lineage by tracing a web of as-sociation from the natives in *National Geographic*, to the poet-persona's "years / spreading across [her] dark behind," and then to her child, who has "her father's hips, his hair / like the miller's daugh-ter, combed gold" (42). This difference is also sameness, however. "[H]her lips are mine," she remarks of the daughter (42). The irre-ducibility of genetic lineage to any one line or connection becomes clear in the image of homemakers who stare at them "because of that ghostly profusion" of genetic material.[5] The poem ends with an image that evokes the genetic expedition and also the limitlessness of expe-rience. Looking at her daughter's gaze, the poet-persona feels "sucked into, sheer through to / the gray brain of sky" (42). She thus offers a gray (i.e., complex) view of genetic lineage and rejects it as fixed.

Likewise, in "Pastoral" Dove describes a potentially sentimental moment of breast feeding. The scene is indeed pastoral, mother and baby "lying / outside on a quilt," with the baby "milk-drunk" (38). Yet the poet-persona intrudes on the scene, adding a final sentence that refuses this aspect of identity as totalizing or absolute:

> . . . I felt then
> what a young man must feel
> with his first love asleep on his breast:
> desire, and the freedom to imagine it. (38)

Ekaterini Georgoudaki describes the scene as an example of Dove's "crossing boundaries" ("Rita Dove"). Dove actively refuses having her identity (or writing) reduced to any one racial, gendered, or national perspective. In a moment many might applaud as being intimate mother-child connection and fulfillment of identity for the mother, Dove introduces two shifts that force the reader away from that narrow reading. One shift is to a male subject position, and the other is the introduction of sexual desire. By opening the experience of nursing to accommodate an analogy to seemingly contradictory experiences, the poem refuses identity reduction and invites a plurality of perspectives. The final line of "Pastoral" provides a self-reflexive warning as Dove comments on introducing a male perspective of romantic love into the poem: She had "the freedom to imagine it" (38).

The final poem of the section, "Backyard, 6 A.M.," signifies on home, fixity, death, and flying; it also sings the weary blues of a nomad. The speaker is "home, [facing] jet lag and laundry" (43). "Backyard" implies a more intimate place for the identity, restricted as it is to the family in residence (unlike the front yard, which puts on a public face for the neighborhood). Although the poet-speaker has experienced and presumably enjoyed international travel, there seems some degree of relief in being back to "the floor of the world," where "space is stapled down with every step" (43). Fixity, the poet suggests, has its moments, even for a nomad.

Dove's rhythmical turn to death at the end of each section appears in an avoidance of death: "I swore to be good and the plane didn't / fall out of the sky" (43). Given that section three focuses mostly on the poet and her daughter and children more generally, it is appropriate that death is deferred in this section alone. Hence there are fewer poems in the section—the future, including death, is unwritten for children. Yet referencing death, even in a section on children, maintains the volume's momentum toward archetypal patterning. Flying, a motif threaded throughout *Grace Notes,* is parlayed through mention of transatlantic flight and is also in the imagery of the final stanza, where the poet-persona hears "wings" (43). The gnarled beauty of the final lines suggests a potential blues contemplation afforded by being home. The insects

> quickening in the forgotten shrines,
> [are] unwinding
> each knot of grief,
> each snagged insistence. (43)

A home, however temporary, allows reflection about pain and loss and how to unknot them.

After such an intensely personal section the volume turns toward Dove's professional identity as a poet, another home, enacting her conviction that the personal can be used as a lens through which to view larger issues. Section four positions her as a poet and self-reflexively comments on her place in the tradition. Section five, composed predominantly of persona poems, puts her poetics at play and reveals invention as the mediating force among cages, freedoms, and—continuing the last line of "Pastoral"—"desire, and the freedom to imagine it" (38).

Dove opens section four with two gestures toward the poetic tradition. The first poem is entitled "Dedication" and the second, "Ars Poetica" (47, 48). Both, together, establish some of Dove's most enduring beliefs about the relationship between poetry and the identity of the poet. In "Dedication" she speaks as a poet and begins abruptly with "[i]gnore me" (47). Dove does not value poetry as a self-indulgent revelation of a poet's personal life. She speaks to the limitations of art as "ways / to trap us in rumors" by reducing identity to its representations. She exclaims that such art has "[t]he freedom of fine cages!" (47). Instead of "bad music" and "faulty scholarship," she seeks "that ironic half-salute of the truly lost" (47). Thus Dove privileges irony and uncertainty and depicts the artist self most able to achieve those things as "truly lost" in the flux of existence. That she asks for a "half-salute" seems a call for reaffirmation.

"Ars Poetica" clarifies how she intends this "lost" (i.e., nomadic) artistic identity to function. Comparing her artistic desire to that of two other writers, an "unknown but terribly / important essayist" and an "Australian novelist" (both male), Dove writes:

> What I want is this poem to be small,
> a ghost town
> on the larger map of wills.
> Then you can pencil me in as a hawk:
> a traveling x-marks-the-spot. (48)

In comparison to the two men, whose desires are larger (and, she implies, more ego-centered) than her own, Dove positions her poems as small ghost towns—traces of meaning, discovery, and identity—and continues the mapping metaphor of a nomadic poetic identity. Revising her usual wordplay on her last name and extending the flying motif of the volume, Dove creates herself as a bird of prey, a hawk hunting for moments of poetic revelation. Central to this poetic identity is a nomadic insistence on traveling. No one location—whether physical, emotional, or intellectual—will pin her down for long. The passage's refusal of the "shoulds" of Archibald MacLeish's "Ars Poetica" reinforces the sense of an independent poetic identity.[6]

She does not find herself completely free from others' attempts to cage her, however, and follows the opening pair of poems in section four with "Arrow" (on a lecture by the scholar William Arrowood at her university) and "Stitches" (on a small accident that required her to have stitches). In these titles Dove conveys the risks to her hawk-artist-persona, caught as she can be by others' racism and sexism. Hawks can be wounded by arrows and require healing, a connotation that the red color imagery facilitates. The lecture by Arrowood, presented as being racist and sexist, wounds Dove and her students. She feels "my chest flashed hot, a void / sucking at my guts until I was all / flamed surface"; Becky, a student, "twitched to her hairtips" (49).

"Arrow" demonstrates several strategies that women use to cope with marginalization, including distancing, mastery, illness, and invisibility. Dove senses that she "had to" speak up, phrasing her question as "sardonic, / eminently civil my condemnation phrased in the language of the fathers" (49). Such a response reflects a poem in section one, "Flash Cards," in which she describes her father advising "[w]hat you don't understand, / master" (12, emphasis in the original).

Dove fights racism and sexism by demonstrating mastery of the "language of the fathers" (49). She also distances herself by being sardonic. Two of her students, however, become ill. The third, Janice, protects herself in a fashion reminiscent of Luce Irigaray's concept of "mimicry," in which women in a patriarchy adopt an appearance that allows them to "remain elsewhere" (76). Janice wears "black pants and tunic with silver mirrors" and thus reflects the racism and sexism directed toward her. The poem suggests that she can defend herself in this way; she even wears "pointed and studded, wicked witch shoes" (50). Such a strategy can have a subversive power, although Janice will use invisibility. She wears

> red for three days or
> yellow brighter
> than her hair so she can't be
> seen at all. (50)

That strategy, the poem implies, will be successful in restoring Janice in "three days" (emphasis added) by linking her to the archetypal story of the death and resurrection of Christ, who rose on the third day.

"Stitches," which follows "Arrow," shows the cost of Dove using her mastery of the "language of the fathers" to defend herself from racism and sexism. Wounded, she looks at the open skin and thinks, "'So I am white underneath!'" as if she had been accused of being white "inside" (51). Such a line seems a direct response to the comment that she "writes white." Dove's wound in the poem is not only from the lingering forces of racism and sexism but also inflicted by those who see mastery of traditions other than solely African American as a move away from blackness. After she humorously describes the doctor's "beavery" suturing the wound, Dove interjects a self-critique that reveals how she negotiates such perceptions: "You just can't stop being witty, can you? / Oh, but I can. I always could" (51, emphasis in the original). Thus, she laughs to keep from crying, a typical blues attitude, and uses humor to distance herself. At the same time, she is serious about targeting and acknowledging the wounds those attitudes cause.

Dove responds to such views excluding her from the black experience and uses humor to comment on her privileged position and lack of "brutal experience" typical in blues expression. "And Count-ing," which indicates it was written in Bellagio, Italy, presumably dur-ing a Rockfeller Foundation–funded "magic month at the Bellagio Study and Conference Center, where *Grace Notes* took shape" (*Grace Notes* viii), begins "[w]ell of course I'm not worth it," a reference to being the recipient of a wonderful experience (53). "Someone's got to listen to the fountain" (53), Dove jokes. Although she says, "I came here / to write, knock a few poems off the ledger / of accounts pay-able," she finds herself indulging in pasta and sambuca, day trips, tennis, and dozing over casual reading. Dove, however, does not rest with laughing off privilege. The poem ends with a contrast between "Our Age" of complexity and the "one phosphorescent ball" em-blematic of the comparative simplicity of Christianity's beginnings. It asks, "[W]hen the sky's the limit, / how can you tell you've gone too far?" (53). Such a question reflects the privilege relayed in the first two stanzas, as if to caution against its dangers.

The last two poems of the section meditate on the poet-speaker's fate, both professionally and personally, and tie it to the archetypal patterns of life and death. Immortality, it suggests, might be achieved through art. In "Medusa," the poet takes on the persona of the myth-ical gorgon who killed the men who looked at her directly by turn-ing them to stone. Such an allusion ties her to a lineage of women poets, including H.D. (Hilda Doolittle), Louise Bogan, and Rachel Blau DuPlessis, who have adopted the Medusa persona as a figure of the woman poet.[7] Dove portrays a poetic process that is intensely per-sonal: "I've got to go / down where my eye / can't reach" (55). Such interiority functions as a means to the universal and immortal. The speaker muses:

> Someday long
> off someone will
> see me
> fling me up
> until I hook
> into sky. (55)

Lacking current affirmation, the speaker hopes to someday be seen; such a moment will immortalize her like a star in the sky. Evok-ing the water imagery associated with the blues, the poem closes with

"[m]y hair / dry water," which suggests that Medusa's "hair" of writh-
ing snakes becomes inert, perhaps indicating immortality or an end
to her blues.

The final poem of the section, "In a Neutral City," continues the
water imagery of the blues with "the last sad trickle in a toilet stall,"
"fountains," and "rain"; the motif of a nomadic bird is in "wild birds
defying notation" (56). The section closes with a direct statement on
the fate of the poet-speaker: death. When Dove depicts the end as the
final course of a meal ("the cheese and pears will arrive, / and the
worms" [56]), she is imagining the finish of her own life-cycle. The poem's lush imagery— plants, wildlife, and nature—connotes a rhyth-
mic cycle of life and death. That the "someday" of death will occur in
a "neutral city" is a comment on the final "home" of a blues nomad.
It is just one of many homes and a place that cannot be afforded any
more than neutral status in a life's journey of rhythmical displacements. That the word *neutral* means not taking sides and also having
no particular kind or characteristics underlines the nomadic characteristics of her poetic identity as well as the revisionist universalism of
her poetic.

Dove's nomadism and signifying on home culminates in section
five, where she presents a series of personae who are artist figures
struggling with the tension between freedoms and cages. Thus her
personal becomes universal, as implied in the epigraph from Con-
stantine Cavafy: "Don't hope for things elsewhere. / Now that you've
wasted your life here, in this small corner, / you've destroyed it everywhere in the world" (57). Genie ("Genie's Prayer under the Kitchen
Sink") suffers through physical and emotional cages, finding freedom
in home projects where he invents his dreams. The breezeway he will
build next has "real nice wicker on some astroturf" (61). In "Canary"
(a caged bird), Billie Holiday "can't be free," yet through her art she
can "be a mystery" (64). Even the powerful presence of the island
women of Paris, "each a country to herself," suggests restriction; their
"deft braids carved into airy cages" link art and imprisonment (65).

Throughout, Dove associates mirrors and invention with freedoms and finds multiplicity, deflection, and re-creation as useful responses to cages. Always, the response to cages creates art. Genie, for
example, moves beyond being his mother's "least-loved son," of
whom she disapproves, to put up a mirrored globe (60–61) and build

rooms. Holiday's art, a "mirror" and a "bracelet of song," reflects the "invention of women under siege" by patriarchy and racism (64). In the multiplicity of personae and identities, places, and homes, Dove enacts her "x-marks-the-spot" poetic and positions herself as just one speck among many. The volume ends in a retirement home in Jerusalem, where she sizes up her place in the scheme of things: "So you wrote a few poems. The horned / thumbnail hooked into an ear doesn't care. / The gray underwear wadded over a belt says So what" (73).[8] The poet's footsteps make an "inconsequential crunch" (73). Dove's place, or final home, will be the same—death. As the momentum of the volume demonstrates, it is all part of the archetypal cycle of life and death, and "[e]veryone waiting here was once in love" (73).

Preceding the final poem, and following the blues poem "Lint," are two that counterpoint the volume's existentialism and turn *Grace Notes* and section five toward myth, anticipating Dove's next volume, *Mother Love*. Such a move refuses even an existential abyss as a final position or location as it gestures toward an ancient dimension to the themes of home, nomadism, the blues, identity, racial particularity and the universal, and death. "The Royal Workshops" and "On the Road to Damascus" use events and figures of the early Christian era to link the mostly contemporary poems of the rest of the collection to larger archetypal patterns.

"The Royal Workshops" juxtaposes the experiences of two figures, Zebulun and a slave who is a dyer. The poem shifts between the situations of the two. Zebulun, whose name means "dwelling," is the head of his tribe, which he leads into, and later out of, Egypt. The slave is charged with dyeing holy cloths for a sanctuary, as described to Moses by God on Mount Sinai (Exodus 25–26). Both personae—named leader and unnamed slave—convey ancient and recurring dimensions of the volume's themes.

The poem opens with the dyer's kettles ("dark red, / dark blue"), which convey blue, purple, and scarlet—colors specified in the Bible. The ten linen curtains made with these colors are supposed to have, specifically, loops of blue. The veil or scrim for the arc holding God's testimony is also to be blue. Thus Dove re-casts the blue of her blues in *Grace Notes* and links it with the ancient past and what is sacred. The work of the dyer who "ferment[s this] unpierceable scrim" (70) is "practised" (70), "holy," and "wretched" (69), which suggests brutal experience that is characteristic of the blues and is also deeply significant in that his work is "man's work to adorn the unspeakable" (70). Dove reinforces the volume's blues of death in wordplay around the word *dyeing*, which sounds the same as the word *dying*. That the dyer/die-er is specifically a slave surely signifies Dove's slave heritage and is part of an archetypal pattern across time and culture. The inference is reinforced by the emphasis on (skin) color in dyeing.

Against the uncomplaining slave who is a dyer, the poet places Zebulun, who wails to God about having to lead his tribe across "mountains & / hills, oceans & rivers" in the exodus from Egypt. While others received "countries," all he got was "the snail" (70). With the persona of Zebulun, Dove connects nomadism to the exodus of the children of Israel and links their flight for freedom to her own poetic stance and project. She specifically locates nomadism in the image of the snail, which becomes a figure for the nomadic subject in its ability to recreate a home anywhere. As Braidotti remarks, a nomad "carries his/her essential belongings with her/him wherever s/he goes and can recreate a home base anywhere" (16). That ability, the poem suggests, is far more valuable than having "countries" (70). Typically eschewing nostalgia or fixity, Dove moves the poem into racial difference ("red-haired Thadaeus, / blue-skinned Muhammed" [70]) and "battle" in the last two stanzas, "as God retreats" (70).

"On the Road to Damascus" uses as a segue the fabric and dyeing motif of the previous poem in portraying Saul's conversion ("flames poured through the radiant fabric of heaven" [71]). As related in Acts 22:6–7 (the epigraph), Saul is converted when Jesus speaks to him from heaven and becomes the voice of God and is his witness. Dove ties his conversion to the blues of the volume, especially to the signature blues poem "Lint," in Saul's "first recollection of Unbroken Blue" that he must reject because of his guards' "sworn" testimony (71). Dove renders Saul's conversion as a death that is not an end. Although "a spear skewer[s him] to the dust of the road" and his compatriots find "no one home" when they greet him, Saul has become the voice of the divine (72). He transcends his individual name and experience. That this happens on the road to Damascus suggests nomadism as a potential journey toward a connection with larger archetypal and spiritual truths.

∼

The momentum from the personal into the archetypal in *Grace Notes* reverses direction in *Mother Love,* which moves from the world of myth into individual and personal manifestations of archetypal patterns. Divided into seven sections, the volume moves generally from the world of myth to individual incarnations of the Demeter-Persephone myth and then into the poet's own voice and experience in a final section that ends again in the mythic cycle. The first and last sections, one and seven, each contain one poem, although "Her Island" (section seven) is long and has eleven linked sonnets. "Heroes" (section one) is a meta-poem about entering, accidentally and unwillingly, the world of myth. Section two details Persephone as a child, the abduction, and Demeter's grief. Section three shows Persephone's young adult life in debased and urban Paris, and section four follows her after her fall to Hades. Section five opens out into a plurality of voices in Persephone-like situations and a scathing critique of patriarchy. Section six expands even more broadly to include persona poems that parallel Demeter's role and poems that reflect on myth and history. The final section, seven, uses Dove's personal travel experience in Sicily.

The movement from myth into individual manifestations of mythic patterns in *Mother Love* is an important part of Dove's revisionist universalism and cosmopolitan stance. Although in *Grace Notes* she demonstrates that the personal—the racial and gendered specific—can be universal, in *Mother Love* Dove seems intent in proving that the process can move in the other direction as well, from myth to the personal, as race- , gender- , class- , and culture-specific as it can be. Especially in the persona poems of sections five and six, Dove demonstrates that the nomadism of her poetic enables her to voice personae from racial, cultural, or class locations not necessarily her own. Although she works to expand the experience articulated in her blues to include middle-class experiences, she does not allow herself to speak exclusively from a middle-class position or only that of race or gender.

Dove presents many Persephones and Demeters and from many different points of view. Hers is an everyday mythic world populated with everyday voices, from the child Persephone being teased at school to the young-adult Persephone enjoying life in Paris. Her world also includes a trucker's girlfriend, a German woman poet, a woman leaving her home (and her man), a child witness to Persephone's abduction, and a community of African American women. "History," in section six (59), describes how Dove moves from the personal to the mythic. In the poem, which follows section five's strongly feminist perspective, Dove suggests that women theorize history from the inside out through personal experience much like the internal experience of pregnancy. She aligns herself with this process of getting to the mythic via the personal. The man in the poem is a "wise / guy," whereas "his" woman is the one who "wisely" knows that "[e]*very wish / will find its symbol*" (59, emphasis in the original). By the end of the poem Dove has described one of her enduring themes, the process of telling "herstory" rather than history, a representation of the unspoken text of history.

Dove does not limit her process, however, to personal experience. In her characteristic crossing of boundaries she incorporates a diverse range of experiences and perspectives into reimagining of the Persephone-Demeter myth, a range, notes Georgoudaki, that includes the African American vernacular tradition. In *Mother Love,* a black maternal voice is associated with wisdom and comfort. In "Grief: The Council," the persona appears to be a member of the black community who is planning how to help Demeter through her grief. She agrees with others that "it's a tragedy, a low-down shame" but has told Demeter "enough is enough. / Get a hold on yourself" (15). She rallies the other women, saying, "[W]e gotta see her through." A similar voice, although younger, appears in "Rusks," where the persona describes the self-healing that came from the wisdom of her mother. She has decided to "[l]et someone else have the throne of blues for a while" (61). She points out, "As my mama always said: / half a happiness is better / than none at goddam all" (61). Persephone and Demeter, for Dove, also inhabit the upper-class realm of a Parisian bistro, where a mother goes to meet her daughter, who has been seduced by Hades. "The Bistro Styx" presents an affluent and well-educated mother persona whose vocabulary includes words such as *anachronism* and *demimode* and whose aesthetic sense deplores the lover's "appalling canvases" (40, 41). All of these voices, Dove insists, inhabit the same mythic realm and are in dialogue between the contemporary and the eternal.

In *Mother Love,* Dove reprises signifying on going home and her interest in the potentially productive tension between cages and freedoms, both of which began in *Thomas and Beulah.* She no longer simply signifies and enlarges upon the idea of home. "But, ah, can we ever really go back home, as if nothing had happened?" she asks directly in the introduction to *Mother Love.* In the case of Persephone—and, by implication, for everyone—the answer is no. Persephone's partial homelessness is thus emblematic of a feminist nomadic subjectivity.

Steffen links Dove's theme of breaking away from home and family in *Mother Love* to notions of "exile and migration" ("Beyond Ethnic Margin" 238). Those terms, although partially helpful to understanding Dove, do not convey her project as accurately as the concept of the nomad. Braidotti addresses all such terms and observes that the notion of exile can be "an evasive tactic" associated with race and class privilege (21). An exile is someone who leaves a country, usually for political reasons and with some degree of class privilege, such as that promulgated by Virginia Woolf in *Three Guineas.* "[A]s a woman, I have no country. As a woman I want no country. As a woman my country is the whole world" has become, according to Braidotti, a "*topos* of feminist studies" (21).

Aligning with Adrienne Rich's call for a "politics of location," Braidotti argues that Woolf's observation does not seem to be an accurate generalization about the status of women, either in 1938 or now, and also that such "generalizations about women should be replaced by attention to and accountability for differences among women" (21). Furthermore, Braidotti asserts, "[I]ssues such as exile and the right to belong, the right to enter, the right to asylum, are too serious merely to be metaphorized into a new ideal" (21). Braidotti also problematizes using the term *migrant*—usually among "the most economically disadvantaged groups" (22)—as inadequate to describe the subjectivity she wishes to articulate. "The migrant is no exile," she maintains, "s/he has a clear destination; she goes from one point in space to another for a very clear purpose. Europe today is a multicultural entity; the phenomenon of economic migration has created in every European city a set of foreign 'sub-cultures,' in which women usually play the role of loyal keepers of the original home culture. I do not think that effective links exist between the 'white' intellectual women and the many 'domestic foreigners' that inhabit Europe today" (22). In contrast to the exile and the migrant, Braidotti's nomad does not move only once and from one place to another, nor is a nomad fixed in one class identity or cultural location. The point of being a nomad is being able to make repeated moves among locations; it is about "crossing boundaries" and "deterritorialization" (21–23).[9]

Dove's view of her role in the transition to the twenty-first century positions her similarly to the idea of the nomad. In discussing W. E. B. Du Bois's "the problem of the twentieth century is the problem of the color line," Dove responded to the suggestion that she makes the line "a dot-dot-dot or a blur" with, "A demilitarized zone. . . . I make it permeable" (Appendix, page 190). Dove self-fashions her poetic identity as a deterritorialization of the color line and, by implication, of other such boundaries. That is nomadic; a migrant or exile would make only one such crossing and in only one direction.

Dove's nomadism in *Mother Love* carries a trace of the nomadic figure she uses in *Grace Notes,* the snail. The snail is introduced in "Protection," where a Demeter voice—specifically African American, as the reference to "good" hair versus black hair "in clusters" attests—comments on the lost of Persephone as "the snail has lost its home" (11). Imagery and direct reference to the snail occur in three more poems (25, 45, 59). In "Persephone in Hell," Dove links it directly to her surname wordplay when Demeter mutters (interspersing her remarks with Persephone's experiences in Paris), "[M]y dove my snail" (25).

In "History," Dove deploys the snail imagery of "tracking" used also in the poem "Blue Days." As the creature that carries its home on its back, the snail is symbolic of Dove's cosmopolitan resolution to the challenge of writing her way back home. The snail figures prominently in "Blue Days," the key blues poem in the volume, which opens section five's persona poems (45). In "Blue Days" Dove sings the blues of a woman who lives in a patriarchal world of violation and debasement that men say she "ask[s] for." The "blue days" of the title carry a double valence typical of the blues—the day is both peaceful and violating, beautiful and disgusting—just as the blues has a "tragicomic lyricism." The sky is a beautiful "Arizonian / blue," yet the day becomes suffused with the blues as misogyny is revealed.

The blue of the title also connotes men, because blue is the color traditionally used to signify a boy. Thus negative male attitudes toward women are targeted in *Mother Love* as an agent of women's blues. While the volume focuses on the loss at the core of the mother-daughter relationship (as depicted in the Demeter-Persephone myth), that loss is brutal—and thus worthy of the blues—because, the poems suggest, the daughter falls into the world of male dominance and patriarchal subjugation.

Mother Love is Dove's most feminist volume. As such, its view of male-female relationships under patriarchy is bleak: "the two of us forever: / one who wounded, / and one who served" (52). The nomadic "snail" in "Blue Days"—women's genitals tracking slime on the floor—becomes an oppositional, ironic figure of feminist subjectivity. Although men might view the snail (and women's bodies) as "tracking slime," snails, for women, offer a nomadic image of independence and freedom from patriarchy and misogyny.

In entering myth and rewriting it from a feminist point of view, Dove aligns herself with the modernist American poet H.D., whose revisionist mythmaking of figures such as Helen and Eurydice revealed the hidden patriarchal assumptions of male perspective and male dominance behind myths. Dove admits that she avoided rereading H.D. while working on *Mother Love* because, "I did not want to approach myth in any way like that she approached it, so I wanted to forget" (Appendix, page 181). Such a comment suggests the strong influence of H.D.'s mythic poetry on Dove, one perhaps not successfully forgotten. Like H.D., Dove reinvisons myth from an untold female point of view and critiques male dominance. In traditional versions of the Demeter-Persephone myth the interiority of the two female figures is markedly flat; readers learn of Demeter's grief at her loss and Persephone's surprise at being abducted. The reigning and more complex perspective is that of Zeus, who must contend with a cycle of nature gone awry and complaints from lesser gods. In negotiating with the various interested parties he becomes the hero in the tale and thus its dominating figure. In Dove's version, Demeter's point of view is enlarged and fully rendered. Her quest to rescue her daughter—and then heal from the daughter's unwillingness to be rescued—make her the hero of the tale.

Mother Love's central theme is the repeated loss that parents experience as they let go of their children and also the children's loss of innocence as they move into the world. As Dove notes in her introduction, "An Intact World," the myth on which she centers the volume tells of "a violated world." Section six, which struggles to come to terms with this "fragment[ed]" reality (52). The fragments refer, of course, to the fragmented women's bodies in the preceding section, five. They are also the fragments of the violated world that the music, blues, and poetry attempt to express lyrically and thus make whole again.

The cycle Dove depicts is a fall from innocence (with the mother) to experience (the world of men) and the eventual acceptance of the fall as necessary to the fertility cycle of life and death as paralleled in the cycle of the seasons. Although Dove traces a loss specific to mothering a daughter—the loss of the daughter to the "Law of the Father" and the debasement of patriarchy—it remains, in her rendering, much like T. S. Eliot's *The Waste Land,* a continuous parallel between the modern world and the world of myth, making the universal of gendered specifics. Throughout *Mother Love* the modern version of the cycle is portrayed as degraded and corrupt through a motif of waste imagery. From dog droppings in Paris to a racetrack built on an ancient site on Sicily, modern waste permeates the fertility cycle represented in the Demeter-Persephone myth and is in tension with it. Waste and disease, furthermore, are strongly associated with patriarchy and how it debases women. Dove focuses in particular on the psychological effects of male domination of women in her persona poems.

Mother Love's strong critique of patriarchy and its depiction of men as domineering or abusive depart from the majority of Dove's work, which represents males fully and empathetically, as in the portrayal of Thomas in *Thomas and Beulah* or Dove's father in *Museum.* In contrast, Hades in *Mother Love* is a one-dimensional, dominating male, as are Mick, Diego, and the men in the margins of "Exit," "Afield," and "Lost Brilliance." Such a negative depiction of males emanates from the book's perspective of mother love, a lens through which no man seems worthy. Dove counters this monofocal depiction of males in the final, autobiographical section of the poem, where she and her husband share a marriage of equals. Perhaps the characterization of Hades represents every mother's worst fears for her daughter and the representation of Dove's husband a possible and better reality.

The first poem in *Mother Love*, "Heroes," places readers squarely into the world of myth. Heavily ironic in its title and tone, the poem plays with poetic control of the specifics ("make it a poppy") as it demonstrates how people are drawn into archetypal patterns not necessarily of their choosing (3). The sense that "there's nothing to be done" about a fall into the fate of myth is enhanced by the epigraph to the section ("One had to choose, / and who would choose the horror?"), which is from James Hillman's *The Dream and the Underworld*.

The poem also contains a number of links to "In the Old Neighborhood," which furthers the idea that Dove's movement from the personal into myth and then from myth into the personal should be read as a balancing of the race- , gender- , or class-specific with the unmarked universal and part of her revisionist universalism. The imagery of "Heroes"—weeds, flowers, a garden, and a white boulder—is shared by the family-of-origin poem "In the Old Neighborhood." The poems also share the speaker's "why me?" or "it could have been me!" perspective. Both also focus on death, that of a bird in the earlier poem and a flower in the later one. But the poems write the relationship between the personal and the archetypal from opposite directions. "In the Old Neighborhood" writes from race, class, and gender specifics (closely aligned with Dove's family of origin) that can be linked to larger archetypal patterns. "Heroes," however, writes from the "meta-story" of mythic patterns that can be made individually specific to a reader. Using the same materials, Dove demonstrates that her poetic can work in both ways.

Section two of *Mother Love* focuses on Persephone as a child and Demeter's grief upon losing her. Dove reinforces connection among the Persephone poems with a series of titles that begin with *P* words ("Primer," "Party," "Persephone" [twice], and "Protection"). The poems detail such typical childhood experiences as being taunted at school, attending a first grown-up party, and admonitions from parents and highlight their "universal" character. At the same time, they allow racial specifics such as black hair ("Mine comes out / in clusters," 11) and class markers (a "Caddie" [7]). The voices of Persephone and Demeter slip nomadically among personae, maintaining consistency of perspective, and at the same time are not locked into any one "real" figure. Across several poems in section two, for example, Demeter can be linked, variously, to black hair (11), a Cadillac (7), a neighborhood where women wear pink foam curlers (10), the blues ("How done / is gone?" 11), cotton-picking slaves (13), international travel (18), drinking martinis (18), and a community of black women (15). Such plurality of specifics maintains particularity while emphasizing the universal behind the particulars.

Rendering Persephone's fall as a rape in "The Narcissus Flower" ties it into the waste motif that views her fate as a loss because it is a fall into patriarchy and female subjugation. Her protected virginity is conveyed by her "foot in its frivolous slipper" and the echo of "chaste" in the word choice of "chasten" to depict "the plunge" (12). The penetration of Persephone is violent "as a knife easing into / the humblest crevice" (12). The incident moves her from innocence to experience and myth and to the archetypal pattern of the cycle of life and death. As she realizes one of life's mysteries:

> you can eat fear
> before fear eats you,
>
> you can live beyond dying—
> and become a queen
> whom nothing surprises. (12)

Although she has fallen and is hardened by experience, Persephone is now also immortal. She has entered a cycle akin to life and death—six months in the underworld and six months on earth.

Demeter's response to Persephone's fall sings a blues of mother loss in "The Search" and "Protection." "The Search" is a negative portrait of a neighborhood similar to the one represented in "Ozone": "Blown apart by loss, [Demeter] let herself go" (*Grace Notes* 10). Her "indifference" to markers of conformity such as "proper" clothing and combed hair leaves her vulnerable to attack by neighborhood women who feel that "an uncombed head [is] not to be trusted" (10). Dove shows the brutality that can accompany such judgmentalism. When, in stanza two, it appears that Demeter may have been raped during frantic wanderings in search of her daughter ("one with murmurous eyes pulled her down to size"), community reaction commits a second brutality: "Sniffed Mrs. Franklin, ruling matron, to the rest: / *Serves her right, the old mare*" (10, emphasis in the original). Dove depicts a neighborhood that fails to support unconventional women.

Such a view points out that conformity, and the communities that enforce it, participates in the mindless waste of modern society.

Demeter's blues is voiced directly in the first-person "Protection," where Dove employs blues vernacular in the final lines, "Are you really all over with? How done / is gone?" The poem also brings up the issue of "good" versus "bad" hair that resonates throughout black women's writing. Speaking of Persephone's hair, Demeter sees

> the stubborn baby curls . . .
> I know I'm not saying this right.
> "Good" hair has no body
> in this country; like trained ivy,
> it hangs and shines. Mine comes out
> in clusters. (11)

Dove applauds the body and curls of black hair and points out the limits of "good" hair (typically associated with white women) through phrases like "trained ivy" and "hangs." Thus she weaves racial particulars into a poem about an archetypal loss of a daughter by a mother to convey her persistent belief that the universal can be marked as black without losing its universal character. That "Protection" also reintroduces the snail figure of nomadism—and comments on Persephone's abduction as "the snail has lost its home"—makes the poem a centerpiece for key themes in the volume (11).

Dove's revisionist universalism is foregrounded by the structure and personae of "Grief: The Council," which is also in section two. She places two voices in counterpoint: a black woman summoning other black women to help Demeter and a disembodied, imagistic voice of nature's fertility that is associated with Demeter. The black woman employs a decidedly black vernacular, including such common phrases as "a low-down shame"; voices lessons about life ("you still got your own life to live"); and shares figures of speech ("like / a dog with a chicken bone too greedy to care / if it stuck in his gullet and choke him sure" [15]). That her audience is the other black women of the community, who are possibly associated with a church group, is apparent in her directions: "Sister Jeffries, you could drop in / tomorrow morning," and "Miz Earl can fetch her later to the movies" (16).

Such a depiction of support and nurturing counters the negative representation of neighborhoods elsewhere in Dove's work. The distinctly black voice is balanced by a voice that depicts Demeter's loss in terms of nature images. She "let[s] the garden go to seed" and bemoans the loss of "tender cheek [and] ripening grape" and "the last frail tendril snapped free" (15, 16). The voice has no markers of race or even embodiment. It is a voice of seasons and emotions. By placing the voice in counterpoint to one that is distinctly raced, classed, and gendered Dove balances the particular and the universal in a way that celebrates both. The poem moves toward some degree of comfort for the Demeter persona by its final two lines (*"at last the earth cleared to the sea / at last composure"* [16, emphasis in the original]), which suggest that the black female voice has been an effective site of comfort and support for Demeter in her loss.

The extended poetic sequence "Persephone in Hell" (section three) shows her fallen life in the underworld. Persephone here is a junior-year-abroad persona in a run-down, contemporary Paris of dog droppings, promiscuity, arrogance, racism, and sexual predators. The downward imagery of the first stanza (replayed throughout the sequence) reinforces the setting as a fall into waste and degradation. Persephone relays, "I was not quite twenty when I went down / into the stone chasms of the City of Lights" (23). She is an innocent on the verge of sexual awakening, which is imaged in "nipples gleaning on the innocent *beignets*" and the "chaste white wrapper" of the bread she buys (23, 24). In the chill of late fall turning into winter, Persephone "was doing everything and feeling nothing" (25) and seems to be looking for "[w]hich way is bluer?" (28). Hades targets and seduces her handily.

The sequence closes with a compelling duet of loss between mother and daughter reminiscent of Julia Kristeva's "Stabat Mater" in poem seven. Lines indicating the daughter's voice are justified on the left margin; those that indicate the mother is speaking are justified on the right. Dove moves back and forth between the two (each side is fourteen lines), singing the daughter's loss ("the garden gone") and partial desire ("I entered for warmth / a part of me had been waiting") alongside the mother's grief ("I part the green sheaths / I part the brown field / and you are sinking") and acknowledgment of archetypal patterning ("I am waiting / you are on your way") (23). The ending places the specifics of Paris into the larger mythic cycle of the volume.

Paris is also the setting for section four, as evidenced in "The Bistro Styx," which is situated as the apex of *Mother Love* and is almost exactly in the middle of the volume's seventy-seven pages. Having fallen for "Hades' [p]itch," Persephone is presented in the poem as being distanced from the fecundity that her mother, Demeter, represents. She is "gaunt" and wears "gray" clothes and "graphite" shoes (40). Her mother comments that she is "blighted," a word associated with agriculture (blighted crops) (40). Her fall into waste is represented emphatically as a fall into a patriarchially defined role for women: female object and male artist's muse. She has become, her mother thinks, "the brooding artist's demimonde" (40), posing "nude for his appalling canvases" (41).

Such a debased role for women is paralleled in debased art. Dove describes paintings of "faintly futuristic landscapes strewn / with car-wrecks and bodies being chewed / by rabid cocker spaniels" (41). Persephone's role as art object ("me, he drapes in blues and carmine") does not nurture or fulfill her. When she eats at the bistro, "Nothing seemed to fill / her up" (42). Demeter's loss of her daughter becomes final in the last stanza, when Persephone "bit into the starry rose of a fig— / [saying,] 'one should really try the fruit here.' / *I've lost her*, [Demeter] thought, and called for the bill" (42). The fruit recalls the pomegranate seeds that Persephone eats in the underworld to ensure she will always have to return.

Section five turns the volume's focus into individual manifestations of the myth through an array of personae who are in Persephone-like situations. Dove emphatically connects the fall into experience to the fall into male-female romantic love, which damages women. The signature blues poem of the volume, "Blue Days," appears in this series. Amid imagery of waste, the personae in this section reveal how heterosexual romantic love situates women as "ask[ing] for" abuse and degradation (45). Love is like "a skull" (47) rather than the source of fecundity it should be. Male-female relationships under patriarchy— from a mother-love perspective—are based on forced dependence of women ("he can't give / you up, so you give in until you can't live / without him" [50]). The enjambment and rhyme in these lines play provocatively with alternate possibilities on which women miss out. The word *give* evokes desired reciprocity in the relationship, and *live* calls up a fertile and fulfilling situation, neither of which is the case for this woman.

The forced dependence in "Afield" taps into the waste motif of the volume by depicting such a relationship as a wound that becomes infected:

> Like these blossoms, white sores
> burst upon earth's ignorant flesh, at first sight
> everything is innocence—
> then it's itch, scratch, putresence. (50)

The final poem of the section, "Lost Brilliance," portrays the loss of women's light and possibility to a darkened, diminished expectation, albeit one of "plush privilege" (51) that is the reward for going along with patriarchy. The poem also stratifies men and women into set roles of the "served" and the "wounded" (50).

Poems on myth and the archetypal cycle appear in section six, which begins to move into a catharsis in which the fragmented women's bodies of section five are healed and the dominant blues motif in the volume is resolved. The epigraph, from Muriel Rukeyser's "The Poem as Mask," begins the process: "Now, for the first time, the god lifts his hand, / the fragments join in me with their own music" (53). The lines echo, again, Eliot's *The Waste Land:* "These fragments I have shored against my ruins."

Section six comments on the preceding poems and sections in a unifying movement toward closure and acceptance. The first poem, "Political," places the fall into experience into a larger cycle, suggesting that one must move beyond being stuck in the loss of the fall into experience. Using the situation of a man imprisoned—perhaps to suggest that men are also prisoners in a patriarchal system—the speaker asserts, "[Y]ou must talk yourself to death and then beyond, / destroy time, then refashion it" (55). Rather than being stuck in the downward part of the life-cycle, one must complete it and move beyond the time-bound and into myth (and thus into universal immortality). Even waste, the poem advises, is part of the fertility cycle. The man did wrong and "paid in shit, the world is shit and shit / can make us grown" (55).

"Political" draws together the waste imagery throughout *Mother Love* and places it into the larger cycle of life and death depicted in the Persephone-Demeter myth. Excrement is, after all, a fertilizer that helps plants grow; likewise, sores are the body's attempt to heal. That seasonal, cyclic rendering of waste imagery moves the poems toward a more accepting view of the process of loss as part of necessary regeneration. The final lines of "Political" connect that process to the blues: "Our wail starts up / of its own accord, is mistaken for song" (55). The lyrical expression of these painful experiences is a cathartic and healing part of the process. The beauty of the song makes the painful process one of art.

The blues of *Mother Love* and Dove's several preceding volumes is resolved in section six in "Demeter, Waiting," "Lamentations," and "Rusks." Demeter's pain of loss moves from an emphatic no to an accepting yes in the reverse-structured sonnet "Demeter, Waiting," in which the octave follows the sestet rather than the usual sestet-octave pattern. Although Demeter, at the beginning of another period without Persephone, first feels unable to bear her loss, by the end of the poem she enacts her grief and then "sit[s] down to wait for" Persephone (56). That the poem ends with "Yes" suggests a positive resolve and an acceptance of the larger cycle on the part of the mother. The yes affirms life, even life with pain. Moving beyond the blues continues in the next poem, "Lamentations," which urges that people "[t]hrow open the shutters / to [their] darkened residences" (57). Not to do so is to "deny this world" and deny life. As the final lines spell out,

> *To refuse to be born is one thing—*
> *but once you are here,*
> *you'd do well to stop crying*
> *and suck the good milk in.* (57, emphasis in the original)

If the third part of the blues process is indeed a reaffirmation, as Craig Werner and Albert Murray assert, Dove's blues in section six of *Mother Love* enters the final phase of the process and reaffirms life. "Rusks" finalizes her blues process and abjures any further blues. The persona takes on the attitude of a blues queen who, stepping down, declares:

> I got tired of tearing myself down.
> Let someone else have
> the throne of the blues for a while,

let someone else suffer mosquitoes.
As my mama always said:
half a happiness is better than none at goddam all. (61)

Section seven uses the individual experience of the poet to make a mythic quest back into myth; it also presents a positive relationship between a woman and man. The epigraph, Satan's lines in *Paradise Lost* comparing hell's "mournful glow" to heaven's "celestial light" continues Dove's depiction of the modern world as a degraded version of archetypal patterns (65). The imagery (island, lake, and racetrack) and structure (eleven linked sonnets) of circles attempt to turn the world counterclockwise from waste back to myth. Throughout, the poems counterpoint modern and ancient, waste and potential fertility.

In turning back toward the ancient myth, the poems seek to regain suspended fertility. Climbing through a city dump and led by a wizened guide, the poet-persona and her husband find an ancient site—seven Doric columns, albeit surrounded by weeds, roosters, and speeding traffic (72). They move counterclockwise around the island of Sicily, bringing together fragments of ruins, a "most exalted litter" (74). In attempting to track (perhaps like the snail) back to "one infernal story" of a girl pulled into a lake, the speaker seeks to "[turn] time back" to a purer mythic past (74). The irony is, of course, that when they find the lake that is the setting for the myth they find that a racetrack has been built around it, complete with advertising billboards (75). There is no going back to a purer time or an original myth. Instead, "[N]o story's ever finished; it just goes / on" (77). This is the story of the "Earth—wild / mother we can never leave," humanity's one and only home (77).

Dove treks into the mythic cycle by foregrounding the personal, lived experience and racial particulars of the poet and her husband. As the poem opens, they are clutching guidebooks in Agrigento, an ancient city in southern Sicily. Their encounter with a local man-cum-guide specifies his reaction to Dove's race: "His touch trembles at my arm; / hasn't he seen an American Black / before?" (69). Echoing Adrienne Rich, the poem details, "We find a common language: German" (69). The lines enact Dove's revisionist universalism in which she gets to the universal through particular experience (which is sometimes inflected by race, class, or gender). Her blackness affects the situation but does not determine or restrict it. The poet, her husband (who is specified as German a few poems later), and the guide cross the boundaries of their races and cultures and find a common language that can help guide them toward the archetypal myth. The scene does not erase the potential for schisms of racism or sexism, however. In the next poem Dove reports, "The way he stops to smile at me / and pat my arm, I'm surely his first / Queen of Sheba" (70).

Dove's revisionist universalism does not paint a fuzzy, warm world of unity. At the same time, however, she does not see race, gender, or class differences as barriers to perceiving shared life patterns. Ending *Mother Love* with a poem sequence based on the specifics of the poet's life, Dove completes her cosmopolitan demonstration of the interrelation of the racial particular and unraced universal.

Notes

1. Therese Steffen sees Dove as "conflat[ing]" the personal and the mythic in *Mother Love* ("Beyond Ethnic Margin" 227), a different way of seeing the relation between the two terms.

2. Lynn Keller and Susan Van Dyne also remark on Dove's attentuated acceptance in African American letters.

3. Among these are Therese Steffen, Peter Erickson, Helen Vendler, Robert McDowell, Susan Van Dyne, Ekaterini Georgoudaki, and myself. Other than Arnold Rampersad's early essay on Dove and some reviews of individual volumes by critics such as Houston Baker, I can identify only one critical article that has been published on the African American cultural expression in Dove's work by an African American scholar: that on folk idiom by Kirkland Jones. My appreciation goes to Jennie Mussington for assistance on this question.

4. Steffen's book on Dove was published while this book was in manuscript form and under review. Consequently, most references in this volume are to Steffen's articles and an interview with Dove published before 2001. Although Steffen shares my interest in Dove's crossing of boundaries (*Crossing Color*), we differ greatly in characterizing Dove's oeuvre. Steffen's book discusses Dove's work interchangeably across twenty years, whereas I emphasize her developmental process.

5. The lineage has poetic, European dimensions as well, as the allusion to Tennyson's "The Miller's Daughter" in the line about her daughter's hair suggests.

6. Thanks to Tony Jackson for assisting with the allusions to William Wordsworth, Alfred, Lord Tennyson, and Archibald MacLeish in this volume.

7. Thanks to Susan Stanford Friedman for assistance in identifying one of these writers.

8. Fred Viebahn relates that this poem "refers to the minor German-Jewish poet Harry Timar who had emigrated/fled to Palestine in the 1930s and whom we'd met and befriended first in Jerusalem in 1979; by the time we returned to Jerusalem two years later, in 1981, he had become very frail and was living in this old folks' home, where he died a few years later, alone and lonely and forgotten" (personal communication, Feb. 8, 2002).

9. Braidotti is quoting Gilles Deleuze.

Conclusion

In more than a quarter century of published writing Rita Dove has produced a body of work that challenges received ideas about race and literature. She has moved readers from the end of the twentieth and into the twenty-first century and a new conception of the relationships among race, identity, gender, nationality, and aesthetics. As a poet whom critics have identified as unyielding in her close observations and unswerving in her refusal of sentimentality, Dove's most observed and least sentimental aspect has been her cosmopolitanism and how it interacts with the influence of racial protocols on the reception of her work.

Dove's early poetry tries to remain out of the fray, although *The Yellow House on the Corner* thematizes her literary anxieties about being perceived as culturally mixed. Instead, her literary criticism, fiction, and drama bear the brunt of the pressure Dove felt to adhere to black nationalist conceptions of her art. The repression of anxieties about being perceived as a cultural mulatto, however, creates the symptomology of an incest motif throughout her work, some of which creeps into the poetry of Beulah's section in *Thomas and Beulah*. In her first major poetic volume, *Museum*, Dove presents a cosmopolitanism that defines and participates in one of the prominent black poetic aesthetics of the final two decades of the twentieth century. In *Museum*, Dove insists on the universal dimensions of her perspective as a black woman.

After *Museum*, Dove plays more freely and confidently with conceptions of identity, race, and gender, throughout which she signifies on the idea of home and neighborhood. She also deploys a blues nomad poetic identity, her mature reinvention of a cosmopolitan identity. The volume *Thomas and Beulah* puts the source of her nomadism in her family roots. The blues that begins in *Thomas and Beulah* and continue through *Grace Notes* and *Mother Love* has multiple layers, including Dove's partial sense of loss due to her nomadic identity, inclusion of middle-class experiences in the blues, lack of affirmation from the African American literary community, loss caused by death and children's eventual separation from their parents, and the painful debasement of patriarchy. Following Dove's excavation of her roots in *Thomas and Beulah,* both *Grace Notes* and *Mother Love* demonstrate an ongoing cosmopolitanism that balances the racial particular and the unraced universal in an interplay between the personal and the archetypal.

On the Bus with Rosa Parks lacks the focus and cosmopolitan tensions characteristic of Dove's earlier work. She admits that its poems are an assortment written over a number of years (Appendix, page 183), which might explain their disparity and lack of unity. Furthermore, she comments on the theme of the volume as being similar to Wittgenstein's "To take yourself as the case," rendering the personal as an existential eye in the universe (Appendix, page 183).

Such comments suggest that Dove's tensions regarding the emergence of cosmopolitanism are resolved and do not affect the poems of *On the Bus with Rosa Parks,* perhaps making it less artistically interesting than her earlier work. The volume does, however, offer a vantage point from which to reconsider her body of work. In it, Dove remarks upon ideas about home, identity, and freedom as part of an interest in journeys. Sections such as "Freedom: Bird's Eye View" and poems such as "Lady Freedom among Us" celebrate freedoms both real and symbolic. Dove places in counterpoint to this the experiences of those who have not had full access to freedoms, particularly Rosa Parks and other founders of the civil rights movement. In sections such as "Cameos" and "Black on a Saturday Night," she positions herself as a black poet who is on the bus with Rosa Parks (in the sense of participating in the same culture and quest for freedom as well as resulting fame).

As in the poem "QE2. Transatlantic Crossing. Third Day" (chapter 5), Dove demands that readers know of her lack of the brutal experiences of many of her forebears. Comparing her luxurious ride on the *Queen Elizabeth II* with that of many bus-riding blacks during the civil rights movement, Dove writes of the ship:

Aviva Dove-Viebahn, Fred Viebahn, and Rita Dove. (© 1999 by Fred Viebahn. Used by permission of Fred Viebahn. All rights reserved)

> This is a journey for those who simply wish to be
> *On the way*—to lie back and be rocked for a while, dangled
>
> between the silver spoon and the golden gate. Even
> I'm thrilled, who never learned to wait on a corner,
> hunched in bad weather, or how many coins to send
> clicking into the glass bowl. I can only imagine
> what it's like to climb the steel stairs and sit down, to feel
> the weight of yourself sink into the moment of *going home*. (84)

Dove cannot claim an experience such as that of Rosa Parks. She cannot claim economic lack or participation in the fight for civil rights that grew up around the symbol of a bus. She cannot, furthermore, even claim the experience of not having a fixed home. Dove expects readers to know that. At the same time, she asks them to admit her version of African American experience.

Reflecting in the final poem of the volume on her journey "back home," she comments,

> I've missed the chance
> to put things in reverse,

> recapture childhood's backseat
> universe. Where I'm at now
> is more like riding on a bus
> through unfamiliar neighborhoods. (88)

The lines can be read in several ways, including as a reflection on the journey of the volume, a comment on the "backseat" years of the black experience in America, and a personal musing on the circumstances of her life.

In light of a long-range view of Dove's on-going signifying on ideas of home and returning to the old neighborhood, the lines relay almost apologetic regret. She seems most eager for nostalgia and most wishful "to put things in reverse" and return to the old neighborhood. Instead of having a neighborhood, however, the poet-persona appears to be a perpetually transient explorer, a placeless nomad. The poem's ending, however, turns partly away from loss:

> . . . . I know
> I vowed I'd get off
> somewhere grand; like that dear goose
> come honking down
> from Canada, I tried to end up
> anyplace but here.
> Who am I kidding? Here I am. (88)

Speaking from her Charlottesville, Virginia, home that overlooks a pond, Dove parallels herself with the internationally migrating goose. The poem suggests that where she "get[s] off" the bus "for the purpose of *"going home"* (84) is a combination of "vow" and accident. Likewise, readers' identities, the home they carry with them, are also a combination and contradiction. Finally, Dove asserts "here I am" as a statement of present home and a state of identity.

Such a statement echoes Dove's comments about Langston Hughes's essay "The Negro Artist and the Racial Mountain" in a 1995 interview with Steven Bellin. Asked how she felt about characterizing African American writers as either Afrocentric or Eurocentric, she responded:

> I don't find the terms Afrocentric or Eurocentric useful. I think
> they're divisive; they're the province of frightened people who need

to put things in categories in order to know who and what they are. . . . I'm in favor of nothing that walls out knowledge in the name of purity. There is no way to keep yourself "pure," be it race-specific, gender-specific, or caste-specific. The most fascinating thing about life is its flux.

Some critics persist in trying to define me, and it's tricky answering those kinds of questions. Newspapers are looking for a sound bite—something snappy—and they won't quote the entire answer because it's too complex, like life—so they will try to shorten the answer and they will get it quite wrong. My favorite response to that line of inquiry comes from Langston Hughes, who published an essay in 1926 called "The Negro Artist and the Racial Mountain," in *The Nation*, I believe. The "new Negro" artists of the Harlem Renaissance, he says, intend to express their "individual dark-skinned selves without fear or shame"; if white people liked the results, that was great, but if they didn't that was fine, too. He then takes it one step further: it would be wonderful if other black people liked what the Renaissance artists were doing, but if they didn't, that wouldn't matter, either. He ends with a declaration: "We build our temples for tomorrow, strong as we know how, and we stand on top of the mountain, free within ourselves." (30–31)

When Dove proclaims "here I am" at the end of *On the Bus with Rosa Parks*, she accepts her cosmopolitan identity within the African American literary tradition without fear or shame. In the face of regret, loss, and resistance from those committed to a specious idea of cultural purity, she embraces the poetic truth of her complicated and cosmopolitan experience.

Appendix:
Interview with Rita Dove

We met at Dove's home on the outskirts of Charlottesville, Virginia, on January 12, 1998. In an open, spacious living room lined with musical instruments (including Dove's custom-made viola da gamba), contemporary paintings, and Dove's folk art collection of black dolls, we had tea and Girl Scout cookies while our conversation ranged across a number of Dove's works, beginning with *The Darker Face of the Earth*, an oedipal drama set in the antebellum South. The protagonist, Augustus, unacknowledged son of the white plantation mistress Amalia and her black slave Hector, returns to the plantation unaware of his parentage. Ignoring the possibility of a romantic relationship with fellow slave Phebe, he becomes Amalia's secret lover while, unbeknown to her, he joins a group of rebel slaves who are plotting an overthrow.

~

Malin Pereira: There's been a lot of excitement recently about your play, *The Darker Face of the Earth*, being performed at the Kennedy Center. I understand you have made several revisions to the play and Story Line Press has issued a revised edition. What kinds of changes did you make? How substantial are they?

Rita Dove: Well, the ending is different. The revision actually came about after seeing some of the scenes kind of put on their feet, as they say in the theater, which means actually having actors read the lines and try to walk through them. The history of the play is very strange for a play. I wrote it without knowing what the theater world was like, and there were other things happening in my life, so I finally decided no one will do this play because it's too big, etc. And so I put it away. It's only because my husband kept bugging me every five years or so to do something that I finally rewrote it and Story Line Press published it in 1994. At that point I really did assume that that play was going to be on the page and that was it, and maybe someday when I was dead someone would do it out of pity or whatever. When Oregon Shakespeare Festival was interested in the play, I realized I had this opportunity now to see if what I *thought* would work onstage would indeed work onstage. A lot of the revisions came about from just not feeling comfortable with some of the scenes and the pacing. I did add a couple of scenes as I realized that certain characters were more stock than essential and that we needed to feel that they had a full life, even if you didn't know what the life was. This is a complicated human being who is bringing everything from their past to the pressure of that moment. For instance, there is now a scene between Phebe and Augustus because Phebe just kind of became embittered over being left, and I actually liked her as a character. I was exhausted by the time I finished that version. I thought, "Okay, that's enough." Also, I did change the ending. It's essentially the same tragedy except that Augustus does live at the end of this one, it's just not a life worth living. With this version what happens is that Amalia kills herself; also Phebe is now in there, too, because I thought this is essential to have her there. As the three of them piece together, in this moment of craziness, what exactly the story is, that indeed Amalia's his mother, each reacts in a different way, and his mother then kills herself to try to save him, which means that the revolutionaries think that he did what he was supposed to do and he's a hero. But what kind of hero is that who's just realized that he's lost everything that could make him happy? That change came about because of my daughter, who had participated in all of the sessions at Oregon Shakespeare Festival. She loved it and would sit through all these rehearsals and make suggestions. It was great. And one night I was still perturbed at the ending. I had put Phebe in it, but I still just didn't like the way the insurrectionists came in, bang, bang, everyone was dead. So I was fiddling with it, and she came down (she was supposed to be in bed), and I said to her, "I was just messing around with this ending." And she said, "You know, I think he should live. There are worse things than death." This is a twelve-year-old who really doesn't know what she's saying, but when she said that I suddenly realized, yeah, that's even worse. It was interesting because in some of the workshops, that was one of the questions that was always presented to me, because in the original *Oedipus*, of course, he does live. People asked, "Why didn't you follow the myth exactly?" I don't follow it exactly because I didn't want it to be a kind of checklist against a Greek myth. I couldn't find the right way I could make it believable that he could live. I hadn't found the plot that would make him live and why that would be worth it for him, not just to fulfill the myth. And that was the moment that did it. So those are the major changes. Hector's part also has been deepened. I didn't want him to be merely a crazy man in the swamp. I really wanted everything that he said to make eminent sense if you knew the whole story. Since no one knew the whole story, he seemed crazy. So he does have a couple of monologues and things like that, but the basic story is still the same. And that all came about working with these wonderful actors.

MP: So it was the putting the play into production that offered these realizations; it becomes apparent that certain things need to be changed. I guess that's very typical in the theater.

RD: Yes, it is very typical in the theater, from what I understand. I found it really exciting because as a poet, someone who's used to doing everything in one circle of lamplight, this was exhilarating. It was also exasperating sometimes: too many voices. I can really understand now how people can lose perspective in the theater because there are a thousand things to think about. Most of the time I had to just simply forget everything everyone said and go back out to my cabin and make my decision. So it was a fascinating experience. As a poet (because I really think of myself as a poet), one of the things artistically that I learned in rewriting the play was how much power in theater a silence or gesture can make. It's very close to poetry and how what you don't say has to be contained in those white spaces but also in the sound of the word. That's one of the essences of poetry that always thrills me and keeps me going back to it.

MP: Your earlier poetry often was dealing with the historical past, but in *Grace Notes* and *Mother Love* you seem to have moved more into the personal present, and you've commented in other interviews about your willingness to now come into the personal a little bit more. You called it at one point "coming home," writing your way "back home." How does *The Darker Face of the Earth,* which I read as a play about the historical foundations of American culture, relate to that?

RD: Well, that's a great question. There are two parts to my answer. First of all, because *Darker Face of the Earth* has such a long history, in a very interesting way it's an early work that I came back to. I began working on that play actually about the same time that I just finished my first book, *The Yellow House on the Corner.* So in that sense all of the themes of *Darker Face* were very close to the slave narratives of *Yellow House on the Corner,* filling in the past, trying to get into the past as a person and to humanize it so that eventually I could get to my own past without being self-indulgent. However, trying to go back to the play and rewrite it for production felt like another kind of coming home because now I had to inject a lot of my own emotions and takes on things in characters to make sure they were alive and not just mythic representations walking around saying their lines and getting off the stage. The first version of the play is clean but it's very quick, and it's more pageant than personalized. So there's a little bit of me in every one of those characters that wasn't necessarily there in the first version, particularly Amalia, and it was very important to allow her to speak. In the end I didn't want any easy answers; I didn't want anyone in the audience coming away thinking, "These are the bad guys, these are the good guys, slavery is bad, slave owners are bad, look at the noble savage" and all that. I wanted every one to be fighting for their own individual realization against the system. The big bad guy is the system, obviously. But that's all the kind of stuff I learned by finally coming around, coming home in the previous volumes.

MP: Interesting. So do you think that in some way the personal present and national history end up being connected for you?

RD: They've always been.

MP: Why or how?

RD: I think they both have something to do, a lot to do, with being female and being black. From as early as I can remember, I always felt that there was a world going on with lots of "historical" events going on and that my viewpoint was not a direct one, but I was looking at it from the side. I'm talking about when I was small. First it started out as a female issue, because I think most kids when you're growing up, there's a point when you're in a minority when you realize you're a minority. It's very strange. It's kind of, "Oh, really, I'm not like you?" It usually comes from the outside somehow. But as a *girl*, growing up in a really traditional family, with a mother who is a housekeeper and a father who is a chemist, I always felt that there was this view of how the world should run, and then I was supposed to fit into this somehow and I didn't think all the rules were quite right. Both my parents would say "education is the key" and "you can be anything you want to be," and then I'd look at the magazines and say, "I can't be everything I want to be unless something's going to change." So that meant that I didn't take the historical at face value. Ever. And, of course, W. E. B. Du Bois talks about the double vision when you're a minority. You see what the mainstream is immersed in, which is reality, but you also see the other reality. He talks about what advantage this kind of binocular vision gives you; it gives you perspective, it gives you depth. As I grew up I felt enormously lucky that, because of my circumstances, I had this vision. I always felt underneath it—I never believed that the newspapers were true necessarily—that was just one version of the truth and it's interesting, it's pretty good, but I'll wait to see what judgment is going to come in. So that's why the personal present and the historical past have always been connected for me. I think it's truly a part of my environmental influences. On the other hand, language was always fascinating to me, even from a young age. I think with most children it's fascinating at a really existential level; the sounds that you make are wonderful, regardless of whether they make sense. There were several kinds of ways in which language was stylized in my life. I'm talking about storytellers in the family, the good ones, the ones who could tell the story you've heard three thousand times and suddenly it's a good story, from those to the kind of oral games you play on the street as a black kid, from the dozens to what that implies and how the language becomes plastic, all of that and then also the literature. To read someone like Shakespeare and think this language is part of the emotion, and there are all these different levels to language and different tones and qualities. All of that, too, was experience which is perceived directly as one part of life, but if you're going to be a writer or are going to be an artisan, you choose a medium. The trick is to use this essentially artificial, made-up medium to try to imitate that immediacy, which it can never do because it's never immediate, but you give the illusion of immediacy. I was fascinated by that from a very young age. It was probably part of the reason why, and I've talked about this in other interviews but I've never really talked about it in this kind of way, when I was in second grade I wrote this silly novel called *Chaos* where I took my spelling words and wrote chapter by chapter according to the list of spelling words. And part of the fascination with that was to see how the words themselves, the language, these symbols would build the reality.

MP: So in some ways writing your personal present is rewriting national history, adding the version that wasn't represented or writing from the center that was marginalized.

RD: That's one part of it. That's absolutely one part of it, with the understanding that my personal history is only one personal history. That is part of it. Also, I think that because I was acutely aware, even at a young age, that my perception of an "official" historical event was very different than that "official" version, I thought that this must be the same for every person if you really stop to think about it. There's a war, and people can talk about casualties in the war, but if you've had someone die in the war it takes on a completely different cast, and if you're a refugee from that war it takes on a completely different cast. All these kinds of things I think are really fascinating, and in the end, unless you have a writer, or artist, or an oral history, the only version left is the one that is the official version, and I really resist that. I just feel that all of us cannot ever forget that the official version is merely a construct that we may need to order our timeline, but we can't forget that there are human beings, all sorts of individual human beings to punctuate this.

MP: Which of course is what you're doing in *Museum,* writing poems of "unofficial" history. It reminds me of James Baldwin and how he

talks about how the sad thing about white America is they often believe their own myths, they believe the official version of history, and
I find that somewhat true when I teach. So many of my students just
hang on to those official versions of history.

RD: And they can be utterly devastated when they realize that it's not
true. I think that's why Vietnam and the sixties were so explosive and
powerful. It was the moment when we realized that the myth didn't
hold. Then the seventies and the eighties became this retreat to "it's
just me and I'm going to do this."

MP: How does it feel now *not* to have all of those responsibilities of
being poet laureate?

RD: It feels wonderful actually. That's a terrible thing to say. It does
feel wonderful. It also is not completely over, either, and I think that
one of the hardest periods of time for me was right after it was over
because I naively assumed that Bob Haas was going to take this over
and I could go back to my life, and I couldn't go back to my life. There
are residuals and the letters and the requests keep coming, but you
don't have the outside justification to say, "Well, I'm going to go on a
half-time teaching load." So it took me, and it's still taking me, a lot
of time to just to figure out how to conduct my life so that I have one.
And since I was raised to be a dutiful daughter I am someone who answers letters, and I think Toni Morrison is the same way. We're mid-
western. We know how our parents raised us. In a way you get raised
to try to fit into the northern world. The southern roots are very close;
my grandparents came from the South. They came to the North and
went into these factories and then had to build a new neighborhood,
a new home, and the rules of social behavior were fairly rigorous. They
say to the children, "This is how you have to be," and you do this because you honor yourself as well as your community, which really puts
a double-whammy on you. So there I was, trying to answer these letters, and finally—I really think it took until about last year—I realized I don't have to answer all of these letters. I can actually just not
answer, and they'll write again.

MP: Oh what a relief! [Laughter.] It's apparent that music, your training in classical music, has been important for your work. It comes up thematically in so many ways. One thing that I'm curious about is how does that training influence your work structurally? Have you thought about that at all?

RD: Oh, I've thought about it. I haven't thought about it in any kind of critical way. First of all, at a very basic level, I believe that language sings, has its own music, and I'm very conscious of the way something sounds, and that goes from a lyric poem all the way to an essay or to the novel, that it has a structure of sound which I think of more in symphonic terms for the larger pieces. I really do think that sonnets to me are like art songs. That's one thing. I also think that resolution of notes, the way that a chord will resolve itself, is something that applies to my poems; the way that, hopefully if it works, the last line of the poem, or the last word, will resolve something that's been kind of hanging for a while. And I think musical structure affects even how the poems are ordered in a book. Each of the poems plays a role. Sometimes it's an instrument, sometimes several of them are a section, and it all comes together that way, too.

MP: What we were considering in my class on your work, and I think we were applying this to *Yellow House on the Corner,* was that you sometimes have five sectioned works, and we were wondering if you were structuring things along the idea of five movements for longer symphonies. You have moved away from that, of course, in more recent volumes, but especially since it was your first work structuring a longer piece like that I was wondering if you just went to that structure.

RD: This is fascinating because the book I'm working on now has five sections, and I remember feeling like, "Oh, I like these five sections."

MP: Yes, comfy.

RD: Yes, really comfy. [Laughter.] I think that three-sectioned books put too much emphasis on that middle section being solid and holding onto the ends, and when you have five sections it kind of takes the edge off of putting such great importance into the beginning. One of the things about when I'm ordering and structuring the books is to try to thwart people's notions that the first poem is going to give you the key and now here we go! But all it is [is] just an opening.

MP: Actually, I teach it that way. [Laughter.]

RD: There's also this sense that if you take it as the key, then what doors does it open further down. It's more like: Here's an opening motif, and then it's going to be embellished, and then it may change, and then it may go minor, and then it does all these kind of things, so it isn't like this is the truth, but this is just one truth.

MP: Very true of *Museum* too. You play with the opening motifs along the whole way. It's really diverse; it's not just like the answer is at the beginning. Well, you've published a lot besides poetry: short stories and essays and plays, and a novel, and I know from other interviews that crossing genres, you feel, is very necessary and a good thing as a writer. I've wondered whether you find that there is a specific relationship between your poetry and your non-poetry that you'd be able to articulate. Do you think, for example, are certain subjects inappropriate for poetry that then you turn to other venues?

RD: Well, actually, when an idea occurs to me, sometimes it's an idea, sometimes it's a line, sometimes it's a word, sometimes it's a character, but at the moment when a piece begins, gets its genesis and I feel that something is going to happen and become a piece of writing, I know what form it's in already. I can't think of an instance where I've tried it out as a poem and said, "Oh no, this should be a short story," or something like that. The only case I can think of where there are almost duplicates is the scene in the novel on a beach playing the guitar, and then also in the poem "Summit Beach," but I deliberately decided to try it both ways. It was willed. The story came first, and then I thought I really would like to try this from a different angle, just that moment. So there hasn't been that kind of crossover where I've said, "Oh, this didn't work, or that didn't work." I think it must happen further back in the brain, a series of thought processes that by the time it comes to my consciousness all those decisions have been made. I think that has something to do with the way that the language itself then gets used in various genres, the weight of each word, too. Because I remember when I was working on the novel, at first, and I knew it was going to be a novel, and I thought, "Oh I don't want to write a novel—too big, too many words, it's such a waste." This is just how you think as a poet. Then, until I could figure out how the weight of each word and the weight of each sentence wove the story, I was just writing a lot of verbiage. Once I figured out two things, the key signature and the time, then it became much easier. I figured out how each individual note—you've got me talking in musical terms!— how much weight each different note had, what kind of time signature I was going to have in this piece. All artists can fall into the traps of whatever we do well, and that for me is to write a poem. To write in other genres offers stretch and a counterbalance to that trap. The other genres help remind me that there's a value to length, there's a value to overload; there's something to lushness, too, and it can be just as powerful as something austere.

MP: Which is mostly your aesthetic in your poetry.

RD: It is.

MP: You don't tend to go on and on and on.

RD: No I don't, but someday. . . . [Laughter.] The thing is that if you go on and on, it has to have a purpose. I get really frustrated with poems that go on, but the words can be kind of sloughed away. I think there's a way to go on and on and still have it—the intent. But I do find, in relationships between the genres, that when I'm writing poetry I very often read prose and vice versa.

MP: You don't want to be influenced by the poets when you're writing poetry.

RD: It's not just that I don't want to be influenced because when writing a poem I will go to the bookshelf and take a book up because I know there's something in there that I need to read again. But I don't want to sit down and read lots of poetry books while writing poetry. It muddies the water. It must have something to do with the musical training because when I'm in another country I can pick up languages fairly quickly; I do it mostly I think through imitation and the into-nation of the language, the way it falls. For example, I speak German fluently, but I have a great difficulty if we go somewhere and some-one speaks German with an accent, like a Swiss-German, or someone who speaks English with an Afrikaans, South African dialect. After an hour I start to talk like that, and I have to go away! Wales and Ireland were a nightmare because I would start doing that, because I also loved the way it sounded, too, so that tendency in me would mean that if I were reading exclusively Adrienne Rich for days then I would start to write like Adrienne Rich. That's not necessarily me. That's not my voice, that's her voice. So I have to not read much poetry while writ-ing it, for self-protection.

MP: I've been interested in your recent focus on the work of Breyten Breytenbach. You just translated his Li Po poem, and I noticed you dedicated a poem to him as well in *Mother Love*, called "Political." I was curious, first of all, how you picked up Afrikaans. Did you go to South Africa or how did this all come about? And I'm curious what interests you in his poetry as well.

RD: Well, a lot of it is just circumstance. First of all, I don't know Afrikaans. I know German, I know a little bit of Dutch. If I listen to Afrikaans long enough I can get into it. The way that the translations came about was that I was at a poetry festival last summer in Rotter-dam called the Poetry International, and this has been going on for twenty years; I've been there once before. And each year they've had writers come from all over the world and have this week-long festival, just poetry day and night. But also sometimes in the mornings they have a translation workshop for the week, and they choose a poet who is either Dutch or Dutch-related in the language, and all the other writ-ers come in and translate the work, and the idea is to try to bring some of these works to their respective languages. So Breyten Breytenbach was the poet for this last summer, and it was great because he was there, and they also had provided literal translations in a host of lan-guages, in English, in German, in French, in Spanish. And he gave a reading. So I used the French and the German and the Dutch and the Afrikaans and the English, of course, to try to put it together. Again it gets to my fascination to try to find the approximation in the language.

Breyten Breytenbach I find interesting because of his linguistic standpoint, he knows so many languages. I like a lot of his poems, but there are also others that I'm not that crazy about.

MP: Yes, he's published a novel in French as I recall.

RD: Right, and he's lived in Paris all these years, and I've met him at several conferences. When you go to these international conferences you meet the same people all the time. I think he lived in Spain sometime, too. So I can't help but feel all those languages influenced his work. So that's really where all that came from, and it's less a fascination with his work as it is just the way the circumstance presented itself. With dedicating "Political" to him, that occurred after I think the first time I met him in Mexico and as I was working through those poems about mothers and daughters. I remembered a description from his memoirs, his *Confessions of an Albino Terrorist,* when he talks about the black political prisoners singing as someone's being led to execution, and that really was powerful. I was trying to get into the sense of Demeter going down into hell and what's going to sustain you if your daughter is going down into hell. That image came back up to me.

MP: I remember reading in an interview, it must have been at least ten years ago, that you were interested in going to South Africa, but I guess you never got there yet.

RD: I have never gotten there. Actually, I'm going this May [1999]. There's going to be a writers' conference in Durban, so I'm going to go this May.

MP: Are you going to get to go around a bit?

RD: A little bit but not enough. I can't stay long because of my stupid schedule—I'm only going to be there for ten days. But I'll probably go back some time next year to the University of Cape Town. There were a couple of instances when I was supposed to go to South Africa through USI [the U.S. Information Service or Agency], but they could not assure me that I and my husband could travel together and that I would be speaking in front of mixed audiences. So I didn't go.

MP: A writer you've mentioned throughout your work is Derek Walcott. What would you say has been important for you about Walcott and his work for you as a writer?

RD: It's interesting because I'm still trying to figure that out. I love his work, but I don't think that he is influencing me. I mean, I find that his work is *very* different from mine, but I love his work. The first time that I came in contact with his work was through his play *Dream of Monkey Mountain.* I read the play—I must have been a junior in college—and I just thought it was phenomenal; I just never know that theater could be like this. I was surprised to discover that he was a poet as well. I thought, "Whoa! I get a double treat here." Part of it is the fact that he's always dealing with this, I don't want to call it dilemma, but with this *position* of being in love with this island, in love with his people but feeling also separate from them because he's gone off to school and that he's writing these amazing poems that they won't read. And also wanting to honor where he comes from but at the same time not wanting to be another colonizer of the experience, and he's always very conscious of that. I think he is even conscious of it all the way to the level of language because he has earlier poems particularly where he puts in a lot of patois, and even in later poems where in the middle of this absolutely gorgeously constructed English, this British turn-piece sentence, comes one of those "he no be this," which happens in the culture a lot. I just think that he is an exquisite writer.

MP: But technically you don't feel that there is a debt there or any kind of influence?

RD: Well, I think technically there is a debt in the sense that I wish that I could write that well. I think that the language is just gorgeous, and it's not my voice, it's not my style. But, in general, I admire his trying to mix in all levels of the language, because this is what he has grown up with, and his making it work on the page. That was something that I aspired to. Trying to get the more syncopated rhythms into the more classic iambic pentameter.

MP: So it's that mixed heritage and the mixing of the traditions that you like.

RD: I think it's a wealth rather than a problem, and it's so ass backwards to say that there is a black way of writing and then there is a white; this is madness. Every black person that I know speaks at so many different levels all the time, and why not use all of that? All of it. Why not? I do believe that people will come along; even if they haven't heard it that way they can think of it. We've done it so long with other ethnic groups. If you think about all those attitudes and expressions that we've gotten from Jewish Americans, for example. . . .

MP: It should be a both/and not an either/or.

RD: Exactly.

MP: Which brings me to one of my favorite poems.

RD: Which one is that?

MP: "Upon Meeting Don L. Lee in a Dream" from your first volume, *The Yellow House on the Corner.*

RD: Oh.

MP: Critics have noticed this poem.

RD: I know.

MP: You can't help but notice this poem. Arnold Rampersad points out that this might show a bit of hostility to the black arts movement. It's an early poem of yours, and I wonder if you've moderated your stance toward some of the black arts movement aesthetic views or prescriptions over time.

RD: Yeah, moderated is a difficult word. It implies. . . .

MP: Extremism to begin with.

RD: Right.

MP: Well, you do fry him alive in the poem. [Laughter.]

RD: He and I are friends, too, you know.

MP: Have you come to a broader prospective now?

RD: I think of it more as a generational poem as opposed to a one that deals with aesthetics; that as a young girl, insecure as a writer, in a sense I was doing that killing the father thing. I remember having someone ask me, "Well why do you say, 'in a dream,' why don't you just say it directly?" I answered, "No, I want it to be dreaming because it is a psychological poem, it is a poem that works on that kind of psychic landscape." It wasn't an excuse for the surrealism in the poem but a way to say not to take it at face value, it's not that. I *do* think that when I was beginning to write or beginning to contemplate putting the writing out into the world (which is a different thing altogether) when I was in college, just beginning to think seriously about writing for publication and stuff like that, I *was* terrified that I would be kind of suffocated before I began. That I would be pulled into the whole net of whether this was black enough or whether I was denigrating my own people and all this kind of stuff. This is a pressure, not just from the black arts movement, but this is a pressure of one's whole life, to be a credit to the race. When I was in my twenties, I think I knew instinctively I was not strong enough to be able to take that, that I would probably just stop writing, and I didn't want to stop writing. Which meant that I didn't publish for a while and that I really kept back and didn't want to get out into the fray, so to speak. I didn't want to get into the political stuff because I felt like I had to figure out what I was doing artistically, and if I didn't write my particular take on the world, if I could not find that conduit before I got out into the fray, then I was lost. So that poem, which is a very early poem, in fact I wrote it in college, was kind of clearing the way. It was this feeling of "I'm gonna be strong enough to stand up to you, at least in a dream. I don't know if I'm gonna be able to do it later." I think I was really lucky that I wasn't born a few years earlier, too, because when I began to develop I *had* to publish, I had to see if it mattered to anyone else, and luckily for me by that time there was more leeway being allowed. I have nothing against anyone in the black arts movement.

MP: Not personally.

RD: No, no, not at all. Not even artistically. I see how it was absolutely necessary, and I think a lot of it is really wonderful, too.

MP: Perhaps it was the hegemony of some of their proscriptions which was upsetting to you.

RD: Yes, that's what it was. It was a "don't fence me in." And yet part of me could also see that given the stereotypical ways in which the mainstream America looked at blacks, it was necessary to build the base first before you started admitting more complexity into that and perhaps even some negative things and negative characters. To me, I feel that it is anathema to an artist to tamp down the truth for any kind of poetical goal. I don't see how you can be an artist at that point; I think you compromise yourself very severely. I think of Seamus Heaney's essay that he wrote about the eastern European writers, the poets, and the way he felt that the pressure of the political situation forced them to find a way to say the truth. And there is something to be said for that. There are ways, if you are dealing with any kind of constricting or restrictive artistic system, to pull through, but it takes an enormous character. It takes a very strong character, and I believe there are writers who have been lost because they simply could not take that. I don't think that it is anything to be ashamed of either. Some people are stronger than others in that sense. *So,* that poem was really when I first put my foot outside of the door. You know, put it in *The Yellow House on the Corner* and said, "Okay." I was tempted to take it out of *Selected Poems,* and I thought, "No, that's not fair."

MP: It's a good poem, too.

RD: It is a part of how I developed, and so I thought I had to be honest.

MP: There is another place in your work where it seems like you're answering back to something that could be read as a black arts movement proscription. The opening sequence of the novel *Through the Ivory Gate*—the Penelope doll scene—is answering Toni Morrison's *The Bluest Eye* and the whole obsession with the doll that goes on there. But in your novel, Penelope, the white doll, is kept, and the other doll, the black doll that the parents are so eager to give Virginia, is thrown out the window.

RD: Just thrown out the window. [Laughter.]

MP: So what issues were you thinking about in that scene? Did you have some of those things in mind?

RD: Well, it's true that I had read *The Bluest Eye,* and that book really struck me very deeply for several reasons. I stumbled across it in a stack in the library when I was in graduate school. I didn't know who the author was. I take the jacket covers off, so I didn't even know that the author was black. I just saw the title. And I picked up this book, and I started to read it, and I thought, "Oh my God, she's telling my life." It was the first time that I had ever read anything that dealt with blacks in the Midwest. At that point I had felt very alone because I had had so many instances where people assumed that I either came from Harlem, you know, or from the South. You wonder, Do I have to go to the burden of explanation, or can I just start where I am and write this story? Here was someone who was doing that. So I felt suddenly not alone.

MP: It was a bridge.

RD: Yeah, it really was a bridge. The story of the doll was a bridge, too, because that's an autobiographical moment in the novel, although many are not. It was a moment in my life I had always felt ashamed of, that I had thrown the doll out the window. Why did I do it? It's not a justification for why did you throw the one doll out, but what does this show you about how society's expectations and judgments impinge upon a small child. In a way it was, for me, it was confession. And it *was* an answer to Toni Morrison, but it was more like an "Amen." It's like saying, yeah, I know where people are coming from. This has happened to a lot of us.

MP: An "I've been there too."

RD: Right, exactly.

MP: What's implied in Toni Morrison's novel is that the doll represents the white aesthetic of beauty which can be so destructive for young black girls growing up. You are agreeing with Morrison, then, in your sequence, you feel?

RD: Yes, I am agreeing with her. I'm agreeing with her at that level. There is another part of it, too, and that is that with those two dolls, in my novel, the white doll had real hair that you could comb. And the black doll had painted on curls, and it was one of the first efforts at mass production of black dolls, but it really wasn't a very good likeness. It wasn't beautiful, not cause it was black but because whoever had made it had decided that that's what a black doll looks like. It didn't look like a *person*. When I went back and started to remember the scene and write it I realized that was what disturbed me about that moment. For years I had felt ashamed cause I thought that I had rejected the black doll. But it wasn't that at all. It just wasn't a *good* doll. They made an ugly little doll, and it wasn't useful. I couldn't comb its hair. That's essential! [Laughter.] Obviously, there was not a big market for black dolls, so they felt they didn't have to put in a lot of effort. But at the end of that section of the novel, the protagonist, Virginia, has grown up and runs across that doll, the white doll again, who has gotten waterlogged and who stinks now. She throws her away, and for me that was a moment when she kind of got rid of the guilt and was feeling that she could move on as an individual, which was why it was important to have that at the beginning of the novel.

MP: Yeah, I thought that it was really a powerful scene for her. In relation to this, you might be familiar with Trey Ellis's essay in the winter 1989 issue of *Callaloo* where he talked about the new black aesthetic, an aesthetic born of the black middle class which he sees as combining all kinds of aesthetic influences—white and black, counterculture and high art, and so on. He argued that the central feature of this was the artist, the black artist, as a cultural mulatto. What do you think of his idea that now that we are in the midst of this new black aesthetic? Do you think that's true of your work or of a lot of what's happening now?

RD: Well, my first impulse was it was all sort of "manifesto." [Laughter.] If you have to write a manifesto, fine, go ahead. It gives people something to bounce off against. I tended not to pay much attention. I read it and I thought it was interesting, but it didn't help me. I just don't feel the need artistically to have to take a stand all the time. I think that taking such stance *can* be important in the whole critical history because it gives people points around which to swirl and to fight, and . . .

MP: Publish.

RD: . . . . and publish and to burst out against. But I do think that my artistic temperament is really to be a moving X marks the spot, to keep going. I try not think about the cultural history of literature right now. That doesn't help me as an artist. I would much rather be in the middle of it, totally confused.

MP: I found interesting his reinvention of the term *mulatto*. It has had such a history with it, from the turn-of-the-century and then the Harlem Renaissance "tragic mulatto" who was often depicted as a pathetic soul who self-destructed, to the pejorative use of "mulatto" by black arts movement writers such as Amiri Baraka in the 1960s. Ellis reclaims mulatto as a positive term for contemporary black writers from middle-class backgrounds. It seems an attempt to give voice to something that I think was a closet issue for some black writers that, "Yes, I can freely draw on iambic pentameter," as you were saying earlier. I think it does link back to Derek Walcott.

RD: Yes, it does. I think that is what he is saying, and you are absolutely right. It does pull it out into the open, and it needs to be talked about. I had difficulty with the "mulatto" aspect only because, and this is a poet being obsessed with detail, "mulatto" implies that this only happens to one aspect of humanity. When we say "mulatto" we only think of a black who has white blood in him, or that kind of mixture, but never the other way around. I mean, never that there are whites who have all sorts of ethnic things mixed in. It's the way that it marginalizes again that makes me uneasy with that *term* that's all. Not with what he's saying.

MP: Not pluralistic or truly multiple. . . .

MP: Well, he's claiming this group as *black,* and I see it as actually a kind of pulling toward blackness. I saw Trey as trying to keep blackness a center in the artistic lives of these artists. But you are right, it leaves out a whole other range of possibility, doesn't it?

RD: It does, but it is the nature of manifestos to claim a certain ground and then say, "Okay, come what may," and that's fine too. I mean even the surrealist has to say, "This is what is claimed as the center." I recognize that, given our society, it is hopelessly naive still to imagine that one's own heritage will not disappear entirely or be ignored if we are not constantly reminding people that it's important, and I'm very grateful that there are people who are doing that work, and I'm glad I don't have to do it.

MP: This also reminds me of that short story of yours, "The Spray Paint King," in the collection *Fifth Sunday.* That is sort of your portrait of the artist as a cultural "mulatto." I know you've said elsewhere that he was based on a Swiss guy who was going about doing this graffiti when you were in Germany, but is it possible that you had Jean-Michel Basquiat in mind, or was he not impinging on your world then?

RD: He wasn't impinging on my consciousness then. When I was working on that story there were these graffiti going up all over Germany and Switzerland, and no one knew who was doing them then. I made up a mixed-race artist to do them. In that sense I think certainly that this artist is my symbol of the artist as a cultural "mulatto." I used the word *mulatto* there because "mulatto" also implies an oppression. It implies a psychological oppression. That's one of the reasons why I'm having problems with Trey's use of "mulatto," you see. But in "The Spray Paint King" he has that oppression that he keeps trying to fight against or feel his defiance.

MP: One thing I would like to talk about is one of the very first things we exchanged correspondence over: the incest motif in your work. It transcends your genres.

RD: Yes, it does, doesn't it.

MP: It's *everywhere*. So would you like to talk about this incest motif?

RD: I was baffled about it. I must say that I wasn't even aware it was there, and it's very obvious, once you brought it up. I thought, "Oh, my God!" There is no incidence of incest in my family, there is no autobiographical or even close-friend incidence of it. So it is something that I can't explain. I have decided that eventually I'll figure it out.

MP: And it remains exclusive to your work before *Grace Notes* and *Mother Love*. I was very much looking for it there, and I can't find it. It's in the short story "Aunt Carrie" in *Fifth Sunday;* it's in the novel *Through the Ivory Gate*. It's in the play *The Darker Face of the Earth*, which when you tell me that that is an earlier piece now I see it fitting there. It's in Beulah's life in *Thomas and Beulah*. Now there we really have to look for it, because it could just be physical child abuse but for the mother's righteous anger, "I will cut you down." With Beulah, I wonder how much you *consciously* thought of her as being a victim of incest with the father and then negotiating this marriage with Thomas, or did it just end up in there somehow?

RD: I didn't think about it at all. In fact, I can't say that the poem "Taking in Wash" in *Thomas and Beulah* was ever on a conscious level for me about incest. I knew that it was about that moment when the mother comes in between the father and daughter; whether the mother has always come in between or not was not, for me, the issue. I felt the mother always managed to come in between them.

MP: Except there is evidence to the contrary. I mean, I can't argue with the person who wrote the poems, but Beulah has nightmares where she goes and sees herself in the mirror as this monster figure— nighttime terrors. There's also "Promises" and "Anniversary" which are two poems that have a lot to do with her marriage, but they also suggest she's overly involved with her father.

RD: The father is always there.

MP: What's the father doing in her marriage?

RD: I think there is probably an element of not incest necessarily, but there's that unhealthy attachment of fathers to daughters, or even mothers to sons, that starts really surfacing at the time of marriage. It is almost built into the whole tradition of bridal showers and weddings in the fact that the father can give her away. Give him something to do so that he doesn't freak out or whatever. Part of me also feels, and I think that this is why the Aunt Carrie stories are in *Fifth Sunday* and *Through the Ivory Gate,* that our fear, as a society, of incest and of sex in general fuels excessive guilt when we feel our love toward our children. I'm not talking about sexual love toward children but just that feeling of clinging and then not wanting to show too much because that could be cloying, and that could be interpreted some way. We are really messed up actually. I know I've seen it in me in my feelings with our daughter. As kids grow up they don't want you to touch them just because they are growing up, and we are almost ashamed that we wanted to touch them. That's very natural to want to stroke her hair again. But we've gotten to the point now where we can't do that, and maybe we really should be doing it. I remember I wanted to be on my own, but I wanted to be held, too. It just was unseemly to be held. You are supposed to grow up. That's part of why the incest thing comes up all the time, though it is obviously a very extreme example. I just can't give you any more because I don't know if it's over yet.

MP: It's unconscious.

RD: Yes, unconscious, and I don't know if it's over. I don't think it is going to come up in a poem anytime soon.

MP: I don't want to have you thinking about it because then it might never come up! [Laughter.] Now another writer who comes up on several occasions in your writing is H.D. And it's interesting to me that every time you've cited her you haven't cited her poetry. You've cited her prose. When did you become familiar with her work, and what about her work interests you?

RD: I became familiar with her work in graduate school at, actually, Iowa.

MP: Via Louise Glück?

RD: I'm trying to think if it was Louise or not. I don't know who mentioned it, but I did study with Louise and that would make a lot of sense. But I just don't remember if she was the one who mentioned the book. Well, I'll tell you the first thing that fascinated me about H.D., though I can't remember who said it or who mentioned the book. Someone mentioned *Hermetic Definition,* and I thought "H.D./ hermetic definition—in just that tension between her initials and that. . . ." I just thought, "Oh, I gotta read this person, she must be very strange and wonderful." It's interesting, I do only quote her prose, but I love her poetic work. It's so much itself, if that makes any sense, and it's so very musical in its own insistent phrasing and stuff that I take her in very small dosages, otherwise I'll start sounding like her.

MP: Do you read her poetry now?

RD: I do read her poetry. I haven't read it for a long time now. And part of that was that I wanted to (it sounds so practical but I guess I am in some ways), but when I was working on the *Mother Love* poems I did not really want to reread her because I did not want to approach myth in any way like the way that she approached it, so I wanted to forget and I haven't gotten back to her yet. I will.

MP: She is very intense.

RD: Yes. What I admire about her is the way she could take the outrageous circumstances of her life sometimes and write a poem or sequence which was absolutely beautiful; I thought she could do that and it was not self-indulgent, it was not really confessional in any sense, and I'm glad I don't have that situation in my life.

MP: You've produced a pretty large body of work now, especially in poetry. Do you see any kind of development or phases? Do you feel that things got to a certain point and now you've turned somewhere?

RD: I try not to look to see if there is any kind of development because that'll stop me doing the next thing, *but* the other kind of language you were using about turning corners makes sense and I do see those kinds of directions—like feeling that it is time to turn a corner to stop going down this road. Then there are certain things that I'll do sometimes very deliberately technically to try to pull me down a different road. When I finished *The Yellow House on the Corner,* the next, *Museum,* was on the one hand inspired by my living in Europe at that time, living in Germany mostly, and what that did to my perspective of a history of the world. But the technical thing that happened was that almost every poem had its title first, and in *The Yellow House* it was always the other way around. I had great difficulty with titles, and I despaired of ever being easy about titles. For some reason, in *Museum,* the thing that began to happen was that the titles were almost there first. It was very strange. When *Museum* was finished and I was already working on *Thomas and Beulah,* but I didn't know it was *Thomas and Beulah,* the technical task that I gave myself, it's true, I said, "Okay, you don't want to write an 'I', because everyone was writing an 'I' at that time, you know, and you don't want to write in 'You' because you know everyone was doing that too," and it seemed so weird. What's left is only a "he" and "she," and so I thought I should try to write poems in which there were characters in which there were the "he" or the "she." It wasn't that I would throw something away if it had an "I" or a "you" in it, but I just did that and it happened to come together with these poems. After *Thomas and Beulah,* this expanded narrative, this poetic sequence, I had a great desire to write songs, something that was a lyric, which is what *Grace Notes* came out of. I enjoyed it. The mother-daughter poems in *Mother Love* were both a product of my life, obviously, with a daughter growing up, but also the fact that I had been reading Rilke's *Sonnets of Orpheus*—I suddenly started writing sonnets. There have been other things I've tried. I've said I want to try to write a long-range poem. It just didn't work, I felt. I said, "That's not gonna work right now, I think I'll just wait awhile." This way of assigning myself little technical things is just a means to push me somewhere else, such as the emotional or the artistic. But it's the emotional artist push that I don't want to define. So I'd rather just define the technical and let it fall where it may.

MP: So what are you working on now? You said it was a five-part. . . .

RD: It's a book of poems. I'm still at the point where I can't really give you an idea of it though it's almost finished. In fact, it only has one or two poems that need to go in it. But I don't know what it is exactly, because the poems have occurred over a great period of time as opposed to the other books where they were much more concentrated. There's a point in *Mother Love* where I was only writing those poems, and I had the sense of the book. This book is different. There is a very early poem, a long poem, in it that I've always tried to put in books and it never fit and now it's found its way. Then there are some very recent poems. And because I haven't been publishing a lot of these poems I just didn't publish them. I didn't feel like I wanted to hear where they were going yet. I didn't want someone to start commenting on them before I could figure out where I was going with all of this stuff. A lot of them are short, *Grace Notes*—short kind of thing. A lot of them are really lyrics, but they have a different sense to them. They aren't private lyrics, it's more like Wittgenstein's "to take yourself as the case"—to take it so the personal is more like the existential eye in the universe.

MP: Getting to the universal through the particular.

RD: Getting to the universe through the particular but also assuming that the universe is a particular as well. Sounds kind of big and grand. Some of them I feel are kind of lonely poems. No, not lonely. *Alone* poems.

MP: There is a difference.

RD: Yeah, quite a difference. At the risk of over-interpreting myself, I think that some of my experiences about the schizophrenia of being a private person and a public person has informed these poems. Not in any autobiographical way, but just in that sense that I think every one of us is alive in our skin and at the same time you feel completely insubstantial. I want to get at that.

MP: It's always a shock how people perceive one; you must have gotten a heavy dose of how people perceive you in the last few years. I'd like to pick your brain for a minute on two poems we had very interesting debates about in my class last semester. One of them is "Shakespeare's Say" in *Museum*. What I read this poem as being about is that he, Champion Jack, is creating art out of his sometimes brutal experience, in the blues tradition of lyric expression coming out of this brutal experience, and that he does create art out of this. A couple of my graduate students launched a very interesting counterargument though where they claimed his art actually was false and failed, and they hung their argument on, particularly, the stanza that reads "going down slow crooning," and then Shakespeare said, "Man must be careful, what he kiss when he drunk," and then the repetition of going down and how nobody's listening to him. I wonder how you see Champion Jack in this poem and his art?

RD: I never thought about it consciously this way. At the beginning of the poem we see the façade of Champion Jack and his myth, in a sense, in debt and in his walking suit and all of that stuff, them leading him around. This is the public Champion Jack. Yet they don't understand him at all; the essential Jack Dupree is not there and is never there for his audience because they don't have any reference points. At the moment when he's going down and he's not in good shape physically (the man is a drunk, you know, and he's not at the height of his powers) you could say he's at his worst. But the mistakes sound like jazz. I think at that very moment he comes back to what makes him an artist in the beginning, the blues. He comes back to "my mother told me there would be days like this." At this moment he feels, again, the blues. Before that he's got his act, he's got his little rap, everything is fine, and he can say all this stuff about Shakespeare. I don't think it's great, but at that moment, when he's drunk, he can't hold his piss, "my mother told me there would be days like this," that's where the art and the life come together. The blues lyric fits, and he feels it. So he does the whole trajectory, but in the end, at the moment when to the outside world he's washed up, is really a moment when he found it again.

MP: Which is the blues tradition. It can't be an external thing, it can't be a façade, it can't be a show.

RD: Right. On the very, very physical level he's going down into the cellar, to do this stuff, and it's scary, but to "go down" means to get deeper, get deeper into something. With Persephone and Demeter in *Mother Love* I always thought that going down meant, if this hurts a lot and it doesn't feel good then most people don't want to be there, but you gotta get there in order to be able to know what you are walking on when you're above ground, not to just assume that that's all of reality. In contrast, going up for me is often a place of great loneliness. You know, the only dark spot in the sky.

MP: The other poem is "Roast Possum" from *Thomas and Beulah*. When I taught the poem last semester I talked about how Thomas is in an honored role as the storyteller who's giving the tale to the grandchildren and using the animal tale as that mechanism to talk about race and survival and racism. Two students in the class really wanted the whole issue about Strolling Jim to be brought in a lot more into the reading of the poem than I had been doing. At the end where Malcolm interrupts, which is an important word, "interrupts," asking, "Who owns Strolling Jim and who paid for the tombstone?" and then Thomas corrects him, firmly re-centers him on the main topic which is the possum—"We ate that possum real slow"—I had always read it as being that Malcolm had gotten distracted by the story that was supposed to be for embellishment. Two students pointed out that Strolling Jim brings issues of enslavement and ownership into the poem and that maybe Malcolm is not so wrong to be paying attention to Strolling Jim. So I'm wondering how you read this showdown, man-to-man, between Malcolm and Thomas. What's going on?

RD: It's a complex showdown because it is a generational showdown too. Neither one of them is necessarily right, but they are right for their time, which is why I chose the name Malcolm, too. What Thomas is doing is telling a story the way I'd heard it as a child; you are given all these elements, and you have to decide what is important in the story. All of the tangents are important, too. But it's really up to you, as the listener, to decide which one of the tangents you are going to be frustrated by or if you are going to listen to them, and they kind of change it as the years go by. One becomes more important or one not. So he brings in Strolling Jim, and he tells his story against that possum. It is about a horse who did unique stuff, and remember horseback riding is an elite sport for the rich and for the white. Then he gets buried under the ground like a man, and, of course, "man" is a charged word for African Americans. So when Malcolm interrupts him, it is very important to ask who owned him. It is about ownership, and it's also about who qualifies as a man. Is a horse a man? Is a black man a man? It's a little bit of all that, too. Are you a boy chasing a possum? Thomas doesn't contradict him, necessarily, but he tells him, "Don't forget the possum, that's all. It's not like you shouldn't remember the horse. I'm not going to answer this question because if I answer this question, to tell you who owned him and paid for the tombstone, you're going to get wrapped up in the details of that, or you are going to get so angry about the fact that this horse got a grave as a man, that you are gonna forget how to catch the possum, and you've got to know that, too." Now Malcolm is ready to go and demand stuff, and the grandfather is saying, "Sometime, if you just look really closely you can see that someone is playing the possum, and that's how you catch him." So both of them are right. It's a moment that, hopefully, Malcolm will remember later on in his life. It's probably too early right now for him to like that answer.

MP: Because he wants to be a hothead.

RD: Yeah, he wants to put the count on a man, you know, like Strolling Jim did. And he wanted to be outraged, and he should be outraged because what Thomas has in *his* head, too, is the fact that in the encyclopedia this is what they are saying about black people, and even though he's an old man, at that point, he's seen the changes that are happening in the country with the whole civil rights movement starting up. So things have obviously changed from the encyclopedia saying that black children are intelligent until puberty, then they are lazy. But he's got to let Malcolm figure it out on his own. Malcolm has a different history. Thomas's history goes back; Malcolm's is going forward.

MP: Yeah, looking at it from different directions.

RD: Yeah, and then meeting at this moment. It's so interesting because so many of the stories that should have had morals in my childhood, didn't. They never told us the moral. They just told us a story. You wanted to try to get to the moral, so you'd ask, "What happened to them?" They would say, "I don't know." I can't tell you how many times I asked this. There are a lot of things that could have happened to them, but you go through the story to figure out what paths they would have taken.

MP: You've been living in the South now for over a decade. I don't know if you realize that. Is that right?

RD: Oh my God, it's true. [Laughter.]

MP: And, like me, you were raised in the Midwest. How has being in the South affected you or your writing?

RD: Well, Virginia, particularly Charlottesville, is very strange South. This is the land of contradictions and nexuses, I think, and that's one of the things that I love about this place. You have Thomas Jefferson with all of his contradictions. You've got the cradle of democracy and the constitution; you've got the cradle of the confederacy. . . .

MP: Your assistant told me about Lee/Jackson/King Day, how Martin Luther King Day is used to also honor white Confederate heroes Robert E. Lee and Stonewall Jackson.

RD: It's astonishing, but that's really who we are as Americans. We contain all these contradictions and our whole concept of what this country is, and our great myths about American are just riddled these kind of contradictions. So I like being at this kind of place. I can't tell you what it's doing to my writing yet. It generally takes me a good many years before I start writing about wherever I'm at. I think it will do something to my writing, I just don't know if it's there yet.

MP: The South is a point of origin for so much. Understanding the South helps me understand how everything else got to be the way it is.

RD: That's right because, you know, the really bizarre thing is that we are more racially divided now in this country than we've been in I don't know how long, all because we've never dealt with the Civil War. I really think it's because we haven't done our work. When I was a kid, the South was this land of terror. I had relatives in the South, and we went down to visit them when I was ten and again when I was fourteen. I was absolutely convinced that I was going to be lynched and terrible things were going to happen. What I didn't understand, but really impressed me was that blacks and whites interacted, though there was great caution on both sides. They knew each other better than blacks and whites in the North.

MP: They lived in proximity.

RD: I realized that we didn't live in proximity in the North, where I had assumed that we would be this great integrated dream. That was amazing. I'd say Charlottesville is an academic community mostly. It's a very strange place here. It's really almost Washington, and so it's an odd place to be, in that sense. I taught at Tuskegee for a semester, 1982, and that was much more like being in the South. That was Real South.

MP: I wonder if being in the Real South would do anything for your writing at all. [Laughter.]

RD: I think that, maybe I hope that, one of the ways being here will influence my writing is the interest in exploring our myth of ourselves as Americans, because I do feel that all the time here. I feel we're constantly rubbing up against what we've always, in our hearts, thought America was and how we contribute to this or fight against it and what things aren't resolved. Here Jefferson's everywhere, and the vehemence of the arguments about Jefferson here is just absurd. When I first came here and went to a dinner at the president's house someone stood up to toast Mr. Jefferson, and I was about to make a joke, and my dinner partner said, "Oh yeah, he's gonna toast Jefferson." But I realized they were *serious* and that every official academic function begins with a toast to Mr. Jefferson. That's bizarre. And yet you've got a whole influx of young professors and students who are coming in from all over the place who are kind of amused by all of this. Jefferson is a wonderful man, don't get me wrong; he had talents, but he was also a man. He was also a complicated and fallible human being. What startles me constantly is how it becomes a matter of life and death for people to have the Jefferson they want. Again we're getting back to the public person or the idea of a myth whether you believe it or not. That's why I kind of like being close to all this.

MP: Keep an eye on it.

RD: Keep an eye on it. I don't know where it will go. I've often joked with my husband that some day I'm gonna write this play called *Jefferson* that will get me banned from Charlottesville, and then I'll have to go someplace else.

MP: Kicked out of paradise. Not quite?

RD: Not quite.

MP: It's the end of the millennium, as you know, and people are making a big deal out of this, and we're using it to structure our systems of meaning about all kinds of things. But it's the close to the twentieth century in American poetry. How do you see your work as coming at the end of the century in American poetry? Are there lineages you feel it fits into, and then how do you see it as starting a lineage for the twenty-first century?

RD: Well, first of all let me just say that I'm fascinated by the millennium because it's a boundary that's totally constructed. When I lived in Arizona, my husband and I would often at New Year's have a *ball* because we would just celebrate it every hour. When you have to find these points, to say we've crossed over somewhere. . . . So that's something that is fascinating to me, and though there is no such thing as a new millennium, the fact that we *believe* that there is a new millennium means that there *is* a new millennium, it means that people are working toward it and all that kind of stuff. I haven't really thought of it in terms of a new millennium artistically because I don't believe in these kind of boundaries, but somewhere it's going to, of course, pull it together. I think in my own life of where I'm at because I'm forty-five, and you start thinking about this. At forty-five you still feel like you have a foot in youth, but it's getting there. At fifty you can't do it anymore, or maybe, I just don't know, I'm working toward that. So it is true that there is something that I feel that is starting, not to close down. What I really find exciting is to be a bridge. I have had the fleeting idea thinking, "Gosh, I'm glad that I'm not *seventy-five* at the end of the millennium." I mean, I'm really glad that I'm this age so that I can actually say that, "Oh, yeah, I've got a role." I like the bridge aspect of it. I just like to be going through it, and I'm really kind of excited to see how people are going to react.

MP: Well, you can actually be the one they react against.

RD: That's right.

MP: Or follow.

RD: Whatever, whatever.

MP: You can go back to Du Bois opening the twentieth century with "the problem of the twentieth century is the problem of the color line." If you use that as an arc to construct it on, I think some of your work is a very interesting segue then into the twenty-first century because you're not interested in the line. Maybe you make it more of a dot-dot-dot or a blur.

RD: A demilitarized zone.

MP: You make it permeable?

RD: I make it permeable. And yet the problem is still the problem, the gray zone.

MP: Well, I don't think that people generally know what to do with gray areas.

RD: No, they don't. Unfortunately, Du Bois's wonderful statement (and because it's so beautifully put) still pertains. It is not a line any more, but it's something else. I think that he was also dealing with the concept that people had to make a boundary between them. The fact is that we still think in terms of boundaries between peoples and groups and sexes and all that stuff and it's so depressing sometimes.

MP: The twentieth-century boundaries, have they broken down?

RD: I don't think that the boundaries can be broken down until people go deeper into themselves and admit that there are no unique compartments in themselves. I really think we, as human beings, have had such incredible denial in terms of how much we're certain of. Why can't we admit uncertainty into our lives? I really feel that we don't admit it into our lives, and when someone does it's something very daring when it should just be the way life is. I think that that admitting uncertainty into one's life also allows you to not to be afraid of anything that feels mysterious, something that is unknown, which then translates into the Other. What is this Other? We have others inside of us.

Note

This interview was previously published, in slightly different form, in *Contemporary Literature* 40 (Summer 1999): 183–213. Used by permission of the University of Wisconsin Press.

Bibliography

Creative Works by Rita Dove

The Darker Face of the Earth. Brownsville, Ore: Story Line Press. 1994. Rev. ed. 1996.

Fifth Sunday. Lexington: *Callaloo* Fiction Series at the University of Kentucky, 1985.

Grace Notes. New York: W. W. Norton, 1989.

Mother Love. New York: W. W. Norton, 1995.

Museum. Pittsburgh: Carnegie Mellon University Press, 1983.

On the Bus with Rosa Parks. New York: W. W. Norton, 1999.

The Poet's World. Washington, D.C.: Library of Congress, 1995.

Thomas and Beulah. Pittsburgh: Carnegie-Mellon University Press, 1986.

Through the Ivory Gate. New York: Random House, 1993.

The Yellow House on the Corner. Pittsburgh: Carnegie Mellon University Press, 1989.

Literary Criticism by Rita Dove

"'Either I'm Nobody, or I'm a Nation.'" *Parnassus: Poetry in Review* 14, no. 1 (1987): 49–76.

"Ralph W. Ellison." Trans. Fred Viebahn. In *Kritisches Lexikon zur fremdsprachigen Gegenwartsliteratur.* Ed. Heinz Ludwig Arnold, 1–10. Munich: Edition Text + Kritik, 1984.

"Telling It Like It I-S *IS:* Narrative Techniques in Melvin B. Tolson's *Harlem Gallery.*" *New England Review and Bread Loaf Quarterly* 8 (Autumn 1985): 109–17.

———, and Marilyn Nelson Waniek. "A Black Rainbow: Modern Afro American Poetry." In *Poetry after Modernism.* Ed. Robert McDowell, 217–75. Brownsville, Ore.: Story Line Press, 1991.

Interviews with Rita Dove

Anon. "At the Hands of Fate: Writer Rita Dove Reveals the Genesis and Evolution of *The Darker Face of the Earth*." <http://kennedy-center.org/interviews /ritadove.html.> Accessed on Nov. 19, 1997. 1–6.

Bellin, Steven. "A Conversation with Rita Dove." *Mississippi Review* 23, no. 3 (1995): 10–34.

Dove, Rita. E-mail to Malin Pereira. Feb. 22, 2001.

Cavalieri, Grace. "Rita Dove: An Interview." *The American Poetry Review* 24 (Mar.–Apr. 1995): 11–15.

Hammer, Mike, and Christina Daub. Interview. *The Plum Review* 9 (1996): 27–41.

Lloyd, Emily. "Navigating the Personal: An Interview with Poet Laureate Rita Dove." *Off Our Backs: A Women's News Journal* 24 (April 1994): 1, 22.

Peabody, Richard, and Gretchen Johnsen. "A Cage of Sound: An Interview with Rita Dove." *Gargoyle* 27 (1985): 2–13.

Pereira, Malin. "An Interview with Rita Dove." *Contemporary Literature* 40 (Summer 1999): 183–213.

Rubin, Stan Sanvel, and Judith Kitchen. "'The Underside of the Story': A Conversation with Rita Dove." In *The Post-Confessionals: Conversations with American Poets of the Eighties.* Ed. Earl Ingersoll, Judith Kitchen, and Stan Sanvel Rubin, 151–65. Teaneck, N.J.: Farleigh Dickinson University Press, 1989.

Schneider, Steven. "Coming Home: An Interview with Rita Dove." *The Iowa Review* 19 (Fall 1989): 112–23.

Steffen, Therese. "The Darker Face of the Earth: A Conversation with Rita Dove." *Transition* 74 (1998): 104–23.

Taleb-Khyar, Mohamed B. "An Interview with Maryse Condé and Rita Dove." *Callaloo* 14, no. 2 (1991): 347–66.

Walsh, William. "Isn't Reality Magic? An Interview with Rita Dove." *The Kenyon Review* 16 (Summer 1994): 142–54.

Criticism on Rita Dove and Reviews

Baker, Houston A., Jr. Review of *Grace Notes. Black American Literature Forum* 24 (Fall 1990): 574–77.

Dove, Rita. "Oedipus in America." Kennedy Center Stagebill for *The Darker Face of the Earth* (Nov. 1997): 8–12.

Erickson, Peter. "Rita Dove's Shakespeares." In *Transforming Shakespeare: Contemporary Women's Re-Visions in Literature and Performance.* Ed. Marianne Novy, 87–101. New York: St. Martin's Press, 1999.

Georgoudaki, Ekaterini. *Race, Gender, and Class Perspectives in the Works of Maya*

Angelou, Gwendolyn Brooks, Rita Dove, Nikki Giovanni, and Audre Lorde. Thessaloniki: Aristotle University of Thessaloniki Press, 1991.

———. "Rita Dove: Crossing Boundaries." *Callaloo* 14, no. 2 (1991): 419–33.

Gregerson, Linda. Review of *The Yellow House on the Corner* and *Museum. Poetry* 145 (Oct. 1984): 46–49.

Hampton, Janet Jones. "Portraits of a Diasporean People: The Poetry of Shirley Campbell and Rita Dove." *Afro-Hispanic Review* 14 (Spring 1995): 33–39.

Harris, Peter. "Four Salvers Salvaging: New Work by Voight, Olds, Dove, and McHugh." *Virginia Quarterly Review* 64, no. 2 (1988): 262–76.

Jablon, Madelyn. "The African-American *Künstlerroman*." *Diversity: A Journal of Multicultural Issues* 2 (1994): 21–28.

Jones, Kirkland C. "Folk Idiom in the Literary Expression of Two African American Authors: Rita Dove and Yusef Komunyakaa." In *Language and Literature in the African American Imagination.* Ed. Carol Aisha Blackshire-Belay, 149–65. Westport: Greenwood Press, 1992.

Keller, Lynn. *Forms of Expansion: Recent Long Poems by Women,* 103–36. Chicago: University of Chicago Press, 1997.

McDowell, Robert. "The Assembling Vision of Rita Dove." *Callaloo* 9 (Winter 1986): 61–70.

Pereira, Malin. "'When the pear blossoms / cast their pale faces on / the darker face of the earth': Miscegenation, the Primal Scene, and the Incest Motif in Rita Dove's Work." *African American Review* 36 (Summer 2002): 1–17.

Proitsaki, Maria. "Seasonal and Seasonable Motherhood in Dove's *Mother Love.*" In *Women, Creators of Culture,* ed. Ekaterini Georgoudaki and Domna Pastourmatzi, 143–51. American Studies in Greece, series 3. Thessaloniki: Hellenic Association of American Studies, 1997.

Rampersad, Arnold. "The Poems of Rita Dove." *Callaloo* 9 (Winter 1986): 52–60.

Shoptaw, John. "Rita Dove's *Thomas and Beulah.*" In *Reading Black, Reading Feminist: A Critical Anthology.* Ed. Henry Louis Gates, Jr., 374–81. New York: Meridian, 1990.

Steffen, Therese. "Beyond Ethnic Margin and Cultural Center: Rita Dove's 'Empire' of *Mother Love.*" In *Empire.* Ed. John G. Blair and Reinhold Wagnleitner, 10. Swiss Papers in English Language and Literature. Tübingen: Gunter Narr Verlag, 1997.

———. *Crossing Color: Transcultural Space and Place in Rita Dove's Poetry, Fiction, and Drama.* New York: Oxford University Press, 2001.

———. "Movements of a Marriage; or, Looking Awry at U.S. History: Rita Dove's *Thomas and Beulah.*" In *Families.* Ed. Werner Senn, 9. Swiss Papers in English Language and Literature. Tübingen: Gunter Narr Verlag, 1996.

———. "Rooted Displacement in Form: Rita Dove's Sonnet Cycle *Mother Love.*"

In *The Furious Flowering of African American Poetry.* Ed. Joanne V. Gabbin, 60–76. Charlottesville: University Press of Virginia, 1999.

Stein, Kevin. "Lives in Motion: Multiple Perspectives in Rita Dove's Poetry." *Mississippi Review* 23, no. 3 (1995): 51–79.

Steinman, Lisa. "Dialogues between History and Drama." *Michigan Quarterly Review* 23, no. 3 (1987): 51–79.

Van Dyne, Susan R. "Siting the Poet: Rita Dove's Refiguring of Traditions." In *Women Poets of the Americas: Toward a Pan-American Gathering.* Ed. Jacqueline Vaught Brogan and Cordelia Chávez Candelaria, 68–87. Notre Dame: University of Notre Dame Press, 1999.

Vendler, Helen. "Blackness and Beyond Blackness." *Times Literary Supplement,* Feb. 18, 1994, 11–13.

———. "A Dissonant Triad." *Parnassus: Poetry in Review* 16, no. 2 (1991): 391–404.

Wallace, Patricia. "Divided Loyalties: Literal and Literary in the Poetry of Lorna Dee Cervantes, Cathy Song and Rita Dove." *MELUS* 18 (Fall 1993): 3–19.

Secondary Sources

Abel, Elizabeth. "Black Writing, White Reading: Race and the Politics of Feminist Interpretation." *Critical Inquiry* 19 (Spring 1993): 470–98.

Anglesey, Zoe et al., eds. *Listen Up! Spoken Word Poetry.* New York: Ballantine, 1999.

Apel, Willi. *Harvard Dictionary of Music.* 1944. 2d ed. Cambridge: Harvard University Press, 1972.

Appiah, Kwame Anthony. "Cosmopolitan Reading." In *Cosmopolitan Geographies: New Locations in Literature.* Ed. Vinay Dharwadker, 197–227. New York: Routledge, 2001.

———. *In My Father's House: Africa in the Philosophy of Culture.* New York: Oxford University Press, 1992.

Berman, Jessica. *Modernist Fiction, Cosmopolitanism, and the Politics of Community.* New York: Cambridge University Press, 2001.

Bloom, Harold. *The Anxiety of Influence: A Theory of Poetry.* 2d ed. New York: Oxford University Press, 1997.

Braidotti, Rosi. *Nomadic Subjects: Embodiment and Sexual Difference in Contemporary Feminist Theory.* New York: Columbia University Press, 1994.

Breckenridge, Carol Appadurai, Homi K. Bhabha, Dipesh Chakrabarty, and Sheldon Pollock, eds. *Cosmopolitanism.* Durham: Duke University Press, 2002.

Brennan, Timothy. *At Home in the World: Cosmopolitanism Now.* Cambridge: Harvard University Press, 2001.

Cixous, Hélène. *Illa.* Paris: Des Femmes, 1980.

Clarke, Cheryl. *Living as a Lesbian.* Ithaca: Firebrand Books, 1986.

Coleman, Wanda. Letters to E. Ethelbert Miller. *Callaloo* 22 (Winter 1999): 99–106.

Conniff, Brian. "Answering 'The Waste Land': Robert Hayden and the Rise of the African American Poetic Sequence." *African American Review* 33 (Fall 1999): 487–506.

Crassweller, Robert D. *Trujillo: The Life and Times of a Caribbean Dictator.* New York: Macmillan, 1966.

Daniel, Melissa. Untitled and unpublished paper on Cheryl Clarke. May 1999.

Deleuze, Gilles, and Felix Guattari. *Nomadology: The War Machine.* New York: Semiotexte, 1986.

Derrida, Jacques. *On Cosmopolitanism and Forgiveness.* New York: Routledge, 2001.

———. "The Law of Genre." *Critical Inquiry* 7 (Autumn 1980): 55–79.

duCille, Ann, *The Coupling Convention: Sex, Text, and Tradition in Black Women's Fiction.* New York: Oxford University Press, 1993.

Ellison, Ralph. "The World and the Jug." In *Shadow and Act.* 1953. Reprint. New York: Vintage, 1964.

Ellis, Trey. "The New Black Aesthetic." *Callaloo* 12 (Winter 1989): 233–43.

Farnsworth, Robert M. *Melvin B. Tolson, 1898–1966: Plain Talk and Poetic Prophesy.* Columbia: University of Missouri Press, 1984.

Feher, Michel. "The Schisms of '67: On Certain Restructurings of the American Left, from the Civil Rights Movement to the Multiculturalist Constellation." Trans. Erik Brunar. In *Blacks and Jews: Alliances and Arguments.* Ed. Paul Berman, 263–85. New York: Delacourt Press, 1994.

Freud, Sigmund. "The Case of the Wolf Man." In *The Wolf Man.* Ed. Muriel Gardiner, 153–262. New York: Basic Books, 1971.

———. "The Interpretation of Dreams." In *The Basic Writings of Sigmund Freud.* Ed. A. A. Brill, 181–552. New York: Modern Library, 1938.

Friedman, Susan Stanford. *Penelope's Web: Gender, Modernity, H.D.'s Fiction.* New York: Cambridge University Press, 1990.

Gates, Henry Louis, Jr., and Cornel West. *The Future of the Race.* New York: Knopf, 1996.

Gilbert, Sandra M. "In Yeats' House: The Death and Resurrection of Sylvia Plath." In *Critical Essays on Sylvia Plath.* Ed. Linda W. Wagner, 204–22. Boston: Hall, 1984.

Harper, Michael S., and Robert B. Stepto, eds. *Chant of Saints: A Gathering of Afro-American Literature, Art, and Scholarship.* Urbana: University of Illinois Press, 1979.

Harris, William J. *The Poetry and Poetics of Amiri Baraka: The Jazz Aesthetic.* Columbia: University of Missouri Press, 1985.

Henderson, Stephen. *Understanding the New Black Poetry: Black Speech and Black Music as Poetic References.* New York: William Morris, 1973.

Holden-Kirwan, Jennifer L. "Looking into the Self That Is No Self: An Examination of Subjectivity in *Beloved.*" *African American Review* 32, no. 3 (1998): 415–26.

Hillman, James. *The Dream and the Underworld.* New York: Harper and Row, 1979.

hooks, bell. "Homeplace: A Site of Resistance." In *Yearning: Race, Gender, and Cultural Politics,* 41–49. Boston: South End Press, 1990.

Honey, Maureen, ed. *Shadowed Dreams: Women's Poetry of the Harlem Renaissance.* New Brunswick: Rutgers University Press, 1989.

Hughes, Langston, "The Negro Artist and the Racial Mountain." 1926. Reprinted in *The Norton Anthology of African American Literature.* Ed. Henry Louis Gates, Jr., and Nellie Y. McKay, 1267–71. New York: W. W. Norton, 1997.

Hunter, Tera. "It's a Man's Man's Man's World: Specters of the Old Re-Newed in Afro-American Culture and Criticism." *Callaloo* 12 (Winter 1989): 247–49.

Irigaray, Luce. *This Sex which Is Not One* (Ce sexe qui n'en est pas un). 1977. Reprint. Trans. Catherine Porter with Carolyn Burke. Ithaca: Cornell University Press, 1985.

Jones, Charles. *Global Justice: Defending Cosmopolitanism.* New York: Oxford University Press, 2001.

Jones, LeRoi (Imamu Amiri Baraka). "Home" In *Home: Social Essays,* 9–10. New York: William Morrow, 1966.

Jones, Norma R. "Robert E. Hayden." In *Dictionary of Literary Biography,* vol. 76: *Afro-American Writers, 1940–1955.* Ed. Trudier Harris, 75–88. Detroit: Gale Research, 1988.

Karenga, Maulana. "Black Art: Mute Matter Given Force and Function." 1972. Reprinted in *The Norton Anthology of African American Literature.* Ed. Henry Louis Gates, Jr., and Nellie Y. McKay, 1973–77. New York: W. W. Norton, 1997.

Knox, Bernard. "Introduction to Oedipus the King" In Sophocles, *Three Theban Plays.* Trans. Robert Fagles, 131–53. New York: Penguin Classics, 1982.

Komunyakaa, Yusef. *Blue Notes: Essays, Interviews, and Commentaries.* Ann Arbor: University of Michigan Press, 2000.

Kristeva, Julia. "Stabat Mater." In *The Kristeva Reader.* Ed. Toril Moi, 160–86. New York: Columbia University Press, 1986.

Locke, Alain. *The Philosophy of Alain Locke: Harlem Renaissance and Beyond.* Ed. Leonard Harris. Philadelphia: Temple University Press, 1989.

Lott, Eric. "The New Cosmopolitanism." *Transition* 72 (Fall 1996): 108–35.

———. "Response to Trey Ellis's 'The New Black Aesthetic.'" *Callaloo* 12 (Winter 1989): 244–46.

Lukacher, Ned. *Primal Scenes: Literature, Philosophy, Psychoanalysis.* Ithaca: Cornell University Press, 1986.

Martin, Reginald. "The FreeLance Pallbearer Confronts the Terrible Threes: Ishmael Reed and the New Black Aesthetic Critics." *MELUS* 14 (Summer 1987): 35–49.

McDowell, Deborah E. "Boundaries; or, Distant Relations and Close Kin—*Sula*." In *"The Changing Same": Black Women's Literature, Criticism, and Theory*. Ed. Deborah E. McDowell, 101–17. Bloomington: Indiana University Press, 1995.

McFadden, David. *A Trip around Lake Huron*. Toronto: Coach House Press, 1980.

Meillassoux, Claude. "Female Slavery." In *Women and Slavery in Africa*. Ed. Claire C. Robertson and Martin A. Klein, 49–67. Madison: University of Wisconsin Press, 1983.

Mulvey, Laura. *Visual and Other Pleasures*. Bloomington: Indiana University Press, 1989.

Murray, Albert. *The Blue Devils of Nada: A Contemporary American Approach to Aesthetic Statement*. New York: Pantheon, 1996.

———. *The Omni-Americans: New Perspectives on Black Experience and American Culture*. New York: Outerbridge and Dienstfrey, 1970.

Posnock, Ross. *Color and Culture: Black Writers and the Making of the Modern Intellectual*. Cambridge: Harvard University Press, 1998.

Raymond, Joan. "The Multicultural Report." *American Demographics* 23 (Nov. 2001): 53.

Rich, Adrienne. *Blood, Bread, and Poetry*. New York: W. W. Norton, 1986.

Roorda, Eric Paul. *The Dictator Next Door: The Good Neighbor Policy and the Trujillo Regime in the Dominican Republic, 1930–1945*. Durham: Duke University Press, 1998.

Rushdy, Ashraf H. A. "'Rememory': Primal Scenes and Constructions in Toni Morrison's Novels." *Contemporary Literature* 31, no. 3 (1990): 300–323.

Sollors, Werner. *Neither Black nor White yet Both: Thematic Explorations of Interracial Literature*. New York: Oxford University Press, 1997.

Spillers, Hortense J. "Mama's Baby, Papa's Maybe: An American Grammar Book." *diacritics* 17 (Summer 1987): 65–81.

Sundquist, Eric J. *Faulkner: The House Divided*. Baltimore: Johns Hopkins University Press, 1983.

Tate, Claudia, *Psychoanalysis and Black Novels: Desire and the Protocols of Race*. New York: Oxford University Press, 1998.

Tate, Greg. *Flyboy in the Buttermilk: Essays on Contemporary America*. New York: Simon and Schuster, 1992.

Wannberg, Scott, et al., eds. *Twisted Cadillac: A Spoken Word Odyssey*. Venice, Calif.: Sacred Beverage Press, 1996.

Werner, Craig Hansen. *Playing the Changes: From Afro-Modernism to the Jazz Impulse*. Urbana: University of Illinois Press, 1994.

Woolf, Virginia. *A Room of One's Own* and *Three Guineas*. 1929, 1938. Reprint. New York: Harcourt Brace Jovanovich, 1992.

Index

MALIN PEREIRA is an associate professor of English at the University of North Carolina at Charlotte, where she teaches African American and American literatures.

The University of Illinois Press
is a founding member of the
Association of American University Presses.

Composed in 10.5/12.5 Minion
with Minion display
by Type One, LLC
for the University of Illinois Press
Designed by Paula Newcomb
Manufactured by Thomson-Shore, Inc.

University of Illinois Press
1325 South Oak Street
Champaign, IL 61820-6903
www.press.uillinois.edu